Corporate Governance

OECD Review of the Corporate Governance of State-Owned Enterprises in Kazakhstan

OECD
BETTER POLICIES FOR BETTER LIVES

This work is published under the responsibility of the Secretary-General of the OECD. The opinions expressed and arguments employed herein do not necessarily reflect the official views of the Member countries of the OECD.

This document, as well as any data and map included herein, are without prejudice to the status of or sovereignty over any territory, to the delimitation of international frontiers and boundaries and to the name of any territory, city or area.

Please cite this publication as:
OECD (2024), *OECD Review of the Corporate Governance of State-Owned Enterprises in Kazakhstan*, Corporate Governance, OECD Publishing, Paris, https://doi.org/10.1787/082c508b-en.

ISBN 978-92-64-49718-4 (print)
ISBN 978-92-64-57626-1 (pdf)
ISBN 978-92-64-69172-8 (HTML)
ISBN 978-92-64-55761-1 (epub)

Corporate Governance
ISSN 2077-6527 (print)
ISSN 2077-6535 (online)

Photo credits: Cover © janetheone/Getty Images

Corrigenda to OECD publications may be found on line at: www.oecd.org/about/publishing/corrigenda.htm.

Foreword

The purpose of this report is to describe and evaluate the corporate governance framework of the Kazakh state-owned enterprise sector against the OECD Guidelines on Corporate Governance of State-Owned Enterprises (the "SOE Guidelines"). It was discussed by the OECD Working Party on State Ownership and Privatisation Practices' (the "Working Party"), the body responsible for overseeing the effective implementation of the SOE Guidelines, at its meetings in April and October 2023.

Since their inception in 2005, the SOE Guidelines have provided concrete advice to countries on how to manage more effectively their responsibilities as enterprise owners, thus helping to make state-owned enterprises more competitive, efficient and transparent. They complement and are compatible with the G20/OECD Principles of Corporate Governance and the OECD Anti-Corruption and Integrity Guidelines for State-Owned Enterprises.

This report was prepared at the request of the Republic of Kazakhstan to support its objective of strengthening its ownership and governance framework for SOEs. It falls under a project which commenced with its first phase in 2022, and included three knowledge sharing seminars, organised by the OECD Secretariat, with the purpose of creating a better joint understanding of international best practices and their application in Kazakhstan. In a second information gathering phase, the OECD Secretariat collected information including from a questionnaire submitted to the Kazakh authorities. The report is further enriched from information gathered from two fact-finding missions to Astana undertaken in February and September 2023 including meetings with government officials, representatives of civil society, business organisations, and SOEs, and additional desk research and information gathered from subsequent interaction with the Ministry of National Economy and other relevant authorities.

In parallel with developing this Review, the OECD also provided technical assistance to Kazakhstan's on-going legislative reform aimed at amending the Law on State Property, for which consideration by Parliament is expected in 2024. The new Law – if and when put in place – may address some of the recommendations identified by this report.

This report is structured into three main parts. Chapter 1 provides background information on the Kazakh SOE sector, including the applicable legal and regulatory framework; Chapter 2 provides an assessment of Kazakhstan's existent legislation relative to the standards of the SOE Guidelines. The final chapter provides conclusions and recommendations for improving the corporate governance framework applicable to Kazakh SOEs.

The report was drafted by Talisa zur Hausen and Karoline Irmscher of the OECD Capital Markets and Financial Institutions Division, and Lazzat Borankulova (OECD local consultant). Meral Gedik and Greta Gabbarini provided editorial support and prepared the report for publication.

Table of contents

FIGURES

TABLES

Abbreviations and acronyms

AIFC	Astana International Finance Centre
AGM	Annual general meeting
AFSA	Astana Financial Services Authority
AIX	Astana International Exchange
APDC	Agency for Protection and Development of Competition
BOD	Board of directors
Bn	Billion
CPI	Corruption Perception Index
CSR	Corporate social responsibility
DBK	Development Bank of Kazakhstan
ESP	Enterprise with state participation
FDI	Foreign direct investment
FSD	Forecast of social and economic development
GDP	Gross domestic product
GDR	Global depositary receipt
GNI	Gross national income
GRI	Global Reporting Initiative
GSM	General shareholders meeting
IAD	Internal Audit Department
IFRS	International financial reporting standard
IPO	Initial public offerings
ITRP	Investment Tax Residency Programme
JSC	Joint stock company
KASE	Kazakhstan Stock Exchange
KPI	Key performance indicator
KTZ	Kazakhstan Temir Zholy
KZT	Kazakh Tenge

LLC	Limited liability company
LLP	Limited liability partnership
LSE	London Stock Exchange
M&E	Mergers and acquisitions
MF	Ministry of Finance
MIID	Ministry of Industry and Infrastructure Development
MNE	Ministry of National Economy
Mn	Million
NBK	National Bank of Kazakhstan
NDP	National development plan
NPL	Non-performing loans
SAI	Kazakhstan's supreme audit institution
SWF	Sovereign Wealth Fund
PPP	Purchasing power parity
RMD	Risk management department
SME	Small and medium sized enterprises
SOE	State-owned enterprise
UNCMC	United Nations Convention against Corruption
UNGC	United Nations Global Compact

Executive summary

State-owned enterprises (SOEs) play a crucial role in the Kazakh economy, particularly in sectors such as energy and mining. They are present in at least 20 out of 30 sectors of the economy and account for around 6.2% of the national employment. Kazakhstan's ownership structure for SOEs is dispersed across a number of large holding companies, with Samruk-Kazyna being the most significant one.

While there is no centralised or consolidated information available to assess the operational effectiveness of SOEs compared to their private sector peers, the two largest holding companies – Samruk-Kazyna and Baiterek – provide a good indication. Samruk-Kazyna's revenues amounted to 14% of GDP in 2021 and had accumulated a debt of 11.8% of GDP. In 2021, Baiterek's revenues amounted to 0.13% of GDP, and its total debt to 9.8% of GDP.

In light of its large SOE sector, **the Kazakh government has embarked on substantial reform efforts aimed at enhancing the governance and performance of SOEs**. In 2023, the Kazakh President announced a need to reduce the share of the state in the economy and to reform SOEs, in line with the *2025 National Development Plan* and the *2030 Concept for the Development of Public Administration*, including the intention to accelerate the privatisation process. Against the background of this call for reform, the Ministry of National Economy developed a seven-point action plan due for implementation by 2028. The outcomes of the action plan are thus only partially assessed by this Review and, as a result, the main findings summarised below should be read as inputs to support Kazakhstan's reform plans going forward.

The reform plans, which are still underway, can benefit from continued commitment to ensure their implementation. The current legal framework needs clarity in defining ownership rationales, and the lack of an overarching ownership policy results in variance in expectations for and modes of accountability among SOEs. Kazakhstan's legal and regulatory framework for SOEs is complex and is further complicated by frequent revisions.

The development of a unified ownership entity would support informed and active state ownership, and can reduce opportunities for undue interference. Centralisation of ownership would further support more effective oversight of entities like Samruk-Kazyna, which would allow the Government to make an informed assessment of its performance. A clearer separation between government ownership and regulatory functions, can help to ensure a level playing field and foster investor confidence necessary for privatisation plans.

The corporate governance framework should focus on ensuring transparent board nomination procedures, board efficiency and respect of minority shareholders' rights. Despite the existence of a National Corporate Governance Code, SOEs are also guided by another two codes issued by the Ministry of National Economy and Samruk-Kazyna, respectively, thus resulting in conflicting expectations for SOEs. Despite existing legal provisions for stakeholder protection, issues persist due to a gap between written law and implementation. Moreover, stakeholders note concerns relating to the transparency around board nomination procedures. The majority composition of boards by government officials raises concerns about objective decision-making and the need for professionalised, independent and autonomous boards.

Kazakhstan must develop standardised and robust disclosure and reporting requirements to strengthen accountability of SOEs. While some SOEs under national holding companies adhere to stricter reporting requirements, there is still a high level of variability in implementation across individual SOEs, and issues with reporting of material related party transactions, inadequate internal controls and lack of regular external audits are noted.

The government is encouraged to ensure a level playing field for both public and private companies, by clarifying and improving public service obligation requirements. SOEs should be required to maintain separate accounts for commercial and non-commercial activities to ensure competitively neutral compensation for carrying out public service obligations.

Looking ahead, **Kazakhstan should focus on designing a holistic ownership policy, enhancing transparency and implementing reforms in corporate governance to align with international standards and foster investor confidence**. Addressing these issues will contribute to the effective performance, accountability, and transparency of Kazakhstan's SOEs and in the broader economy.

1 The state-owned enterprise landscape in Kazakhstan

This chapter discusses the business and economic environment in Kazakhstan and ownership landscape of the country's state-owned enterprise sector – with information on its size, sectoral distribution and economic and financial performance. It then provides information on the legal and regulatory frameworks bearing on SOE governance, including details on the general corporate governance framework as well as on sectoral laws and regulations applicable to SOEs. It finally describes ownership arrangements and examines how the state and holding companies exercise ownership rights, with a particular focus on policies and practices underpinning board and executive appointments, privatisation and financial oversight of SOEs.

1.1. Economic and political context of Kazakhstan

The Republic of Kazakhstan (hereafter 'Kazakhstan') is a transcontinental country located mostly in Central Asia, bordering the People's Republic of China (hereafter 'China'), the Russian Federation (hereafter 'Russia'), Kyrgyzstan, Uzbekistan, and Turkmenistan. It is the largest landlocked country in the world and the ninth largest territory, with a population of 19.4 million (mn) in 2022. Kazakhstan gained independence from the Soviet Union in 1991 and is now a member of a number of transatlantic organisations[1] (World Bank, 2023[1]). The role of capital city shifted from Almaty to Astana in 1998; since then the population of Astana has more than doubled in size. As of 2021, 42% of the population were living in rural areas, steadily declining since 1991 (World Bank, 2021[2]).

Kazakhstan's administrative division includes a relatively small number of government units compared to the rest of Central Asia, including 14 administrative zones, 17 regions, and 170 districts. In 2022, following the so-called *2022 Kazakh unrest*, the government made changes to the first tier of its three-level administrative division,[2] increasing the number of districts and introducing general administrative and territorial reforms (Smagulova, 2022[3]).

1.1.1. Economy

Kazakhstan underwent significant economic transformation after gaining independence in 1991. Since then, the country's gross domestic product (GDP) annual growth rate averaged 4.57% from 1995 until 2022, increasing per capita GDP 20-fold, from USD 700 to USD 14 000. Its poverty rate[3] was at USD 5.3% in 2020, placing the country's performance above the global average (World Bank, 2023[1]). These gains have been heavily linked to Kazakhstan's valuable resources, the extraction of which account for over a fifth of the country's GDP. Commodity exports, such as energy and metals, represent more than 80% of total exports in Kazakhstan.

In the past ten years, however, Kazakhstan's economy has suffered from multiple crises, including falling global oil prices, the effects of the COVID-19 pandemic, and the war in Ukraine and its related sanctions – all revealing economic vulnerabilities, institutional inefficiencies, and the urgent need to accelerate economic diversification. The pandemic caused Kazakhstan's GDP to contract by 2% in 2020, with a particularly negative impact on small and medium-sized enterprises (SMEs) in sectors such as trade, tourism, and catering, which are estimated to employ around 1.6 million workers. At least 1.5 million citizens are estimated to have been on unpaid leave or have lost their jobs due to the outbreak of the pandemic. Inflation has been rising since, also putting further pressure on public finances.

Fears that the economic consequences of the war in Ukraine might derail the post COVID-19 recovery have not yet materialised for Kazakhstan. Growth in the first half of 2022 was supported by an important boost to consumption driven by public sector wage hikes, and a sharp increase in trade flows – particularly export commodities. The drastic increase in global commodity prices linked to the war in Ukraine in 2022 have allowed Kazakhstan to benefit from a strong economic and fiscal performance, with a current account surplus of 3.9% of GDP in 2022, and an annual increase of government revenues by 3.4 pp to 20.5% of GDP, of which 6.6 pp is attributable to oil revenues only (OECD, 2022[4]).

Kazakhstan is one of the world's largest producers of uranium, and enormous deposits of other metals, including gold, iron, chrome, copper, zinc and vanadium as well as rare earths. Kazakhstan also has the second-largest oil reserves and the second-largest oil production after Russia among the former Soviet republics. It counts China, Italy, Russia, the Netherlands, Uzbekistan, India, Türkiye, and France as its main export destinations. In the first half of 2022, crude oil exports rose by 85% in value, with 89% of this increase attributable to higher prices rather than increased volumes. Although, a reduction in Russian demand for mineral and energy exports is noticeable, especially for iron ores, gold, silver and rolled ferrous metals, Kazakhstan has been benefitting from increased oil exports to European countries (OECD,

2022[4]). The increase in the price of crude oil has thus cushioned a spill-over from Russia's economic collapse as of late 2023.

Table 1.1. Selected economic and social indicators for Kazakhstan (2018-22)

	2018	2019	2020	2021	2022
Output and labour market					
GDP, current prices (USD billion)	179.34	181.67	171.08	197.11	220.5
GDP per capita, current prices (in USD)	9 812.6	9 821.6	9 121.6	10 373.8	11 476.6
Real GDP growth (annual %)	4.1	4.5	-2.5	4.3	3.2
Inflation rate, average consumer prices (annual percentage change)	6	5.2	6.7	8.4	20.3*
Unemployment rate (as % of total labour force)	4.8	4.8	4.9	4.9	5.01
Central government debt (as % of GDP)	22	18.5	26.6	24.5	22.4
Current account balance (as % of GDP)	-1	-3.9	-6.4	-1.3	3.9
Social indicators					
Per capita GNI, PPP (in USD)	22 940	24 030	24 390	25 160	27 080
Poverty headcount ratio	4.3	4.3	5.3	5.2	n.d.

Note: n.d. stands for no data.
* Bureau of National Statistics dated 4 January 2023.
Source: World Bank (2023) except for poverty headcount ratio, https://www.statista.com/statistics/818364/poverty-headcount-ratio-in-kazakhstan/.

1.1.2. Government

Kazakhstan's political system is a Presidential republic, where the President serves as the head of state and is elected by popular vote for a non-renewable term of seven years. The Prime Minister is the head of government. The legislature is a bicameral parliament, consisting of the Mazhilis (lower house) of 107 members and the senate (upper house) of 49 members. The judicial system is independent, with the highest court being the Supreme Court of Kazakhstan. Other courts include regional and district courts. Kazakhstan has a multi-party system, but the ruling Amanat (formerly – Nur Otan) party has dominated the political scene since its formation in 1999 (Ministry of Justice, 2023[5]).

As a unitary state, the Constitution established the central government as the supreme authority with a Presidential system of government. This form of government vests executive power in the President, who, next to the Parliament, holds the sole right to act on behalf of the Kazakh people. In theory, this allows the President to terminate the powers of the government and to remove any of its members or ministers.

The Kazakh Constitution underwent a series of amendments since its enactment in 1993. Several of those changes sought to define the President's decision-making authority more explicitly. Legal provisions were introduced to require certain conditions and specificities to apply before changes delegated by the Presidential administration may be passed. For example, according to resolution No. 47/506 in June 2022, the President is now required to seek approval from local assemblies before appointing mayors and governors. The resolution also prohibits the President's affiliation with a political party during their Presidential tenure (Knox, 2008[6]).

In early January 2022, Kazakhstan experienced mass protests, due to fuel price increases, which escalated into violence. The events are widely reported to have triggered a significant shift of power away from the country's previous political elite. Economic, political, and social reforms have been enacted along with a referendum to approve constitutional changes aimed at limiting Presidential powers in favour of the parliament and significant decentralisation of certain powers.

1.1.3. Legal system

Today, Kazakhstan's legal system is based on a strict hierarchy of sources of law, subject to the supremacy of the Constitution. Upon Kazakhstan's independence in 1991, the Constitution laid out the fundament for Kazakhstan's transformation into a democratic and secular state. On the official website of the President of Kazakhstan, the system is described as that of a "social state".

The judicial system of Kazakhstan consists of the Supreme Court of Kazakhstan, local and other courts established pursuant to the Constitution of Kazakhstan and the constitutional law. It vests power in the Supreme Court as the ultimate judicial authority. Permanent judges and jurors are the only persons to assume the right to exercise judicial power by means of civil and criminal court proceedings, and as administered by the courts.

Article 3 of the Constitutional law "On Judicial System and Status of Judges" No. 132/2000 further describes the various local courts that exist next to the Supreme Court. The local courts include:

1. regional courts and courts equivalent to them (the city court of Astana, city courts of the cities of significance)
2. district courts and courts equivalent to them (a city court, inter district court)
3. other courts, including the specialised courts (martial, commercial, administrative, juvenile, and others) may be founded in the Republic of Kazakhstan, which are formed by the President of Kazakhstan to the status of the regional or district court
4. the court of the Astana International Financial Centre (AIFC), which is not part of the judicial system of Kazakhstan and has a special status.

The judicial system of Kazakhstan co-exists with that of the AIFC. The AIFC Court is an independent common law court which operates to resolve civil and commercial disputes in the AIFC. The AIFC is a regional centre for business and finance based in the capital and operates with the intent to connect the economies of Central Asia, the Caucasus, the Eurasian Economic Union (EAEU), Western China, Mongolia, the Middle East and Europe. As such, the AIFC deals with cases, including arbitration awards, mediation settlements and disputes, that tend to involve a non-Kazakh party.

The AIFC reports that in 97.7% of the total number of cases, at least one of the parties involved had business interest in Kazakhstan and agreed to use the AIFC Court and IAC on a voluntary basis. Kazakh law was applied in 97.5% of the cases, whereas AIFC law was applied in 2.3% of the cases. This suggests that most of the involved parties prefer to have their respective cases be dealt with in the AIFC independent court, rather than the courts of the Republic of Kazakhstan. Most types of commercial disputes concerned contracting (typically non-payment and non-fulfilment of other contract obligations) (43.8%), construction (15.8%), employment (15%), company (10.5%), transportation (6%), property (4%), logistics (3%), and PPPs (2%) (AIFC, 2023[7]).

1.1.4. Business and investment climate

As of January 2023, the stock of foreign direct investment (FDI) totalled USD 169.2 billion, the highest across Central Asia. Kazakhstan adheres to the OECD *Declaration on International Investment and Multinational Enterprises*, meaning it is committed to certain treaty standards, including National Treatment of investors. With the COVID-19 pandemic, Russian military actions against Ukraine, and the mass protests in January 2022, the government was incentivised to further assure investors by removing bureaucratic barriers to trade and investment, with streamlined regulations and tax incentives. The President also announced further privatisations, and the aim to reduce monopolies and oligopolies in the economy. In 2022, this ambition was reiterated through the new *Investment Policy Concept*, which outlined a headline target of increasing the inflow of FDI to USD 25.5 billion by 2026. An active dialogue with foreign investors through the President's *Foreign Investors Council* and the Prime Minister's *Council for Improvement of the Investment Climate* feed into the reform process (OECD, 2023[8]).

There remain challenges to doing business and investing in Kazakhstan. The country's legal framework can be complex or its implementation lacking, and as a result there have been concerns about corruption and lack of transparency in certain areas. Kazakhstan has a relatively open statutory framework for FDI, but regulatory barriers to investment remain. Investment and trade in services is still highly regulated, while key network sectors of the economy remain under state control. Additionally, the extent to which information on legal requirements is readily available to firms and the extent to which public institutions are transparent in their business-related decision-making remain unclear. Investors have thus noted issues including finalising contracts and licensing, uncertainty on legal issues relating to expropriation, ownership titles, and a controversial taxation of dividends for non-residents is in place (U.S. Department of State, 2022[9]) (OECD, 2023[8]). According to Transparency International's Corruption Perception Index (CPI), Kazakhstan ranked 124th out of 180 countries in 2021, indicating a relatively high level of perceived corruption in the country. Corruption in Kazakhstan has been reported in various sectors, including law enforcement, government procurement, and natural resource extraction industries. The lack of transparency and accountability in these areas has created an environment that make these sectors more vulnerable to corruption. Although the government has taken some steps to address corruption, including establishing anti-corruption agencies and implementing various laws and regulations to combat corrupt practices. However, there have been concerns about the effectiveness of these measures, as corruption continues to be a significant issue in the country (OECD, 2019[10]).

1.1.5. Capital markets

Kazakhstan's capital market includes two trading venues, Kazakhstan Stock Exchange (KASE) and Astana International Exchange (AIX). KASE is Kazakhstan's first and oldest stock market. Established in 1997, its opening was accompanied by new legislation and regulation in the trading of securities. Later, in 2017, AIX was created under the legal framework of the Astana International Financial Centre, essentially a special economic zone within the capital, which is based on English common law.[4] Law No. 461/2003 defines a "stock exchange" as a Joint Stock Company (JSC) with at least 25% of voting shares owned by the National Bank of Kazakhstan (NBK), which is wholly 100% state-owned. According to this provision, the law thus requires any legally recognised stock exchange to be partially state-owned. AIX hence qualifies as a "regulated securities market" rather than a stock exchange.

In contrast to AIX, KASE is regulated by Kazakhstan's Securities Market law. However, in some respects KASE's listing rules would appear to be less stringent than those of AIX. For example, KASE requires JSCs that aim to issue with KASE's main or alternative market to implement a Corporate Governance Code that was approved by the general meeting of shareholders. AIX's ongoing disclosure obligations require adherence to the corporate governance principles as set out in AIFC's market rules, a mandatory high-level requirement. The corporate governance principles detail a range of reporting items that an issuer must regularly report on.

While AIX's shareholders mostly consist of non-Kazakh companies and groups,[5] KASE's largest shareholder is the NBK, holding 47% of voting shares. The second largest stake in KASE is held by Moscow Exchange MICEX-RTS, with roughly 13% of voting shares. KASE is thus the only stock exchange recognised under Kazakh Securities Market law, meaning that AIX and KASE are responsible to differing authorised bodies for regulation. Market participants registered with the AIFC are overseen and regulated by the AIFC's independent regulator, the Astana Financial Services Authority (AFSA).

Next to the AIX, the AIFC hosts the AIX Central Securities Depository, which is the centre's clearing organisation, as well as an international court and arbitration centre. The centre's mission is to deliver a fair and transparent capital market environment that connects Kazakhstan's economy with international financial markets. In line with this, AIFC's Investment Tax Residency Programme (ITRP) offers a national long-term investment visa for Kazakhstan in exchange for investments in securities listed on AIX. Despite AIFC operating under its own legal framework, which grants independence to its courts system, several of the financial institutions established under the AIFC are held under the ownership of the National Bank of Kazakhstan. Unlike traditional financial institutions, the AIFC, and by extension, AIX, are overseen by the *Management Council*, which is chaired by the President of Kazakhstan. As the supreme governing body, the AIFC Management Council is responsible for setting the centre's key performance indicators, as well as monitoring its performance on the achievement of those.

KASE initially catered to foreign exchange and treasury instrument markets. Later, it expanded to also cover equity and corporate debt instruments (Akimov, 2008[11]). Today, the exchange can be divided into four trading markets: the "main" market, "alternative" market, "mixed" market, and "private placement" market. KASE categorises tradeable shares into a premium and standard tier part of the "main" market, where companies with a premium tier listing must abide to more stringent listing requirements. The "alternative" market follows a similar structure as the "main" market but is designed to help smaller companies to access capital. They both include shares and debt securities, with bank certificates and deposits only being traded on the "main" market. Markets require different baseline listing requirements, with additional criteria being detailed for each of the sub-sectors.

Despite various efforts to expand capital markets, access to capital remains conditioned to an erratic financial system. Kazakh banks, like those of many Central Asian economies, are exposed to a range of vulnerabilities with ambiguous effects on Kazakhstan's investment environment. Following liquidity issues in the advent of the COVID-19 pandemic, Kazakhstan underwent a range of regulatory relaxations for banks (Asian Development Bank, 2020[12]). Whilst in line with recommendations provided by prudential regulation standard setters recognising the severity of the economic downturn, this further resurfaced issues of longstanding, unrecognised credit losses and poor risk management. The set of capital and liquidity relief measures, while easing SMEs' and individuals' credit burden, increased the ratio of non-performing loans (NPLs) that already weakened capital buffers were forced to bear (OECD, 2022[4]).

Furthermore, a high reliance on foreign credit poses risks for Kazakhstan's governmental spending capacities. Kazakhstan issued its first sovereign bond in 1996, which continuously profited off favourable borrowing costs until the end of 2021. However, with increasing investor concerns about Central Asia's economic involvement with Russia (OECD, 2022[4]), annual bond yields for Kazakhstan jumped from 10.6% to 14.3% from February 2022 to February 2023 (Investing.com, 2022[13]). This increase in borrowing costs creates a hurdle to continue Kazakhstan's expansionary public spending trajectory. With promises to revise the 2023 budget to increase public spending by 3% of GDP to meet social demands arising from the war on Ukraine, Kazakhstan thus excavates a historical economic dependence on exporting fossil fuels, which afforded high revenues due to fuel price freezes introduced in January 2022 (IMF, 2022[14]).

1.2. Overview of Kazakhstan's state-owned sector

1.2.1. Number and type of state-owned enterprises

Kazakhstan lacks a clear classification of state-owned enterprises. In accordance with Article 201 of the Law on State Property[6] No. 413-IV/2011, public entities are required to register with the public state registry. The requirement however applies only to "legal entities with the participation of the state" while organisations in which there is no state share do not fall under the object of accounting.[7] OECD interviews revealed that the distinction is not always clear. Even when clear, entities that should register with the public state registry often fail to do so without repercussion, since enforcement is lacking.

According to the budget Code, the *quasi-state* or *quasi-public sector*[8] comprises state enterprises, LLCs, JSCs, as well as national management holdings, national holdings or national companies – the founder, participant or shareholder of which is the state – as well as subsidiaries, dependent and other legal entities affiliated with them in accordance with the legislative acts of Kazakhstan. The government and holding companies manage the state property on behalf of Kazakhstan, and local executive bodies manage the communal property on behalf of their administrative-territorial units.

In Kazakhstan, entities that would be characterised by the OECD as SOEs can take various legal forms. The most common ones are:

- Joint Stock Company (JSC) - a type of company that issues shares to raise funds to finance its activities.
    - Non-commercial JSC - non-profit organisations can adopt a joint-stock company structure, but with limitations: no preferred shares, dividends or convertible securities. Unlike regular companies, these non-profit organisations cannot transform into business partnerships or production co-operatives.
- Limited Liability Company (LLC)[9] – a company in the form of a partnership, such as a limited partnership or a general partnership established by one or more participants. The participants are not liable for obligations and bear the risk of losses associated with the activities of the partnership, to the extent of the value of their contributions.
- State enterprise – a commercial organisation endowed with property by the state with the right to manage it. This type of enterprise is further subdivided into two groups:
    - Enterprises with a portion of their revenues stemming from non-state sources titled as "state enterprises with economic management";
    - Enterprises fully reliant on state revenues titled "state enterprises with operating management".
- State institution is a legal form of a non-profit organisation created by the state that provides public services, socio-cultural or other functions of a non-commercial nature. They could be, if they generate most of their income by selling goods and services, considered as SOEs. These institutions are directly funded by the state and are not allowed to generate profits.
- With an aim to effectively manage state enterprises, the government assigned 22 state-owned joint-stock companies with additional management functions and assigned them specific titles as:
    - National management holdings, national holdings and national companies. National management holdings (2 JSCs)[10] which were established for the effective management of national development institutions, national companies and other legal entities. National holding[11] (1 JSC) was established for the effective management of national companies and other JSCs and LLCs. National companies[12] (19 JSCs) were established to operate in key national economy industries.

According to the Kazakh ministry of finance (MF) the quasi-state sector includes a high number of autonomous institutions:[13] 18 819 non-commercial bodies and 5 469 commercial enterprises (see Figure 2.2. in Chapter 2). This is subdivided into state (the funds of the state treasury, and property assigned to state legal entities, including enterprises of holdings or the so-called quasi-state sector) and communal (the funds of the local treasury and property assigned to communal legal entities) property.

It is important to note that, according to information obtained from the World Bank, not more than 5% of the 5 469 organisations are in fact commercial (thus officially titled SOEs), since more than 95% of them are non-commercial entities – with the majority of their revenue being the state budget, or their activities are related to the provision of public services. Thus, the majority of the 5 469 commercial enterprises – while they may or may not meet the OECD's definition of an SOE – are generally not covered by the SOE Guidelines. The SOE guidelines note an JSC or LLC should be considered as an SOE if the state is the ultimate owner. However, if these SOEs are largely non-commercial then the SOE Guidelines generally do not apply to them. This report thus acknowledges that most of the quasi-public entities at the level of the central government probably do qualify as SOEs, even as the current report disregards them. This report also notes that there is no rational behind the choice of legal form for SOEs.

The data from the MF as of March 2023 finds that the state, directly and via state-owned holding companies, holds 700 enterprises at the central level of government (see Figure 1.1). All 700 enterprises are classified as SOEs by the Kazakh MF. A broad definition is applied: in 139 of these enterprises, the state and its holding companies own 50% or less shares. 58 entities are registered as "non-commercial" JSCs. Thus, chapter 1 of this report applies a "broader" definition of a state-owned enterprise, more in line with that of Kazakhstan.

The first part of this review focuses its an"lytical"work on the following group of enterprises:

- State property: 320 enterprises that are comprised of 132 JSC, 29 limited liability companies, and 159 state enterprises. In 6 JSC and LLCs, the state owns 50% or less shares.
- State-owned holding companies (SOHC): 89 JSCs, 291 LLCs that are assigned to Samruk-Kazyna (178), Baiterek (12), Kazakhstan Engineering (17), social entrepreneurial corporations (96) and others (77). In 133 joint-stock companies and limited liability companies, the holding companies own 50% or less of shares.

The 23 615 entities that are communal property and officially non-commercial enterprises fall outside the scope of the report. Most large SOEs are within the portfolio of Samruk-Kazyna and Baiterek, which display better disclosure practices than those under the government. Part II of the report relies on the analysis of 20 SOEs selected across different ownership entities, in order to assess them on an individual basis. More information on the selection can be found in Annex A.

Figure 1.1. Kazakhstan's state-owned sector

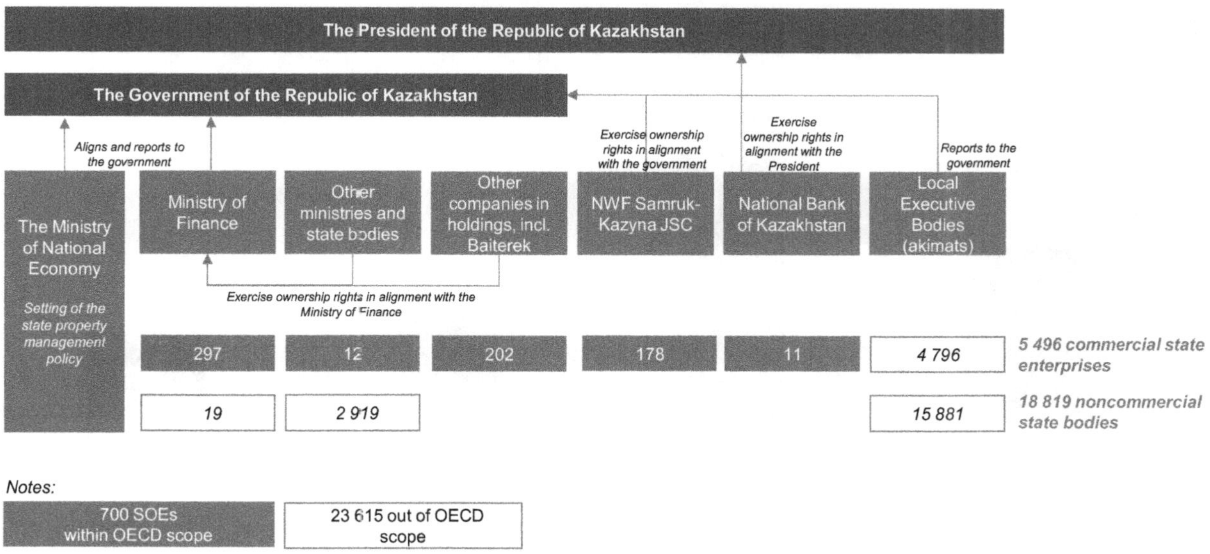

Note: Figure based on the law on State Property, the law on the Sovereign Wealth Fund (SWF) and National Bank of Kazakhstan.
Source: The Ministry of Finance data as of March 2023, analysis of the OECD team.

Key actors in the process of exercising ownership rights are the Ministry of National Economy (MNE) that defines the state property management policies and the MF, that exercise certain controls and supports other state bodies and holding companies to exercise their ownership rights. The legal provisions for the execution of ownership of fully incorporated SOEs are outlined in the Civil Code and State Property Law, while the JSC and LLP laws offer further, detailed indications of divisions of ownership. The more weakly incorporated state enterprises are governed by the law on State Property. SOHCs such as Samruk-Kazyna, as well as the NBK, are also subject to special laws that among other things establish their direct reporting lines to the government and the President.

The government also has a practice of establishing SOEs in corporate forms/holding companies (JSC, LLC) to fulfil the functions of ministries. These organisations do not perform economic activities and are mainly funded by public funds; with more than 90% of government revenues stemming from the state directly or through public procurement channels. This trend is possibly linked to the efforts to pay more attractive salaries and offer budget flexibility/independence.

1.2.2. Sectoral distribution of SOEs

Figure 1.2 shows the number of state and holding properties as of March 2023, noting that SOHC own only JSC and LLCs, while state property also has economic and operating management enterprises. LLC is the legal form most selected by the state and holdings. The Kazakh government makes the distinction provided below, noting that all SOEs in Figure 1.2 are officially under state control.[14] The only distinction which can be made lies in the direct oversight, where 'state property' is directly managed by ministries, while holding property is managed by the SOHCs. In many cases, property managed by holdings enjoy special privileges.

Figure 1.2. Kazakh SOEs by legal forms as of March 2023, number of enterprises

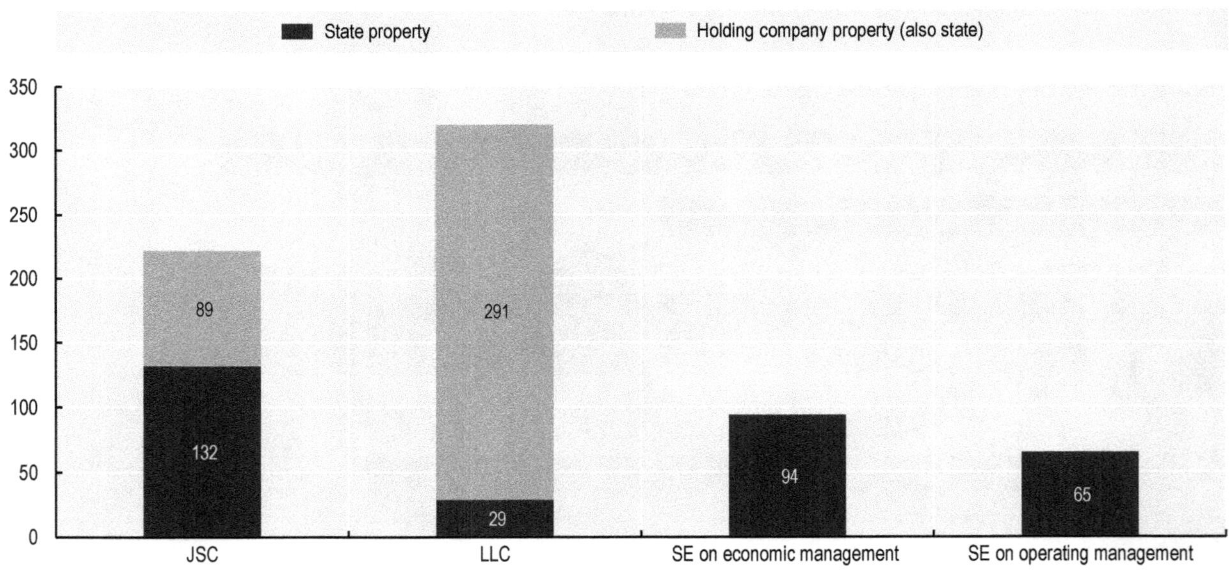

Source: The data from the MF as of March 2023.

Figure 1.2 indicates that state participation is largest within professional, scientific and technical services, education, mining and quarrying, art and recreations, and information and communications – cumulatively adding up to 55% of all SOEs.

1.2.3. SOEs share of the economy

In Kazakhstan, SOEs represent a large portion of the economy, as a legacy of its Soviet past. According to the selection of SOEs for this report 500 669 Kazakhs are employed in the state-owned sector, or 6.18% of the total dependent population – high in comparison to OECD countries, as noted in Figure 1.3. Moreover, the agency for the protection and development of competition in Kazakhstan finds that the participation of the state in entrepreneurial activity is expanding with new monopolies with state participation emerging.

Figure 1.3. Kazakhstan's SOEs' share of total dependent employment compared with other countries and OECD average

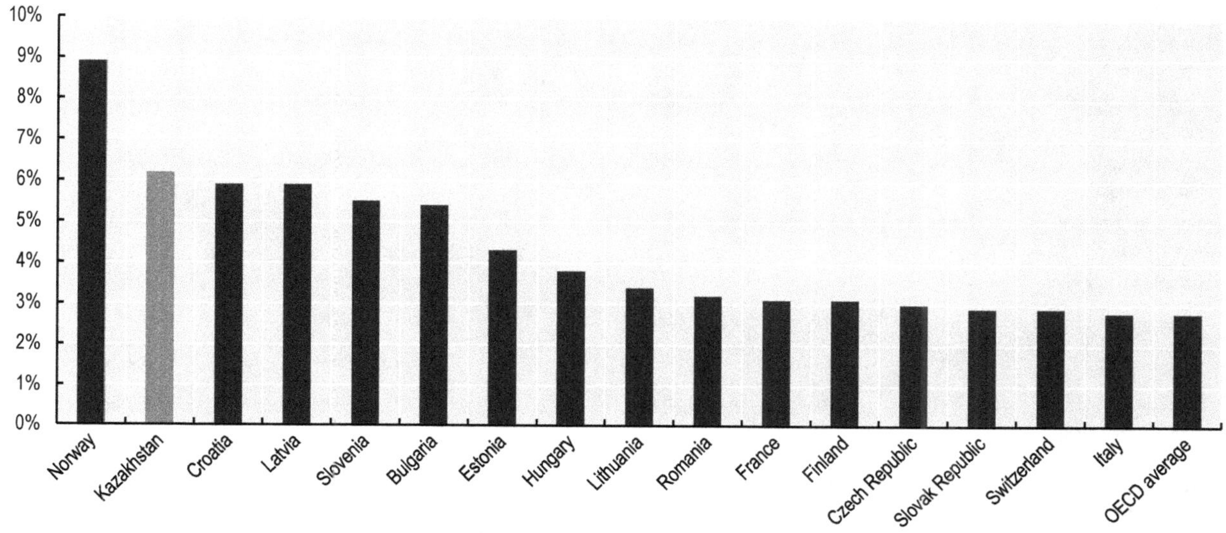

Source: Questionnaire responses from the Kazakh authorities; OECD Secretariat estimates based on data collected for (OECD, 2017[15]); ILOSTAT. Calculation of total dependent employment made based on assumption of 90% out of total employment.

The state is present in at least 20 out of 30 sectors of the economy, with education (51 518), health (20 635), professional, scientific and technical activities (40 142) dominating in terms of employee figures, compared to financial and insurance activities, education, and transport and warehousing in terms of total assets (see Table 1.2). Sectors including education, art, entertainment and recreations, information and communication, health and social services mostly function as state property enterprises, while SOHC enterprises are mostly concentrated on more commercially driven sectors, such as mining and quarrying, manufacturing, transport and warehousing, agriculture, and power and gas.

Table 1.2. Kazakhstan's state-owned sector by sector/number of enterprises and employees/total assets – excluding and including SOHC owned entities

Sector	Excluding SOHC-owned entities			SOHC-owned entities		
	No. of enterprises	No. of employees	Total assets, 2021, USD	No. of enterprises	No. of employees	Total assets, 2021, USD
Financial and insurance activities	15	1 655	36 640 742	14	48 462	35 501 723
Power, gas, steam and air conditioning	3	363	260 220	27	16 142	5 498 207
Health and social services	28	20 635	422 098	6	1 819	59 004
Agriculture, forestry and fisheries	7	1 856	8 317	28	1 597	136 481
Transport and warehousing	7	7 555	914 256	35	119 826	21 192 067
Manufacturing industry	4	1 318	158 531	39	38 171	9 021 685
Information and communication	28	11 980	493 874	19	27 736	2 406 051
Arts, entertainment, recreations	49	8 878	596 966	2	163	6 203
Mining and quarrying	2	13	1 131	58	37 651	10 921 286
Education	59	51 518	1 191 301	7	2 538	5.60
Others	43	31 004	5 175 024	59	13 809	31 939 509
Professional, scientific, technical activities	75	40 412	879 654	86	15 839	4 132 568
Total	**320**	**176 916**	**46 742 120.5**	**380**	**323 753**	**120 814 795**

Note: Data provided by the MF of Kazakhstan is non-consolidated. In addition, inconsistency of data could be detected: total assets seem lower than equity, and the unit measure is underestimated. When fact-checking the figures on the company websites, inconsistencies could be detected.
Source: The data from the MF as of March 2023.

Table 1.2 indicates that SOHC-owned enterprise participation in the economy is significantly larger in terms of employment and asset value than state-owned ones. The largest number of employees in state owned entities are in the sector of education, while under SOHC ownership the largest one is in the transport and warehousing sector.

According to the MNE,[15] in 2021, the volume of net income of SOEs amounted to Kazakh Tenge (KZT) 1 889.1 bn, and the volume of debt obligations at KZT 17 267.1 bn (USD 40 bn). The net income relies on a relatively small sample of profitable SOEs, whereas many other enterprises are consistent recipients of fiscal transfers. Dividends in 2022 were transferred to the budget in the amount of KZT 239.4 bn, which is 2 times more than the level of 2021. In total, the share of dividends paid and deductions from net income amounted to 12.7% of GDP.

1.2.4. SOEs listed in stock markets

Presently, the two trading venues of Kazakhstan, AIX and KASE, offer different incentives for companies to go public. AIX positions itself as a provider of access to equity capital, especially for Kazakh SMEs. In its role as an international financial centre, it seeks to increase the visibility of Kazakh businesses to international investors. In general, there is no clear minimum free-float requirement that companies are asked to maintain while being listed with AIX. Instead, companies are eligible for being enrolled in a simplified regulatory regime if their free-float market capitalisation does not exceed USD 200 million.[16]

Despite this, AIX has hosted the initial public offering (IPO) of one of the largest SOEs controlled by Kazakhstan's sovereign wealth fund Samruk-Kazyna, which is the national uranium trading company Kazatomprom. At the time of the IPO in 2018, Samruk-Kazyna sold an aggregate of 14.92% of Kazatomprom's issued share capital on the AIX and the London Stock Exchange (LSE). From 2018 to 2020, the free-float of Kazatomprom has climbed to a total of 25%.

In contrast to AIX, KASE is regulated by Kazakhstan's Securities Market law. This law warrants several exceptions regarding national SOHC:

- The law does not apply to national management holdings.
- A member of the Kazakh government applying to the position of CEO is not required to have the same amount of working experience as indicated in the law.

As detailed in his annual address of 2023, the President of Kazakhstan has proposed plans to unite the two stock exchanges of Kazakhstan under one management. The merger of AIX and KASE is envisioned to remove any duplicated functions the two stock exchanges may have, while noting that in certain circumstances, the two stock markets appear to compete. There is no concrete and timely roll-out proposed which details how the merger should ideally occur, and there are several issues that may arise and prolong the overall process.

Currently, a number of SOEs are listed with KASE. Amongst them are the Kazakhstan Housing Company, KazTransOil, Kcell, KazMunayGas, Kazakhtelecom, and KEGOC. As one of the largest companies listed on KASE, the national oil company KazMunayGas has issued 3% of its total shares on the market. Similarly, KEGOC, Kazakhstan's Electricity Grid Operator, currently administers a 10% free float on KASE. Kazakhtelecom, KazTransoil and Kcell showcase a higher free float on KASE, ranging from 10% to 20%.

Table 1.3. SOEs Listed on AIX or KASE

Company	Ownership structure			Listed on trading venues
	Shareholder	% of shares	Number of shares	
Kazatomprom	Samruk-Kazyna	75.00%	194 517 456	LSE, AIX, KASE
	Citibank, (nominal holder) (free float)	24.34%	63 118 392	
	Minority shareholders (free float)	0.66%	1 720 760	
KEGOC	Samruk-Kazyna	90.00%	234 000 001	KASE
	United Pension Fund JSC (free float)	7.25%	18 856 931	
	Minority shareholders (free float)	2.75%	7 143 068	
KazMunayGas[1]	Samruk-Kazyna	87.42%	533 395 161	AIX, KASE
	National Bank of Kazakhstan	9.00%	58 420 747	
	Minority shareholders (free float)	3.00%	18 303 585	
Kazakhtelecom	Samruk-Kazyna	79.24%	8 655 561	KASE
	First Heartland Jusan Bank JSC	9.00%	983 350	
	Banks	0.09%	10 235	
	Insurance companies	0.77%	84 165	
	Investment companies	2.86%	312 018	
	Nominal holders	0.82%	89 542	
	Other legal entities	3.64%	397 781	
	Treasury shares (buy back)	1.99%	216 852	
	Individual shareholders	1.59%	173 372	

Company	Ownership structure			Listed on trading venues
	Shareholder	% of shares	Number of shares	
KazTransOil	KazMunayGas	90.00%	346 172 040	KASE
	Individual shareholders (free float)	7.91%	30 405 531	
	United Pension Fund (free float)	2.04%	7 841 477	
	Market makers (free float)	0.05%	216 551	
Kcell	Kazakhtelecom	51.00%	102 000 000	KASE
	Essenov Galymzhan	14.87%	29 745 215	
	First Heartland Jusan Bank	9.08%	18 167 753	
	United Pension Fund (free float)	7.06%	14 116 287	
	Minority shareholders (free float)	17.99%	35 970 745	

Note: We cannot strictly know whether they are all free-float, since there could be a non-state strategic investor holding part of these shares.
1. Ownership structure does not take into account the acquisition of KazMunayGas shares by the National Fund.
Source: https://kase.kz/en/issuers, questionnaire responses from the Kazakh authorities.

Figure 1.4. Change of share prices/GDRs since companies participated in the privatisation programme, in percentage as of 2 October 2023

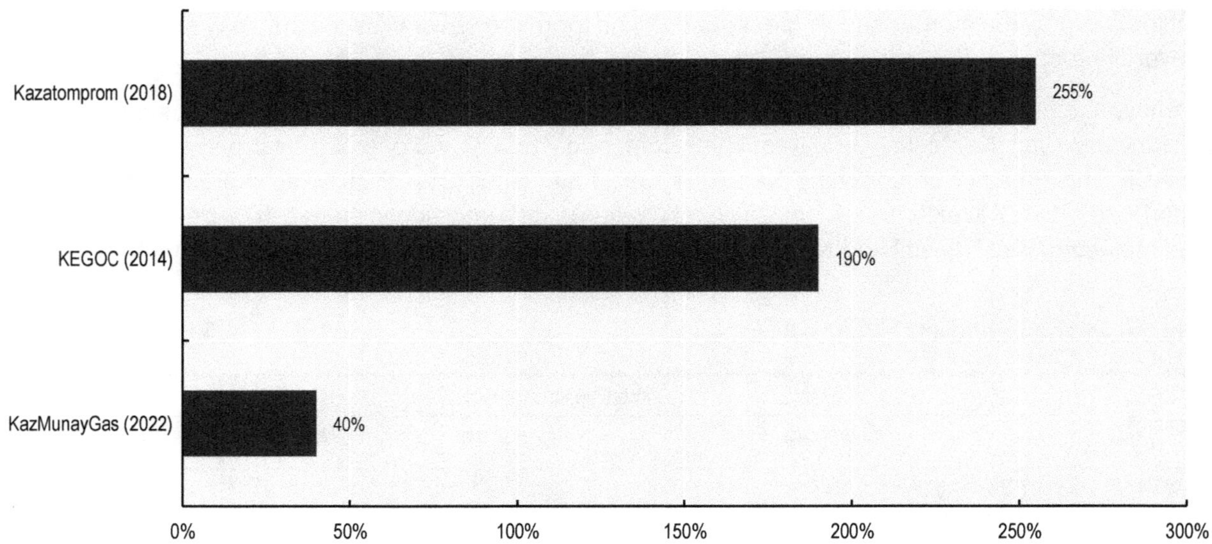

Note: the year of IPO is shown next to company titles.
Source: Company websites, KASE.

1.2.5. Operational performance of SOEs

In general, it remains difficult to assess the financial performance of SOEs given the size of the quasi-state sector. The government does not issue consolidated reports on the quasi-state sector that assess analytical information on the operational effectiveness of SOEs and benchmark them against the performance of private entities. However, due to their large stake in the Kazakh economy, the overall operational performance of the national (management) holdings Samruk-Kazyna and Baiterek are estimated to offer a good indication for the overall SOE sector performance.

Samruk-Kazyna is a major or sole shareholder of many of Kazakhstan's biggest and most important companies. The sovereign wealth fund's (SWF) revenues amounted to 14% of GDP in 2021, comparable to central government revenues (17.1%), and had accumulated a debt of 11.8% of GDP (IMF, 2022[14]). Its subsidiaries include KazMunayGas, Kazakhtelecom, the country's largest telecommunications company, and KEGOC, Kazakhstan's electricity grid operator. KazMunayGas is by far the most significant asset managed in Samruk-Kazyna's portfolio, constituting roughly 42% of Samruk-Kazyna's total assets,[17] based on financial information provided by KASE and Samruk-Kazyna's website. In contrast to this, other large portfolio firms from the same sector, such as Samruk-Energy, the national atomic company Kazatomprom, and KazTransOil, are contributing a substantially smaller part, from around 3% to 6% of the total assets managed under Samruk-Kazyna as per recent data provided by Kazakh authorities (KMGZ, 2023[16]; IMF, 2022[14]).

The sovereign wealth fund's overall operational performance is thus highly dependent on that of KazMunayGas. As detailed on the company's website,[18] 87% of its shares are owned by Samruk-Kazyna, while 10% are attributed to the NBK. Three percent of the shares are in free-float on the KASE and AIX stock exchanges (KMGZ, 2023[16]). KazMunayGas is Kazakhstan's national oil and gas company and transports more than half of Kazakhstan's oil, accounting for 80% of the country's refining capacity. According to Fitch ratings, the current credit rating as of June 2023 stands at BBB, thus denoting good credit quality with relative deviations in the probability of default towards the "speculative" rating tier.

The political and financial implications of a default of KazMunayGas are strong and impactful for Kazakhstan's economy and beyond. KazMunayGas is among the largest Kazakh borrowers in the Eurobond market, thus acting as a proxy issuer of national debt with increasingly complex international financial positions. Tensions in Russia pose an additional threat to the company's export capacities. Currently, the majority of Kazakh oil departs from the Russian port Novorossiysk, connected with Kazakhstan through the Caspian Pipeline Consortium. Said pipeline experienced temporary slowdowns for a month after Kazakhstan announced to balance the European energy market demand for oil and gas upon Russia halting its supply.

Figure 1.5 summarises financial information of portfolio companies of Samruk-Kazyna grouped into different segments as of 31 December of the respective financial year. It details the total profit or loss data derived from 2013-2022, net of tax, of their portfolio companies as grouped under segments of their operations, as reported in the consolidated financial statements of Samruk-Kazyna, largely represented by the "oil and gas" segment operational result. It illustrates the large relative share of equity derived from KazMunayGas in the SOE portfolio of Samruk-Kazyna, which follows a fluctuating trajectory across the examined timeframe.

Figure 1.5. Segment reporting of Samruk-Kazyna - Total net profit/(loss) for the year

In thousand KZT

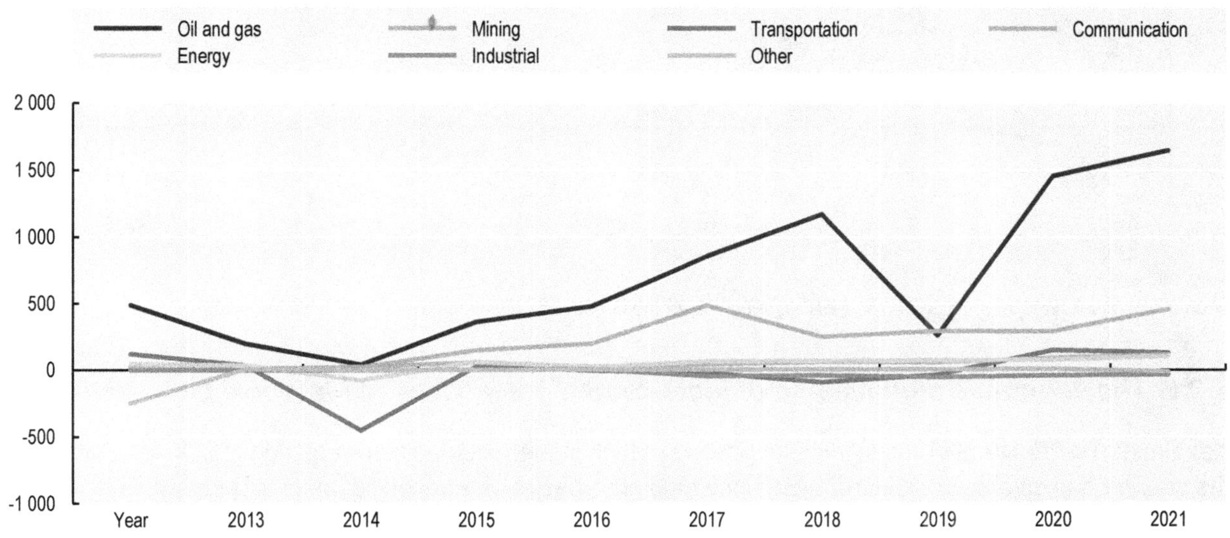

Note: monetary values are not adjusted for inflation.

Source: Unconsolidated information about operating segments of the Group without elimination of intragroup transactions.

After not meeting growth targets in line with Kazakhstan's 2050 Strategy *New Political Course of the Established State*, Samruk-Kazyna entered a transformation programme in 2014-2015. The purpose and aim of the programme are dispersed across two mandates, becoming a top-30 developed nation by 2050 and reforming portfolio companies to attract capital to modernise the domestic economy. On a macro level, the programme was designed to support Kazakhstan in becoming a top-30 developed nation by 2050. On a micro level, the programme sought to reform portfolio companies to attract capital to modernise the domestic economy (Dixon, 2020[17]). The programme is currently inactive, and it remains unclear whether the programme met performance targets and intended outcomes.

In 2021, Baiterek's revenues amounted to 0.13% of GDP, and its total debt to 9.8% of GDP (IMF, 2022[14]). The consolidated financial statements provided on the Baiterek website reflect the consolidated financial position of the Holding as of December 2021, as well as its consolidated financial results and cash flows in accordance with international financial reporting standards. The operational performance of subsidiaries is presented in the financial statements of each subsidiary.

The holding does not provide a breakdown of the different assets that contribute the segment reporting below. The overall profits and losses derived from SOEs under Baiterek's portfolio, appears to be volatile, with a rather large share of overall profits attributed to the "affordable housing" segment. The remaining segments, which are constituted from the portfolio companies under Baiterek's ownership, follow a slightly increasing, though increasingly volatile profit/loss trajectory from 2018 until 2022.

Figure 1.6. Segment reporting of Baiterek - Total net profit/(loss) for the year

In million KZT

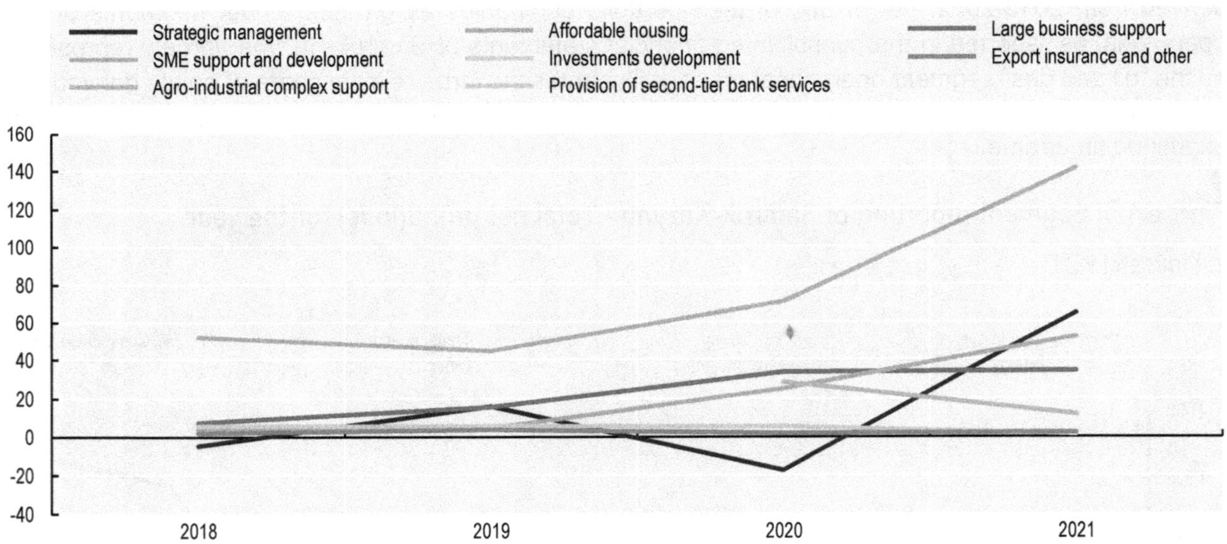

Note: monetary values are not adjusted for inflation.
Source: Unconsolidated information about operating segments of the Group without elimination of intragroup transactions

1.2.6. The economic significance of state-owned enterprises: a historical perspective

Kazakhstan's President holds significant powers, which influences decision-making for SOEs. Additionally, the country has diverse social structures, including clan-based or tribal affiliations that play a role in shaping societal dynamics. Kazakhstan's contemporary SOE landscape evolved from a period of post-Soviet reform and state building. In the early to late 1990s, Kazakhstan embraced a set of pro-market reforms to distance itself from the Soviet central planning model that had priorly formed its economic systems (Dixon, 2020[17]). Initial efforts to distribute ownership through coupon privatisation were unsuccessful, with less than 70% of coupons being redeemed by the Kazakh people, and investment funds absorbing 10% of all property (Narziev, 2021[18]). On top of this, Kazakhstan faced an indebted oil and gas industry and faced difficulties to attract foreign investment. Overall, the top-down restructuring process was stunted by lacking state capacities, which left the real economy unstimulated.

The importance placed on attracting investment during later stages of the privatisation programme effectively changed Kazakhstan's course of development to one of what has been termed 'state financialisation'[19] (Dixon, 2020[17]). While experiencing slow economic growth, financialisation gave way for the foundation of large holding companies of state shares in national companies. Collectives which started as industrial groupings in extractive sectors and banking, developed into state-led strategic investment funds (OECD, 2017[19]).

In parallel to efforts to liberalise markets, Kazakhstan was exposed to pronounced Presidential powers affecting economic policy and decision-making (Pomfret, 2012[20]). Combining the increased power of the state with the new ownership models in the extractive sectors gave way for innovative forms of managing development finance. Kazakhstan's sovereign wealth fund, Samruk-Kazyna, was created by Presidential decree No. 669 in 2008. The majority of SOEs today are managed as part of a portfolio under large holding companies, with Samruk-Kazyna being the most significant one.

Holding companies centralise ownership, making it easier to delegate, co-ordinate and monitor interactions between the state ownership entity and portfolio companies (OECD, 2020[21]). Centralised ownership should establish a clear command chain, which should organise the modes of communication between the government entity down to individual SOEs in a transparent manner. However, centralisation within holding companies entails a risk of cross-subsidisation within the holding structure, between loss and profit making enterprises. Normally a loss-making SOE in Kazakhstan has to consult with the Ministry of Finance, but the mission team was not provided with sound evidence that this is done consistently in practice. It is thus theoretically possible, within a group like Samruk-Kazyna, to conduct a loss-coverage operation using the earnings of (dividends from) profitable group companies such as KazMunayGas.

Furthermore, centralised ownership requires strong public sector governance and SOE accountability. These factors call for a high level of state capacity as well as a clear separation of mandates between that of the state and the corporate SOE. As per the reforms announced in President Tokayev's state of the nation address in 2022 and 2023, Kazakhstan is still amid the process of developing the necessary groundwork to successfully implement centralised ownership.

1.3. Legal and regulatory environment in Kazakhstan

1.3.1. Main laws and administrative regulations concerning the corporate sector

Kazakhstan has a comprehensive legal framework for the regulation of companies, their business activities and interaction with the government, including the entrepreneurial Code, the law on national security, the anti-corruption law, the law on the security market, the criminal Code of Kazakhstan, and the law on rehabilitation and bankruptcy. These company laws are applicable to the entirety of Kazakhstan's private sector, nearly always including clauses for state-owned enterprises. Compliance with the laws and regulations is monitored by various state bodies, including the agency for civil service and anti-corruption, the General Prosecutor's Office, and the courts.

It should be noted that, according to information obtained by the OECD team, safeguards to avoid legal and regulatory overlaps, duplications and inconsistencies are generally not strongly developed. Consequently, there is a multitude of regulatory documents, laws, decrees from a number of entities and rules dedicated to both the public and private sectors that in many cases renders compliance and monitoring difficult. Numerous laws thus apply to SOEs depending on their form, be it the Entrepreneurial Code, State Property Law or, depending on the legal form, the JSC and LLP law.

The **Entrepreneurial Code** No. 375-V LRK/2015, which was amended close to 100 times since then, defines (Ministry of Justice, 2015[22]):

- the legal, economic and social conditions to ensure the freedom of entrepreneurship in Kazakhstan, and thereby defines the rights and obligations of entrepreneurs and companies, sets out the requirements for their registration and operation; and
- regulates government support for entrepreneurship, including investment, tax preferences and investment subsidies.

Article 192 of the Code also refers to the state-owned sector, by providing the rationale for state participation in the economy. It outlines that the competition protection and development agency has to consent with the establishment of a legal entity with more than 50% of shares/stakes. Important to note is that the competition agency's consent is not required if the entity will operate outside the country. The Code also mentions the list of activities carried out by state enterprises with 50% and more shares/stakes, which is approved by a government decree. The consent of the competition agency is also essential when expanding or altering the scope of activities of an pre-existing entity with more than 50% of shares or stakes owned by the state.

The **law on National Security** No. 527-IV/2012 (1) defines the list of strategic objects transferred to the authorised capital and (or) owned by national holdings and companies, as well as legal entities/individuals not affiliated with the state; (2) defines which actions are a threat to national security (Ministry of Justice, 2012[23]).

The **Anticorruption law** No. 410-IV LRK/2015 provides the framework to combat corruption and implement the anti-corruption policy in Kazakhstan and establishes the principle of transparency in the management of state assets. The law provides for an external and internal evaluation of corruption risks, and requests state bodies and SOEs to develop anticorruption standards in line with the standard procedure defined by the anticorruption agency. SOEs are obliged to establish an anticorruption compliance service in the form of a structural unit or responsible person (free from conflict of interest), that operates independently from the executive body and is accountable to the BOD/other independent management body (Ministry of Justice, 2015[24]).

The **law on Security Market** No. 461/2003 was adopted in 2003 and amended 92 times since. The law regulates the process of issuing, placing, circulating and redeeming emissive securities and other financial instruments. It further determines the procedure for regulating, controlling, and supervising the securities market to ensure a safe, open and effective functioning of the securities market, in order to protect the rights of investors and holders of securities (Ministry of Justice, 2012[23]).

The **law on Rehabilitation and Bankruptcy** No. 167 V/2014 regulates relations when a debtor fails to fully satisfy the claims of creditors, and explains the process for debt restructuring, rehabilitation, and liquidation procedures. The law also refers to state enterprises, by noting that in case entities classified as strategic objects face bankruptcy, the state has the right to establish special conditions and procedures to sell the property, or acquire it through one of the national companies (Ministry of Justice, 2014[25]).

1.3.2. Legal and regulatory framework as applied to state-owned enterprises

In most cases SOEs operate in a similar legal framework as private companies. However, every legislative regulation and law contains special provisions that grant specific conditions or exceptions related to the type of state enterprise. The legal and regulatory framework applicable to SOEs is further split between: 1) laws; 2) government decrees; and 3) responsible ministry decrees, administrative regulations and guidelines and internal regulatory documents approved by the governing bodies of the entity. Each layer represents different level of details and descriptions of provisions/processes, the ministry decree and internal regulatory documents being the most detailed.

The key legal framework for SOEs is provided by the law on State Property that covers important aspects of state property ownership and management, from creation of the entity until its liquidation. In parallel, Samruk-Kazyna, the NBK and the Development Bank of Kazakhstan (DBK) have separate laws that covers similar aspects and regulate their operations.

The law on State Property

The **law on State Property** was adopted in 2011 and has been amended 126 times since. The law is the main SOE ownership policy of Kazakhstan, noting the state's rights and obligations regarding the management of state property and the transfer of ownership. It provides the legal framework and basis for state property management, including property assigned/owned by the state, the legal grounds for acquiring and terminating rights to state property. It aims to ensure the effective exercise of the ownership function. The provisions of the law are also applicable to Samruk-Kazyna and its group of assets, unless otherwise stated in the law dedicated to Samruk-Kazyna.

The law defines state property as property that belongs to the state or is under state jurisdiction, including natural resources, land, buildings, equipment, and other assets. The law sets out the rules for the transfer of state property to private ownership, the use of state property by individuals and legal entities, and the protection of state property from illegal use or disposal. It also establishes procedures for the valuation, registration, and inventory of state property, and notes the rights and responsibilities of state authorities and officials involved in state property management. It provides for the creation of state property registers, which contain information on the location, status, and use of state property. Notably, Kazakhstan's 'state enterprises' derive their legal personality exclusively from this law.

The law on Joint Stock Companies

The **law on Joint Stock Companies** No. 415/2003 is the primary legislation to regulate the legal status, creation, operation, reorganisation and liquidation of JSCs, including companies listed on stock markets. The law was amended 76 times and covers the rights and obligations of shareholders; the management of the company; and the procedure for election and responsibility of its officials. The provisions of the law are also applicable to Samruk-Kazyna (Ministry of Justice, 2003[26]). The JSC law is complemented by two further regulatory documents, including the memorandum of association and the charter, which covers key norms, rights and obligations of founders, the list of possible activities, authorised capital requirements, and the process of creating corporate bodies of JSCs.

According to the law, JSCs are managed by 1) the supreme body: the general meeting of shareholders (in a company, all voting shares of which belong to one shareholder – the sole shareholder); 2) the management body: the BOD; and (3) the executive body: a collegial body or a person solely performing the functions of an executive body (determined by the charter). It further allows for state officials to participate in governing bodies of any JSC for which state ownership is at least 10%. The law also notes that state bodies cannot act as founders or shareholders of the company, with the exception of the government represented by the state property committee of the MF, local executive bodies, as well as the NBK. The company is obliged to disclose financial statements online (Ministry of Justice, 2003[26]).

The law on Limited Liability Companies

The **law on Partnerships with Limited and Additional Liability** No. 220-1/1998 notes the management of LLCs,[20] and the rights of participants, liabilities and obligations (Ministry of Justice, 1998[27]).

LLCs are managed by 1) the supreme body of the partnership: the general meeting of its participants (general meeting); and 2) the executive body of the partnership: collegiate and (or) sole. The exclusive competence of the general meeting of participants is to approve/amend the company charter, appoint the executive body, elect members of the supervisory board, approve the financial statements and profit distribution, and reorganise/liquidate the LLC and others. Any participant in an LLC has the right to make proposals on the agenda of the general meeting.

Members of the executive body are elected by the general meeting for a fixed term, but not more than five years and they may not be a participant of the LLC. The responsibilities of the executive body encompass all issues of the partnership that are not within the competence of the general meeting or supervisory bodies. To exercise control over the activities of the executive body, LLCs may establish a supervisory board, with members elected for not more than five years.

Budget Code

The **Budget Code** No. 95-IV/2008 regulates budgetary relations and establishes the basis for the National Fund of Kazakhstan. The description of the exact annual budget approval process is presented in Chapter 1.4 of this report. The Budget Code describes the role of participants, the process of budget development and its approval. The state budget is approved by the law (Ministry of Justice, 2008[28]). The Budget Code provides further guidelines on the budgetary procedures, fiscal policies and financial management practices in Kazakhstan. Regarding the state-owned sector in particular, the budget Code typically contains provisions related to the financial management of SOEs, including aspects such as:

- Budgeting and Reporting: The Budget Code specifies how SOEs should prepare their budgets and financial reports, and outlines the procedures for SOEs to submit their budgets to the government for approval and how they should report their financial performance;
- State Subsidies and Transfers: It includes provisions related to government subsidies, transfers, or financial support provided to SOEs, covering the criteria for receiving subsidies, the process for allocating funds and the reporting requirements associated with these transfers;
- Profit Distribution: The Code addresses how SOEs should manage their profits and surpluses, including guidelines on reinvesting profits, distributing dividends to the government and using funds for specific purposes;
- Debt Management: The Budget Code outlines rules for SOEs regarding borrowing and debt management, by specifying limits on debt levels, conditions for taking on debt and reporting requirements related to debt; and
- Financial Oversight: Provisions related to financial oversight and accountability may also be included, which involves auditing and reporting mechanisms to ensure transparency and accountability in SOE financial operations.

Dedicated laws for state-owned banks

The **law on the National Bank of Kazakhstan** No. 2155/1995 regulates the activities of the National Bank of Kazakhstan, its legal status, goals, functions, areas of responsibilities, authority structure, composition and appointment process of members of the BOD and executive body, and the co-ordination with other state bodies and enterprises. NBK develops a strategic plan for a 5-year period, that is approved by the Chairman of NBK in agreement with the President. Staff headcount, the annual report, appointment of the Chairman and deputy Chairman is approved by the President, while the Chairman appointment also requires consent from the senate of the parliament. NBK is independent in its activities, as the state representative and executive bodies are not entitled to interfere in the activities of NBK. At the same time, NBK co-ordinates its activities with the government and holds regular consultations (Ministry of Justice, 2017[29]).

The **law on the Development Bank of Kazakhstan** No. 178/2001 adopted in 2001 regulates the objectives, goals, functions, activities, and accountability of the DBK and its relationship with other state bodies and enterprises. DBK is a national development institution authorised to implement the state investment policy and industrial development policies. DBK finances investment projects for five years. The DBK is the operator of government programmes, including the development of the manufacturing industry. Within the framework of such state programmes and national projects, DBK provides concessional financing for large (capital-intensive) manufacturing projects by mixing state funds with other funds raised in the capital market.

Other SOE related laws and regulations

The **law on State Procurement** No. 434-V/2015 regulates the procurement of goods, works, and services necessary to ensure the functioning of SOEs, except national management holdings/companies and legal entities affiliated with them, and the NBK. It sets out procedures for conducting procurement, defines the roles and responsibilities of procurement participants, and establishes anticorruption measures, such as the prohibition of the conflict of interest and the requirement for transparency (Ministry of Justice, 2015[30]). Procurement in the SOE sector is also governed by the Law on Procurement of Individual Entities of the SOE sector No. 47-VII/ 2021.

The **law on Public Service** No. 88-V/2013 regulates the public service and the management and administration of SOEs (Ministry of Justice, 2013[31]). It establishes the principles of transparency, accountability, and integrity in the public service, and sets out measures to prevent corruption. The state corporation "Government for Citizens" is a legal entity in the form of a non-profit JSC in order to provide public services via a one-stop-shop, and if possible, electronically. The sole shareholder of the state corporation is the government. The register of public services is approved by the decree of the minister of digital development, innovation and aerospace industry of Kazakhstan and consists of 1 323 public services conducted by different state entities (Ministry of Justice, 2020[32]).

The **law on State Monitoring of Property in Sectors of the Economy of Strategic Importance** No. 490/2003 regulates state monitoring (observation, collection and analysis of information) of property in sectors of the economy of strategic importance. The sectors of the economy of strategic importance are mining and processing of fuel and energy minerals (coal, oil, gas, uranium and metal ores), mechanical engineering, space activities, agro-industrial complex, water management, chemical industry, transport and communications, electricity generation and transmission, military-industrial products' production. The list of property subject to state monitoring is approved by the government decree and consists of 133 entities. The results of the state monitoring contain proposals and recommendations, including on the legality and expediency of exercising the rights of ownership/use/disposal of strategic objects and measures on improvement of efficiency of economy sectors (Ministry of Justice, 2003[33]).

The **Rules for the Assessment of Corporate Governance in State-Controlled JSCs** No. 247/2011 note that the assessment of corporate governance should be based on the OECD SOE Guidelines. The results should define the level of shareholder intervention within company governance systems and provide recommendations for improvements. These rules do not apply to Samruk-Kazyna, since the Fund has its own Code with alternate corporate governance rules.

The **state planning system of Kazakhstan** No. 790/2017 regulates the system of state planning, defines principles, processes and participants of state planning and refers to activities of SOEs. The documents of the state planning system include: 1) development strategy of Kazakhstan until 2050; 2) National priorities (with 1-2 measurable indicators); 3) national development plan (with strategic indicators) and national security strategy of Kazakhstan; 4) plan for territorial development of the country; 5) the concept of industry development; and 6) development plans of state bodies, regions, cities of republican significance, the capital, national management holdings, national holdings/companies (Ministry of Justice, 2017[29]).

The **procedure of appointing officials by the government and the Prime Minister of Kazakhstan** No. 784/2002 defines 1) the list of positions of political civil servants and other officials; 2) the rules of appointment; and 3) the list of 41 national management holdings, national holdings/companies, non-profit

JSCs, development institutions, state organisations of higher/postgraduate education and other organisations, the CEO of which is appointed by the government and the Prime Minister of Kazakhstan.

Kazakhstan's Codes

Based on Article 182 of the law on State Property, **the Model Corporate Governance Code** is developed by the MNE and approved by a Minister's Decree. JSCs with 50% state ownership are subject to the Code. Every SOE is obliged to develop their own Code, and have no permission to change/delete anything, but have the liberty to add provisions. There are no sanctions noted neither within the State Property law, nor the model Corporate Governance Code. Compliance with the Codes does not seem to be controlled, although the MNE can randomly send a request to an SOE and assess their Code.

The MNE is currently amending the Code, which was firstly proposed in 2015. In 2018 it became compulsory for all JSC to have a Code in line with the model Corporate Governance Code. This Code does not apply to Samruk-Kazyna, as Samruk-Kazyna has its own Code, which it updated in July 2023 and applied in all subsidiaries and companies within its group where Samruk-Kazyna owns more than 50% of shares. The key elements of the Code are:

1. the segregation of functions of a shareholder and a regulator (state function) to prevent conflict of interest
2. state-shareholder ensures full operational independence and eliminates interference in operations and investment decisions
3. co-operation between the state body and SOEs is carried out through the BOD (shareholders note KPIs, SOEs create development plans thereon)
4. provisions to protect the rights of all shareholders, including minorities
5. annual self-assessment and an independent assessment of the BOD and its committees every 3 years.

1.4. Ownership arrangements and responsibilities

1.4.1. Ownership arrangements and co-ordination

Ownership policy and framework

In practice, the ownership arrangements for SOEs in Kazakhstan are largely dispersed, with individual ministries simultaneously exercising state ownership and regulatory functions over respective SOEs. To this date, the government of Kazakhstan has not developed a comprehensive and high-level state ownership policy. However, there are elements of what typically constitutes an ownership policy within Kazakhstan's legal framework on state property management, which consists of four main legislative instruments (OECD, 2015[34]).

The overall objectives and motivations behind state ownership are set out in the concept of State Property Management and Privatisation in Kazakhstan (hereafter the 'Concept'), created on 21 July 2000 by decree No. 1095, as well as the law on State Property, which explains the rights and obligations of the state on administering state property and the transferral of ownership. Art. 192 of the civil Code recognises state property as communal property, which may be held at the local government and self-governance levels. Further, article 192 of the entrepreneurial Code provides several rationales for state participation in entrepreneurial activities of the economy:

1. national security, the defense capability of the state or society interests protection;
2. use and maintenance of strategic facilities under state ownership;

3. state monopoly;
4. the absence or low level of competition in the relevant product market;
5. the state can participate in entrepreneurial activities through SOEs that have already been established (OECD, 2015[34]).

A property of the state, such as a JSC and stakes of LLC, may be owned by legal state entities on various forms of regional and district levels, or may retain ownership based on self-governance. Ownership of state property may shift between various state entities, or between state entities and non-state entities. Ownership may be changed by decision of the local executive bodies and moved across the various level of local government. While the State Property law details the legal conditions of changes of ownership, the execution of it remains to be managed across the various state entities involved. Kazakhstan's key legal SOE ownership instrument is thus laying out terms of assigning ownership dispersed across various levels and authorities, rather than providing clear rationales or principles for the management and oversight of ownership.

State authorities defining and exercising state ownership

Several Kazakh state authorities are currently tasked with the management of state property under the delegated authority of the government. They are tasked with enforcing policy on effective state property management, the publishing of regulatory legal acts, as well as the exercising the right to state property. Next to these main responsibilities, the government is also charged with taking decisions regarding the organisation, creation, encumbrance, and privatisation of state property and thus also SOEs. In addition to the government, the NBK, Samruk-Kazyna, Baiterek, other national management holding companies and national holdings as well as local authorities hold stakes in managing ownership.

The main governmental bodies exercising state ownership rights, in particular over SOEs that take the legal form of JSC, are the MNE and the MF. They possess special rights in the ownership function that distinguishes them from other governmental actors. As the main penholder of the drafting of legislative documents and policies surrounding SOEs, the MNE holds responsibilities that impact the ways in which other line ministries practice their ownership. The MF mainly monitors and implements changes in the legal text which influence SOEs and the management of such. In addition to the MNE and MF, line ministries oversee SOEs with sectoral relevance.

Table 1.4 details responsible line ministries, their SOEs' main activities, as well as the co-ordinating ministries that practice legal ownership over them. The table shows that the MF has legal ownership over the bulk of SOEs (297). However, they tend to delegate their ownership to other entities through specific decrees and rules.

While companies with state ownership are typically held under the MF and defined in their ownership rights in the law on JSC, specific decrees regulate reporting lines with both the government and the President for Samruk-Kazyna and the NBK. In combination with the delegation of ownership tasks from the MF to line ministries, ownership challenges may occur, particularly if SOEs gain in relevance through their activities. In practice, as far as the mission team has been able to establish, the ownership arrangements work as follows: Provided that a given SOE operates within the framework of the relevant laws, regulations and government policies, and is not unduly loss making, the ownership powers reside largely with the line ministry in charge of the section in which the SOE operates. The influence of the two economic ministries is noticeably greater in the case of SOEs in operational or financial difficulties.

Table 1.4. The number of SOEs by line and ownership ministries and main activities

Responsible line ministry	Main activities	No. of enterprises	Legal ownership
Ministry of Culture and Sport	Film/video/television production, producing, concert/theatre halls, museums, sport activities, university, high school/technical secondary education, building construction, financial services	57	Ministry of Finance 54, Ministry of Culture and Sport 3
Ministry of Science and Higher Education	Universities, ancillary educational and other services, market/public opinion research, research institute	47	Ministry of Finance
Ministry of Healthcare	Hospitals, post-graduate education, social insurance, scientific research, pharmacy, financial leasing	32	Ministry of Finance
Ministry of Ecology Geology and Natural Resources	Collection/treatment/distribution of water, data hosting and processing, botanical gardens/zoos/nature reserves, research and development, forestry, marine aquaculture	20	Ministry of Finance 19, Ministry of EGNR 1
Ministry of Industry and Infrastructural Development	Data hosting/processing, production of non-ferrous metals, free-economic zone operating, engineering surveys, technical advice, road construction, air and water transport services	19	Ministry of Finance
The President Office	Hospitals, film/video/television production, recreation and entertainment, preschool (pre-primary) education, real estate management, professional/scientific/technical activities, building construction, air passenger and land transport	15	Ministry of Finance 10, the President Office 5
Ministry of Education and Science	Secondary education, university, research and development in natural sciences/engineering/social sciences/humanities, other financial services	13	Ministry of Finance
Ministry of Information and Public Development	Creation/broadcasting television programmes, development and research institutes, real estate management	12	Ministry of Finance
Ministry of Finance	Holding company activities, financial services, mining and quarrying, data hosting and processing, repair/maintenance of aircraft/spacecraft, retail sales, hotel, power generation	12	Ministry of Finance
Ministry of Digital Development, Innovation and Aerospace Industry	Facilities of the Baikonur complex, aerospace activities, satellite telecommunications, computer equipment management, IT consulting services, data hosting and processing, research and development, government public services, transport space system	12	Ministry of Finance
National Bank of Kazakhstan	Central bank activities, collection agencies and credit bureaus, banking service bureau, minting/coins and medals, printing services, payment and financial technologies centre, monetary intermediation, damage insurance	11	National Bank
Others		70	Ministry of Finance 67 Others 3
	Total	**320**	**Ministry of Finance 297** **National Bank 11** **Others 12**

Source: The data from the MF as of March 2023

The government of Kazakhstan and its ministerial bodies

Per the legal text laid out in the legal framework on ownership policy, Kazakhstan's government takes on the highest authority in managing ownership over its SOEs. There are two main branches of the government through which ownership is defined and exercised. First, the MNE's Department of State Assets Management Policy wields influence over SOE's public policy objectives. Second, the MF (in particular, its State Property and Privatisation Committee) is charged with the task of privatising centrally held state property, as well as monitoring KPIs of SOE privatisation (OECD, 2021[35]). However, in practice, Samruk-Kazyna, for which the Kazakh government is the sole shareholder, is the de-facto owner of a large portfolio of partially and wholly-owned SOEs. Similarly, wholly-owned holding company Baiterek oversees companies grouped under the financial sector and is thus practicing a de-facto ownership layer in the state's ownership sphere.

According to the law on State Property the competence of state bodies regarding the management of state property is allocated as follows:

- The government 1) executes a policy and defines regulations for effective state property management; 2) as a sole shareholder makes decisions on the creation/privatisation/reorganisation/liquidation of legal entities, national management holdings, national holdings/companies, and JSCs/LLPs; 3) makes decisions on granting/refusing permission to sell/transfer strategic objects/monopolies; 4) executes the shareholder right to manage SOHCs, JSCs/LLPs; 5) defines limits for general and administrative expenses of SOHCs and Samruk-Kazyna; and 6) makes decisions/grants the right on equity participation and exercises the shareholder rights in legal entities registered at the AIFC.
- The line ministry of the relevant industry 1) carries out the state policy/regulatory frameworks on state property management in the relevant industry; 2) defines the priority area of activities and scope to be financed by the budget for state and communal property state enterprises, determines purpose/goals of activities and approves charters for state institutions; 3) monitors/analyses development plans of national management holdings, national holdings/companies, state enterprises/JSCs/LLPs; 4) manages the state property enterprises, approves their development plans/annual financial statements, establishes prices for their services, approves plans for state budget financing, makes decisions on reorganisation/liquidation in agreement with the MF, and appoints representatives and ensures the inclusion of MF representatives on the BODs of JSCs/LLPs; and 5) prepares the decision for the government to exercise priority rights to acquire a strategic object and approves the decision on the transfer of state property enterprise and strategic objects.

Ministry of National Economy

The MNE's main function lies in synergising strategic planning, tax, and budget related policies. It makes suggestions on legislative frameworks irrespective of ownership (despite ownership being held by Akimats or at the national level, the MNE will be responsible for both). It fulfils a central function in the conjunction between the state-owned and private sectors. As the provider of state guaranteed debt, it has direct influence over corporate lending to the SOE sector. Furthermore, as the main contractor for public-private partnerships, it oversees the delineation of tasks on public and private objectives.

According to the law on State Property, the MNE 1) defines the state policy/regulatory framework on state property management, carries out the assessment of state property management; and 2) and in co-ordination with other state bodies develops regulatory frameworks for SOEs and approves the model Corporate Governance Codes for JSCs (except for Samruk-Kazyna). Besides a broad description of the respective ministerial functions, none of the main governmental conduits of ownership publicise clear ownership tasks with respect to the national SOEs they supervise. Efforts to separate mandates of management and ownership thus remain unseen.

Ministry of Finance (Committee of State Property and Privatisation)

Next to managing the republican state budget, the MF and in particular its Committee of State Property and Privatisation is responsible for exercising control functions over state property. According to the law on State Property, the Committee 1) develops and approves regulatory frameworks, as well as controls, monitors and organises state property management; 2) privatises state property; 3) exercises ownership rights, makes decisions on transfer/rent on state property, and shareholder rights in managing JSCs, and appoints representatives to the BOD of JSCs/LLPs; 4) defines the purpose/goals of activities, type of state enterprise, permits on reorganisation/liquidation/sale of state enterprise; 5) ensures timeliness and completeness of dividend payments from state enterprises under state ownership; 6) carries out monitoring of property in sectors of the economy of strategic importance; 7) develops rules and maintains a register of state property; and 8) based on the government decision acts as a founder of JSCs/LLPs as well as state enterprises.

The National Bank of Kazakhstan

The NBK is a state body and the central bank of Kazakhstan. Within Kazakhstan's dual banking system, the NBK represents the top level. It is governed by the Constitution and the law On National Bank of the Republic of Kazakhstan, No. 2155/1995, which establish it with the task to carry out monetary policy of the state while being accountable to the President. NBK acts on behalf of the interests of Kazakhstan in upkeeping relations with central banks and banks of other countries, as well as other financial and credit organisations.

The NBK exercises SOE ownership on behalf of the state through holding voting shares in various companies. As part of the competences of the NBK laid out in Art. 12 of the law on State Property, it issues and co-ordinates legal acts on the state property that has been allocated to it. The Bank is further tasked with:

1. issuing regulatory documents, managing the property, deciding on creation/privatisation/reorganisation/liquidation of entities under its ownership
2. defining rules, monitoring the execution of development plans of subsidiaries
3. and regulating and approving prices for services and distributes the net income of state entities of the group.

There is no centralised store of information which details the companies that the NBK oversees or possesses shares in. However, most notably, it holds 9.58% of shares of the national oil and gas giant KazMunayGas, 68.84% of the central securities depository, which acts as the depository of the NBK, and is the sole shareholder of national JSC investment corporation of the NBK. The latter is a financial entity that functions similar to a commercial investment fund. It diversifies Kazakhstan's international reserves in alternative asset class investments, such as private equity, real estate, and hedge funds.

1.4.2. Description of Kazakh holding companies

The following section outlines the two largest holding companies in Kazakhstan, while noting that there are other national management holding companies and national holdings with sectorial focuses.

Samruk-Kazyna

Samruk-Kazyna, whilst officially referred to as a sovereign wealth fund, is effectively Kazakhstan's largest state-owned holding company, operates under the mission, in addition to achieving adequate financial returns, to fund social welfare and to modernise the Kazakh economy. It was created through the merger of Samruk, a holding company owned by the state, and Kazyna, a national development fund. The companies managed in Samruk-Kazyna's portfolio are predominantly part of the utilities sector, though also provide a range of essential goods and services relating to transport, logistics, and telecommunications. Currently, it manages USD 69 billion in assets and oversees close to 282 companies across six layers, making it a vital – but likewise highly complex – component of the Kazakh economy.

Samruk-Kazyna has its own law, namely the Sovereign Wealth Fund (SWF) law No. 550-IV/2012 which regulates the legal status, activities, goals, functions, and describes the procedure for interaction between Samruk-Kazyna (legal entities of the group) and the state bodies. The law notes the Fund's corporate governance mechanisms, and outlines the role of Samruk-Kazyna in implementing socially significant and industrial-innovative projects. Samruk-Kazyna's shares are the exclusive property of the state and are not subject to alienation. The provisions of the State Property and JSCs laws shall apply to SK and its group unless otherwise provided in the law. According to the World Bank, the SWF law and its policies, standards, rules and regulations apply to all SK companies (at least the controlled ones), with most of these policies and practices being in line with good international practice.

The interaction between the government and Samruk-Kazyna is based on the agreement approved by a government decree from 2012 (Ministry of Justice, 2012[36]). The agreement is based on 1) exercising the sole shareholder rights through the BOD; 2) non-interference of the government and state bodies within the operational activities of Samruk-Kazyna and providing full operational independence to Samruk-Kazyna; and 3) accountability and transparency of Samruk-Kazyna through regular reports to the BOD and reviewing monitoring reports (the government can review company results only at BOD meetings). All decisions on implementation and financing by Samruk-Kazyna of socially significant, industrial-innovative investment projects are taken by the BOD.

By decision of the sole shareholder, SK annually allocates at least 7% of its net income to a non-profit organisation represented by the public fund "Kazakhstan Khalkyna". It is prohibited for the state body representatives to sit at SK companies' BOD. Some of the competencies of the general shareholder meeting of the SK companies can be assigned to their BOD, correspondently some of the competence of the BOD can be assigned to the management boards. The list of assets to be included within the privatisation list is defined by the government, while the privatisation process is approved by the BOD. The smaller assets are then sold to MF on an electronic platform, while large assets are privatised and conducted an IPO by Samruk-Kazyna.

Figure 1.7. Samruk-Kazyna's ownership structure

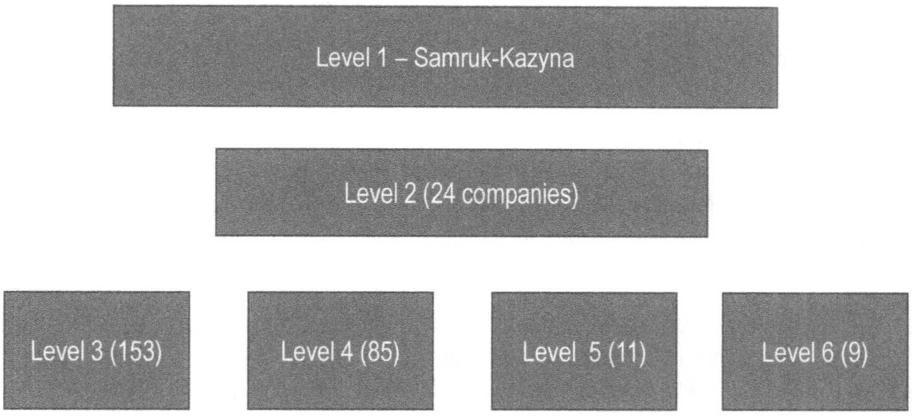

Source: data provided by Samruk-Kazyna as of 01.09.2023.

According to the SWF law, the objectives of Samruk-Kazyna are to 1) increase competitiveness and market value of group assets; 2) ensure best corporate governance practice; 3) stimulate innovative processes and technologies; 4) attract investments; and 5) implement strategic investment projects of national, intersectoral and regional scale.

The corporate governance structure consists of four layers: 1) the supreme body: the sole shareholder, the government of Kazakhstan (the shares owned by the MF); 2) supervisory council previously chaired by the First President of Kazakhstan; 3) corporate board, supported by board committees; and 4) and the executive management. According to the MNE, the government is planning on removing the management council, which was previously chaired by Nursultan Nazarbayev, the former first President of Kazakhstan. This report notes that the supervisory council is removed by the law No 40-VIII/2023 that takes effect from the 1 January 2024.

The exclusive competences of the sole shareholder are to 1) approve documents, such as the charter, annual financial statements, development plans, the Corporate Governance Code; 2) reorganise/liquidate shares of Samruk-Kazyna companies; 3) define the terms/election/termination for the BOD and its Chair/members, including remuneration for INEDs; 4) approve of dividend policy and payments; and 5) decide on financing projects on behalf of the President.

All interaction of state bodies with the SWF and its companies is regulated by legislation, and any additional reporting to state bodies that goes beyond legal requirements is limited by the list, format and process of information supply to state bodies approved by a government decree. This is different to other SOHC and can render communication complicated.

National holding company Baiterek

Baiterek is Kazakhstan's second holding company with the special legal status of being wholly owned by the state. It has a close relationship with the state by being tasked with the funding of economic and institutional development in Kazakhstan, with total assets of USD 28. Upon its establishment based on a Presidential decree No. 571/2013, Baiterek's portfolio encompassed development finance institution such as (temporarily at least) Bereke Bank, the national housing construction savings bank, as well as the "Damu" entrepreneurship development fund. Baiterek positions itself as the operator of all repayable financial support measures through its subsidiaries, particularly in sectors such as business development, agriculture and construction. The aim hereby is helping the country reduce its dependence on traditional sectors like oil and gas and develop a more diverse and sustainable economy. Baiterek works closely with the government to implement economic and industrial policies effectively and thereby often acts as an intermediary between the government and private sector entities.

In the most recent Presidential state of the nation address, the President announced the need for Baiterek to further transform and digitalise. The aim is further to develop AI and big data opportunities and to integrate with the databases of other state agencies.

In March 2021, "KazAgro" JSC was reorganised through a merger with "Baiterek" Holding. As a result, "Agrarian Credit Corporation" JSC and "KazAgroFinance" JSC became subsidiaries of "Baiterek" JSC. In July 2022, "KazAgroFinance" JSC became a subsidiary of "Agricultural Credit Corporation" JSC, which makes Baiterek its indirect shareholder. "Agricultural Credit Corporation" JSC provides credit financing for the agricultural sector, and "KazAgroFinance" JSC provides leasing of agricultural equipment. The companies are tasked to support the agricultural sector of Kazakhstan.

Through managing companies that provide lending instruments, Baiterek, and thus the state, has carved out its position in providing financing solutions to a variety of creditors. Baiterek practices its ownership by means of approving the key performance indicators (KPIs) of its portfolio companies. While monitoring such KPIs lies in the BOD of the various portfolio companies, representatives of Baiterek sit on the boards of all of its 8 subsidiaries (on the first level).

Figure 1.8. Baiterek's ownership structure

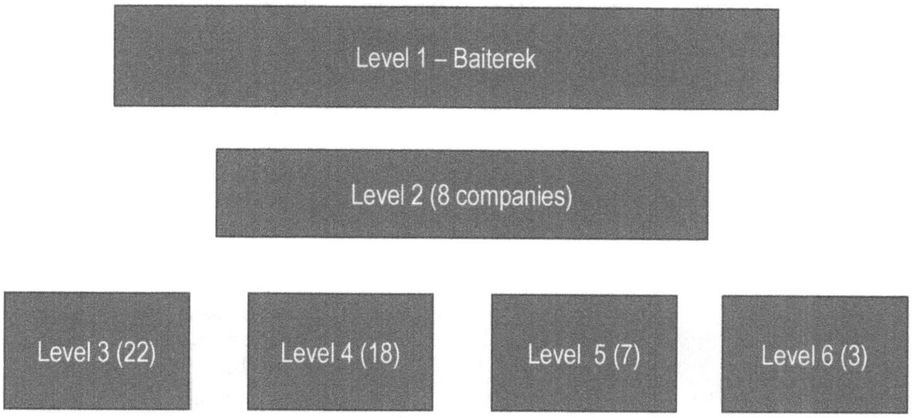

Source: data provided by Baiterek as of 1 July 2023.

Over the course of the past three years, Baiterek has significantly reduced its portfolio from 14 subsidiaries in 2019, to eight subsidiaries in 2022. Overall, however Baiterek reduced its level one subsidiaries, but in total on 5 levels Baiterek still oversees 58 entities.

1.4.3. Boards of directors of SOEs

Structure and composition of SOE boards

Boards in LLCs and state enterprises

In LLCs the composition of a supervisory board is not obligatory, but a number of them still decide to put one in place, as indicated by the selection of LLCs monitored for this report. At the same time, it is impossible to assess how many LLCs have boards, and no government entity monitors this. State enterprises on the other hand are not covered by the model Corporate Governance Code – thus not obliging the composition of a board. However, there are some exceptions for cases when state enterprises are operated in the healthcare and education sectors. Creation of a state enterprise with the supervisory board is approved by the government decree.[21] Usually, state enterprises merely have a head appointed by the ownership entity.

Boards in Joint Stock Companies

In the governance of JSCs, a two-tier board system is employed except where provided otherwise in the corporate bylaws, including a BOD and an executive body (often in practice referred to 'management board'). The Chief Executive Officer (CEO) (often referred to as the Chairman) presides over the executive body and (s)he is the only executive director permitted to serve on the BOD. This is unusual by the standards of OECD countries where executive representation is normally seen only in one-tier corporate boards, and to some extent it runs counter to the "supervisory" role normally associated with a supervisory board. The BOD is responsible for the overall management and supervision of the company, while the executive board is responsible for the day-to-day operations and strategy implementation.

The general guidelines for the composition of SOE boards in JSC are outlined in the law on State Property, the Corporate Governance Code and a number of complementary rules. Article 181 in the law on State Property mandates that SOE boards include representatives of the MNE, MF, the line ministry of the relevant industry and other state bodies.

Table 1.5. Boards across SOE types

Legal form	BOD/supervisory board appointment	Maximum Term	Minimum number	Representation	Board composition
LLC	By general meeting	5 years	No	• Civil servants/ politicians eligible to serve on the board without remuneration • Partners and their representatives are eligible to serve as board members	• Establishment of supervisory board is not obligatory • Representative of the line ministry • Representative of MF • Not permissible for a person to hold a position in the LLC's executive body and serve as a member of the Supervisory Board
JSC	Candidates nominated by the shareholders Appointed and removed by general shareholders meeting or sole shareholder decision	Individuals elected to the JSC's BOD can be renewed without any limitation, the term is set by the general shareholders meeting. Recommended term 3 years and can be renewed for another 3 years. After 6 years special consideration needed. The overall term should not exceed 9 years.	3 members[1]	Civil servants and politicians are eligible to serve on the board without remuneration	• Representative of the line ministry • Representative of MF • 30%-50% of independent directors • Not less than 30% of women recommended by the model Corporate Governance Code • CEO of the SOE • In addition to the above for SOHC: o Representative of the MNE o Representatives of other state bodies by the government decision
Samruk-Kazyna subsidiaries	For 100% owned subsidiaries SK selects and nominates the candidates in collaboration with the SK's BOD, and subsidiary's BOD and remuneration committee Chairs, and appointed by SK For subsidiaries where other shareholders exist candidates nominated by the shareholders and appointed by the general shareholders meeting	Recommended term 3 years and can be renewed for another 3 years. After 6 years special consideration needed. The overall term should not exceed 9 years, in exceptional cases it can exceed 9 years.	7 members	Members of the government and other civil servants are restricted from serving on the BOD (some exceptions noted in SWF)	• Holding representatives • 30%-50% of independent directors • Not less than 30% of women recommended by the Samruk-Kazyna Corporate Governance Code
State Enterprises with supervisory boards	Candidates selected by the Nomination Committee created by the line ministry Appointed and removed by the line ministry	3 years	5 members	Civil servants are eligible to serve on the board without remuneration	• 30% of independent directors • Representative of the Healthcare and Education ministry • Employees of the state enterprise cannot sit on the board

Note: According to the State Property law and the criteria for state-owned enterprises on the right of economic management, state enterprises may establish a BOD, if they operate in the healthcare sector and education sector and fulfil specific criteria, such as number of employees/turnover, etc. More details can be found here https://adilet.zan.kz/rus/docs/V1500010507.

1. Irrespective of whether the company is listed or not, as stated in the JSC law (article 54 item 5), it is required to have a board of directors with a minimum of three members.

Source: JSC law, LLC law, the State Property law, the model Corporate Governance Code, the law on sovereign wealth fund, the Corporate Governance Code of Samruk-Kazyna.

The general meeting of shareholders decides on the size and composition of the BOD. The number of members of BOD must be at least three people, with at least 1/3 being independent directors (INEDs). The model Corporate Governance Code recommends for the number of women to be at least 30% of the total number of members of the BOD, although this figure is at 17% currently. On average, SOE boards consist of six-seven members.

Samruk-Kazyna, Baiterek and their subsidiary companies

This report notes that in line with the SOE Guidelines, Samruk-Kazyna and Baiterek are agencies executing state ownership rights. Their boards are generally not subject to the recommendations, which may explain a larger politicisation of the boards of these (and other) holding companies in Kazakhstan. Baiterek's BOD for instance consists of a number of government officials headed by the Chairman, the Prime Minister of Kazakhstan. Other ministerial members of the BOD are the first deputy Prime Minister, the minister of industry and infrastructure development, the minister of finance, and the minister of national economy. The three independent board members are German, French, and US citizens respectively and possess a range of private sector and public sector experiences. Samruk- Kazyna has the same Chairman, alongside the First Deputy Head of the Presidential Administration, the minister of national economy, and a number of independent directors.

The boards of the subsidiaries of holding companies have different compositions however: If the company is a subsidiary of a holding company, the holding is also represented. For instance, the board of KEGOC (under the SK umbrella) consists of seven members, three of which are independent, three stemming from Samruk-Kazyna, and one CEO. KazAgroFinance's (under Baiterek's umbrella) board is made up of two representatives of Baiterek, three independent directors, the Deputy Chairman of Agrarian Credit Corporation (ACC), plus one CEO.

Eligibility criteria

Article 77 in the State Property law notes that in the selection of candidates the following shall be taken into account: 1) work experience in managerial positions; 2) work experience as a member of the BOD; 3) work experience; 4) education, specialty, including the availability of international certificates; 5) availability of competencies in areas and industries (industries may vary depending on the portfolio of assets); 6) business reputation; 7) the existence of a direct or potential conflict of interest.

However, the lack of transparency and accountability in the selection and appointment of board members has possibly affected board compositions. The process is often opaque, and board members may be appointed based on political connections rather than merit or qualifications. Board members may have business or personal ties to the SOE, which could influence their decision-making and lead to decisions that are not in the best interests of the company or the state.

Board nomination/appointment procedures

Kazakhstan's selection process for board members of JSCs is governed by various laws and regulations, including the law on State Property, the model Corporate Governance Code and, in the case of Samruk-Kazyna its own Corporate Governance Code. The selection process is supposed to involve a nomination committee, which is responsible for identifying and evaluating candidates based on the criteria outlined within the law. Every ministry has its own corporate governance department which shall compile a list of candidates, based on the competence criteria needed for board candidates. The state property committee, as per Article 117 of the law on State Property, receives these lists.

In theory, the State Property law notes that line ministries propose candidates, which are agreed upon by the MF. However, there is no comprehensive document that describes the process how the line ministries shortlist candidates or select them, and based on which criteria the MF agrees with candidates. In articles

68 and 75 of the Corporate Governance Code of Samruk-Kazyna, it is noted the subsidiary board members are nominated by the Fund together with the Chairs of the BOD and the remuneration committee. Baiterek does not specify in its Code how BOD members of its subsidiaries are nominated.

According to the MNE, the human resources and remuneration committee determines the criteria for selecting candidates for members of the BOD, candidates for top managers, develops the Company's policy in the field of remuneration of these persons, and regularly evaluates the activities of members of the board and top managers. The functions of the committee include issues of appointment (election), setting motivational KPIs, performance evaluation, remuneration and succession planning for the head and members of the board.

According to the State Property law, the line ministry of the relevant industry proposes and appoints representatives to the BOD and ensures the inclusion of a MF representative to the BOD of JSCs/LLPs. Representatives of the state property and privatisation committee of the MF are elected based on the committee's management recommendation.

In subsidiaries of holding companies, board members are nominated and/or approved by the holding company. According to the law on State Property, each member of the BOD is elected for a term of up to three years, and the terms of office of the head and members of the board coincide with the term of office of the board. The term of office of the BOD is established by the general meeting of shareholders, and members elected to the board may be re-elected an unlimited number of times, unless otherwise provided by the company charter.

The Chairman of the BOD is elected from among its members by a majority vote of the total number of members of the BOD by secret ballot, unless otherwise provided by the charter of the company. This is unique in the sense that in other countries usually the Chair is usually appointed by the annual general meeting.

The model Corporate Governance Code recommends that the same person not be elected to the BOD of all SOEs for more than nine consecutive years. In exceptional cases, reappointment beyond nine years is allowed, in which case the election takes place annually or at another time determined by the general meeting of shareholders (sole shareholder) of the company, with a detailed explanation of the need to elect this member of the BOD and the influence of this factor to independent decision-making.

The law on JCS specifies that members of the BOD are elected through cumulative voting ballots. The cumulative voting ballot must contain the list of candidates for members of the BOD, the number of votes held by a shareholder, and the number of votes cast by a shareholder for a candidate to the BOD. Shareholders may not enter the voting options "against" and "abstained" into the ballot for cumulative voting. In keeping with normal corporate practices concerning cumulative voting shareholders have the right to cast votes on the shares they own in full for one candidate or distribute them among several candidates for members of the BOD. Candidates with the largest number of votes are considered elected. The minimum threshold to nominate candidates as board members is 5% or more.

1.4.4. Financial oversight in the SOE sector

Budget approval process

The Budget Code No. 95-IV/2008 is the main legal document governing the budget process across all levels of government, including functions such as, public procurement, state audit and financial control, which are subject to separate laws (Ministry of Justice, 2008[28]).

The President determines priorities for Kazakhstan's development in an annual address, and these priorities are taken into account when the republican budget is being prepared. MNE is the central body in the government for state planning, that co-ordinates strategic and economic planning, elaborates budgetary policy, and implements state policy on regional development. MNE also has the responsibility to produce the forecast of social and economic development (FSED). MF is the central body for budget planning, budget execution, accounting, budget reporting and, within its competence, local budgets, and the national fund. MF prepares the draft budget and submits it to the republican budget commission (RBC).

The RBC is chaired by the Prime Minister, who appoints its members, including the first deputy Prime Minister and deputy Prime Minister, ministers, the Chairman of NBK, etc. After consideration in the RBC, the annual law on the Republican Budget No. 163-VII ZRK/2022 is submitted to parliament no later than 1 September, which in turn can approve or amend it. The republican budget goes through separate sequential discussions in the Majilis and the Senate and is to be approved by 1 December. At the same time the annual budget, financial statements and audit reports are scrutinised by the committee on finance and budget and by sectoral committees of the parliament. Corporatised SOEs (JSC and LLC) get their annual budgets and 5-year action plans approved by their boards in December each year.

The authorised body for internal state audit is an agency of the MF that exercises its realising and controlling functions in the sphere of internal state audit and financial control, state purchases, state property, audit activities, accounting and financial reporting. It also reviews the reasons for violations of legislation on the performance of the republican and local budgets and performs control over the execution of decisions that follow from control activities.

Reporting and disclosure requirements

According to the law on Accounting and Financial Reporting No. 234/2007 and the IFRS adoption roadmap for Kazakhstan, all listed companies, including listed SOEs are required to prepare and disclose their financial statements in accordance with International Financial Reporting Standards (IFRS) starting from 1 January 2022. The financial statements must be audited by an independent auditor and then approved by the BOD before they are presented to the general meeting of shareholders. This requirement applies to all SOEs that are listed on the KASE or any other foreign stock exchanges. Samruk-Kazyna companies mostly fulfil these obligations as well.

Law No. 234/2007 further requires that:

- all SOEs follow financial reporting standards approved by the International Financial Reporting Standards Board
- large business entities and public interest organisations prepare financial statements in accordance with international standards
- organisations of public interest[22] prepare financial statements in accordance with international standards.

The government has developed a dedicated digital management reporting system that obliges SOEs (as stated in law 234/2007) to upload regular financial and other reports, apart from the accounting in the register of state property intended for registration and information purposes. The financial reporting depository an electronic database contains annual financial statements and audit reports submitted annually by organisations, lists of affiliated persons of joint-stock companies, as well as information on corporate events of joint-stock companies, with open access to users.

According to the requirements of depository of financial statements, companies have to submit non-financial information as well, which some do. Compliance with the requirements for submission of non-financial information can however be low at times.

Internal and external audit

The law on State Audit and Financial Control No. 392-IV ZRK/2015 regulates and defines the powers and activities of state audit and financial control bodies. The purpose of the state audit is to improve the management and use of budgetary funds, state assets and quasi-state sector. The document describes three types of state audit 1) audit of financial statements; 2) performance audit; and 3) compliance audit. The non-execution of the state audit instructions can lead to administrative offences. On an annual basis, the supreme audit chamber submits a report to parliament on the execution of republican budget and submits reports on activities of the supreme audit chamber to the President and parliament (Ministry of Justice, 2015[37]).

In Kazakhstan, the auditing of SOEs involves several entities. The supreme audit chamber is responsible for conducting external audits of SOEs, compared to the internal audit units of SOEs which report their findings to the management and the audit committees of the SOEs. The supreme audit chamber is the supreme authority of state audit and financial control, executing external audit and financial control over the execution of the republican budget, assessing and verifying the effective and lawful management of national resources. It is directly subordinate and accountable to the President. Finally, the government, through its relevant ministries and agencies, has oversight and regulatory functions over SOEs, including their financial management and reporting.

External Audit

The external audit is generally conducted by an independent auditor, who is appointed by the general meeting of shareholders. The external auditor is responsible for expressing an opinion on the accuracy and completeness of the enterprise's financial statements, and for reporting on any material weaknesses in the enterprise's internal control system. It is also expected that external auditors maintain their independence; however, it is unclear who is responsible for evaluating this independence. Additionally, there are no mandatory requirements for auditors to rotate, and according to the law on Auditing, it is forbidden to provide non-auditing services otherwise the license will be withdrawn. Disclosure of these matters is inadequate. The law regulates related party transactions and conflicts of interest, but its implementation and enforcement are not well-defined. Presently, there seems to be no comprehensive whistleblowing legislation in place. Although there is a lack of comprehensive legislation – holdings and major subsidiaries have in practice established whistleblowing policies.

There are audits conducted for specific purposes pertaining to SOEs or publicly funded enterprises that have received funding from the state budget. These entities are required to submit a report detailing their expenditure, which necessitates entering into a contractual agreement with a financial company and undergoing a specialised type of audit conducted by one of the four major auditing firms.

1.4.5. Competition law and authority

The entrepreneurial Code covers anti-monopoly provisions, and requests a preliminary review by the antimonopoly authority of the market entities' agreement, the right of the antimonopoly authority to send a "notice" rather than conduct an investigation, and the possibility for a company that is subject to an antitrust investigation to launch a review by a conciliatory commission on antitrust compliance.

The 2022 fifth antimonopoly package, notes the:

1. equal access of all business entities to state support measures and procurement;
2. reduction of administrative and economic barriers to enter commodity markets; and
3. price regulation tools.

It also ensures the implementation of the Presidential Decree No. 484/2020 which notes "the active promotion of competition" as a national task.

The agency for protection and development of competition in Kazakhstan - established in 2020 - reports directly to the President, and receives its budget from the MF. Its primary mission is to promote and protect competition within Kazakhstan's economy. It further:

- monitors the behaviour of SOEs and investigates any complaints of anti-competitive behaviour
- ensures that the share of the state is not increasing, by annually proposing which companies to liquidate/privatise
- has a responsibility to ensure that SOEs do not abuse their dominant positions in the market or engage in anti-competitive behaviour that may harm consumers or other market participants
- works with SOEs to resolve any anti-competitive issues that are identified
- has the authority to impose penalties and take other enforcement action if necessary
- provides guidance and assistance to SOEs on competition laws and policies.

The agency also puts in place regular moratoria for establishing new state entities. We observe that as soon as the moratoria have run out, new entities are established. In 2022, the agency issued 508 notifications on the violation of competition of SOEs, up from 430 in 2021.

The agency is further responsible for carrying out an assessment of the country's competitive environment in markets where SOEs operate and update the list of activities carried out by SOEs. The agency is authorised to make recommendations related to shrinking the state participation in the economy, however they may face limitations. For instance, in 2022 the agency recommended to include in the privatisation list 105 assets, out of which only 60 were included for discussion at commission level and 21 assets finally included within the privatisation list.

1. Sectoral regulators

Some of the key sectoral regulators in Kazakhstan include:

- The National Bank of Kazakhstan is responsible for regulating the financial sector, including banks, insurance companies, and financial markets.
- The Ministry of Energy oversees the energy sector, including electricity generation, transmission, and distribution.
- The Ministry of Digital Development, Innovation, and Aerospace Industry oversees the telecommunications sector and is responsible for regulating telecommunications operators, internet service providers, and other technology-related businesses.
- The Ministry of Industry and Infrastructure Development has various agencies responsible for regulating transportation sectors, including aviation, railways, and road transport.
- The Ministry of Ecology, Geology, and Natural Resources oversees environmental protection and natural resource management, including regulation of businesses that may have environmental impacts.
- The Committee on Atomic and Energy Supervision and Control is responsible for nuclear safety and regulatory oversight in Kazakhstan's nuclear industry.

1.5. Privatisation

1.5.1. Legal and regulatory framework for privatisation

The privatisation process is regulated by the law on State Property and the rules for the sale of privatisation assets No. 920/2011 that establishes procedures for sale and liquidation, the sequence of actions and use of proceeds. The list of Samruk-Kazyna assets available for sale and the process of sale is defined by the government and its BOD (Ministry of Justice, 2012[38]), and should be in compliance with the laws on JSCs, LLCs, Securities Market and other applicable laws. The MF provides an electronic database[23] with the objects and assets of sale included within the state property register. However, the current data set has certain limitations and incompleteness, as the OECD team is lacking information and facing data discrepancies in the analysis of the privatisation status of Samruk-Kazyna company groups[24] and communal property.

To ensure national security, the government established restrictions on the transfer of ownership of strategic resources (objects) (Ministry of Justice, 2012[23]). A governmental decree No. 651/2008 released the list of strategic objects under SOEs, SOHC ownership and other legal entities with state participation consisting of 79 legal entities and 78 objects. According to the law on State Property the privatisation of strategic objects and legal entities requires special approval from the government.

The privatisation of state, communal and SOHC property is conducted by selecting mostly one of the following type of sales:

- *Trade sale through competitive procedure.* An auction – proposals declared publicly, held in two ways by increasing and lowering the price, or tenders - proposals submitted in a closed envelope. Both cases of bidding are conducted on the web portal of the MF. If 100% of the shares/stakes of assets put up for auction are not sold after three rounds, these legal entities become subject to reorganisation by affiliation or merger or are subject to liquidation by the BOD decision.
- *Trade sale to a preferred bidder.* Direct targeted sale to a strategic investor[25] subject to government approval.
- *Public offerings via book-building.* Tenders through the two-stage procedures - involvement of an independent consultant, conducting a comprehensive analysis of the privatisation object, forming a list of potential buyers and negotiating the best offer, while the government determines the priority of the price and other conditions of privatisation.
- *Other initial or secondary public offerings.* Trading on the stock exchange - securities to be sold are put up for exchange trading by brokerage companies and carried out in the trading systems in accordance with the rules of exchange trading of the relevant stock exchange.

The valuation of large privatisation assets (book value exceeds 2 500 000 times the monthly calculation index established by the law on the republican budget) is carried out by independent consultants in accordance with international valuation standards, while the valuation of remaining assets is carried out in accordance with Kazakh appraisal activities legislation.

Privatisation arrangements and responsibilities

There are multiple public sector agencies and other actors involved in the privatisation process, including:

1. The government of Kazakhstan is responsible for the approval of criteria and the list of assets for privatisation put forward by SOHCs/SOEs/akimats, by defining all responsible bodies and timelines based on the State Commissions' recommendations. The decision is issued in the form of a government decree.
2. The state commission for the modernisation of the economy is created and its membership defined by a Presidential decree (Presidential Administration, 2007[39]). It consists of the Prime Minister as a Chair, the first deputy Prime Minister, deputy head of Presidential administration, MIID, MNE, MF, CEO and BOD member of Samruk-Kazyna. The main functions of this commission are to make decisions and recommendations on the privatisation list and selling conditions, including of large state entities of SK.
3. As a working body of the State Commission, the MNE is responsible for developing the criteria and list of assets for privatisation, evaluation and consolidate the proposals, the overall programme management and co-ordination, monitoring and reporting of the comprehensive privatisation plan and implementation status. There is no information on whether the MNE evaluates the economic, financial impact or legal aspects (due diligence and valuations etc.) of the proposed privatisation.

The privatisation process faces challenges due to ambiguous criteria when selecting assets. The plans are often residual or rely on independent assessment without considering competition. Thus, unprofitable enterprises, including those providing vital services like education, health, sport activities, become privatisation targets. If they remain unsold after three auctions, legislation mandates their liquidation. This process can force government or local authorities to recreate SOEs for essential services due to lack of alternative providers.

4. Based on the law on State Property and the rules for the sale of privatisation assets requirements, the MF now conducts electronic tenders on its web portal and consolidates the results of the programme on the state registry online platform. It seems however as though the data displayed is not holistic and deviates from official reports on the progress of the privatisation plans delivered by the Ministry of Finance. We observe missing information from holding companies and local municipalities.
5. Service providers and third parties, including external consultants (the "big four", law firms, financial advisors, accountants, consultants, or other investment banks) are hired for valuation and advisory services. Privatisation is then conducted through a two-stage procedure, direct targeted sale, trading on the stock exchange and privatisation of large assets.

Figure 1.9. Actors involved in privatisation in Kazakhstan

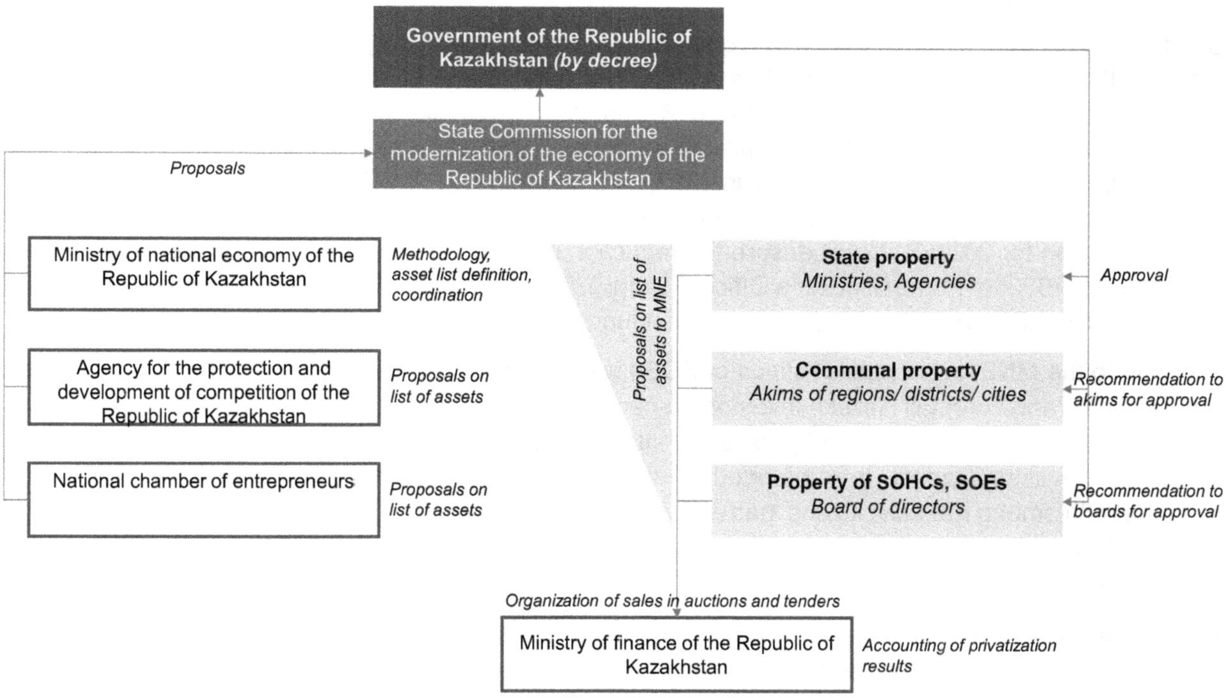

Source: Analysis of OECD project team.

The reduction of the state's share in the national economy to 14% by 2025;[26] takes a central position among Kazakhstan's privatisation objectives. Privatisation efforts of SOEs, however, have created complex ownership structures. According to the current *Comprehensive Privatisation Plan for 2021-2025*, each quasi-state enterprise that is up for privatisation has received a roadmap of privatisation and has been entered into an open database. Said database, which is the register of state property, is designed to act as a platform to facilitate public tenders, as well as to make them more transparent. Furthermore, as part of the privatisation plan, the analysis of activities and economic operability of each SOE is carried out under the supervision of the Supreme Audit Chamber.

Overall, the co-ordination tasks as the owner are yet to be fully defined with the reformed mandate of institutional actors that are undertaking them. To date, the register of state property's "privatisation objects" page remains without any records or entries. Additionally, the Supreme Audit Chamber, which is tasked with auditing the large pool of SOEs in Kazakhstan, is currently undergoing a transformation programme.[27] The implementation of the abovementioned projects creates ambitious work plans for the government and current administration that require reflection on past and current processes. Despite ongoing efforts, the success of innovative approaches to implement the privatisation plan fall back on the current state owner as both the executer and subject of the reform programme.

Rationales for state-owned enterprise privatisation

Article 192 of the Entrepreneurial Code provides several rationales for state participation in entrepreneurial activities of the economy. In line with this rationale, in 2015, the government approved a list entailing 364 activities which justify state ownership. This principle is also called "Yellow Pages Rules". This list is then enforced by the agency for the protection and development of competition or the relevant line ministry to decide on adding an SOE into the privatisation pipeline. Along these lines and since 2014, the government has developed three comprehensive privatisation plans: 1) for 2014-2016; 2) for 2016-2020; and 3) for 2021-2025. Key criteria for being included in the privatisation plan continue to evolve and expand over time in order to keep the list flexible and reflect different aspects and challenges faced during the actual privatisation process (Annex C).

Apart from key criteria for privatisation, the government has defined six key performance indicators (KPIs) to assess the effectiveness of privatisation results. However, the annual reports on the implementation status of the privatisation plans for 2014-2016 and 2016-2020 did not contain information on their implementation. According to publicly available information, the state participation in the economy was 19.1% in 2015, 18.3% in 2016, and 17.3% in 2017, 14.9% in 2019, in 14.6% 2021 (Prime Minister's Office, 2022[40]). Based on a recent announcement of the government, the implementation of the comprehensive privatisation plan for 2021-2025 will ensure the reduction of state participation in the economy to 14% by 2025 (Akorda, 2022[41]; Prime Minister's Office, 2021[42]). The funds received from the privatisation of state property shall be directed to Kazakhstan's national fund.

According to the MNE, initial public listings of SOEs will take place as "People's IPO" programmes which allows a wider range of retail Kazakh investors to participate in the allocation process of listings at a lower price, with the subsequent opportunity to list on international stock markets and attract a wider range of international investors/capital. It is intended to attract resources from the public but also to distribute national wealth among Kazakh citizens, partially via price appreciation. IPOs conducted by SOEs positively influence the development of retail investors and local stock markets, the number of which increased from 111 224 in 2017 up to 491 447 in November 2022 and close to 523 000 in January 2023.

IPOs themselves do not directly impact the decrease of state participation in the Kazakhstan economy unless the placement exceeds the controlling stake of SOEs. Nevertheless, the listing of SOEs' shares in organised stock markets increases the transparency of businesses decisions, and can positively impact operational effectiveness, and ensure compliance of corporate governance with higher (sometimes foreign) stock market requirements.

A brief history of privatisation

The privatisation process laid down in the 1990s, after the collapse of Soviet Union, continues until the present moment. In 1991, the government embarked on a programme of deep economic reforms in which privatisation was to become both the driving force and one of the most important elements in the transformation of the Kazakh economy. Until 2014, the government implemented four stages of privatisation: 1) in 1991-1992; 2) in 1993-1995; 3) in 1996-1998; and 4) in 1998-2000. "The second wave" of privatisation began in 2014 and its implementation is still ongoing.

1. The first privatisation programme of 22 June 1991 (stage I) covered 1991-1992 and focused mainly on the sale of trade, public catering, consumer services and utilities, small industrial enterprises, construction, motor transport, agriculture and other sectors of the national economy, and privatisation of the state housing stock. The primary right to choose the form of denationalisation and privatisation of the enterprise was given to the labor collective, which has priority over other applicants. A coupon mechanism was used to purchase housing by citizens (Ministry of Justice, 2009[43]).
2. The national programme of privatisation for 1993-1995 (stage II) dated 5 March 1993 also covered mass privatisation, privatisation of individual projects and the agro-industrial complex. In 1992, the government introduced the mechanism of corporatisation, namely the transformation of state assets into joint-stock companies with full state ownership of all shares managed through corporate governance structures. During this period, the largest buying of state property was observed, as the state issued coupons to citizens that could be used to participate in the privatisation process. Nearly 11 000 objects were sold, as well as shares of over 1 600 enterprises (Ministry of Justice, 1993[44]).
3. The third stage of privatisation (1996-1998) encompassed sectors such as electricity, oil and gas, ferrous and non-ferrous metallurgy, mining and processing plants, and telecommunications. Starting from 1996, privatisation of any state property was no longer carried out with coupons. As part of these programmes, by the end of 1998, 3 276 JSC and business partnerships were privatised, which is 65% of the total number of established JSC and business partnerships (Ministry of Justice, 2005[45]).
4. The key point of the fourth stage of privatisation (1999-2000) was to ensure the more efficient management of state property through developing the legal framework for privatisation and state property management, improving the accounting of the state property by creating the consolidated register of assets of Kazakhstan and dividing state property into republican and communal property. Management of communal property by local executive bodies aimed to increase efficiency of exercising state ownership and asset management rights. During this period and up until 2013, the activity of the privatisation process began to decline (Ministry of Justice, 1999[46]).

The second wave of reform of assets under state ownership began in Kazakhstan in 2014. Since then, the government has developed three comprehensive privatisation plans: 1) for 2014-2016; 2) for 2016-2020; and 3) for 2021-2025.

According to the MNE, 93% of the 2016-2020 privatisation plan were achieved, bringing forth KZT 629 bn or USD 1.4 bn proceeds (out of 864 assets, 503 were sold, 302 liquidated, 59 transferred to the next plan), the 2021-2025 privatisation plan is still in progress and as of August 2023, notes KZT 307 bln or USD 653 mn in proceeds (out of planned 658 assets, 372 sold,[28] 62 liquidated).[29] The most recent assets' breakdown of the 2021-2025 privatisation plan consists of 5 state properties, 262 of SOHC/SOE property, 152 of social-entrepreneurial corporations and 239 of communal property. Since privatisation begun, we have been observing a fluctuation of the number of assets for sale, the exclusion of assets in the middle of selling procedures, the lack of fixed dates of exit from the asset or the absence of declaring the sale of asset overall – which may be delaying the government's ambitious privatisation plans.[30]

The data on the progress of the privatisation plans on the state register's website does not align with the official government reports. There is a lack of data related to Samruk-Kazyna's group of assets and communal property. The lack of transparent and publicly available reports on the government's progress on privatisation with concrete KPI measures/metrics, as well as the discrepancies in the data raises questions on monitoring methodologies, information disclosure strategies and transparency. This renders it difficult to assess whether the goals of privatisation have been achieved and how the government is evaluating the impact of privatisation to the Kazakh economy.

Selected IPOs

Despite the announcement of potential IPOs of key industrial assets within Samruk-Kazyna since 2014, only 3 out of 8 planned companies have been sold through IPO.

Table 1.6. Selected data of IPOs of Samruk-Kazyna (2014-2025)

Company Title	Announcement date	Initial IPO date and expected listing amount	Latest announcement of date/ actual date	IPO listing platform
Kazakhstan Temir Zholy NC JSC	2014	2025	2025	TBD
Kazatomprom NC JSC	2014	2016 - 10% minus 1 share	IPO of 10% in 2018, SPO in 2020 and 2021 up to 25%	LSE, AIX, KASE
Samruk-Energy JSC	2014	2024	2024	TBD
KEGOC JSC	2014	2014 - 10% minus 1 share	IPO of 10% in 2014, remaining 15% as SPO offered to investors on 27 September 2023 (book building period of 28 September 2023-27 October 2023)	IPO-KASE, SPO-TBD
KazMunayGas NC JSC	2016	2022	IPO of 3% in 2022	AIX, KASE
Air Astana JSC	2016	2024	2024	TBD
Kazakh Gas NC JSC	2022	2025	2025	TBD

Source: https://primeminister.kz/ru/news/kompleksnyy-plan-privatizacii-na-2021-2025-gody-vklyuchaet-675-obektov-gossobstvennosti-i-kvazigosudarstvennogo-sektora-611746; MNE information as of August 2023; https://kapital.kz/finance/119419/ob-yavlen-start-spo-kegoc.html.

KEGOC lists shares under the "People's IPO" programme, while KazMunayGas - the largest local IPO listed on Kazakhstani stock exchanges - satisfied the 48.5% applications from the citizens of Kazakhstan, 47.2% from Kazakh legal entities and 4.3% from foreign individuals and legal entities. SK was only able to place 3% during the IPO of KMG shares instead of the initially planned 5%.

1.6. Recent and ongoing reform

1.6.1. General reforms

The public administration department responsible for reforming the so-called quasi-state sector initiated reforms in particular in 2019, under direct supervision of the President. In May 2022, a package of reforms was approved (Government Decree 654/ 2022), to be followed by an Action Plan with the idea to optimise SOEs fit for privatisation and to shrink the overall state share in the economy. The action plan remains to be implemented, with the provided timeline having expired at the time of writing (January 2024).

In 2019, the President issued a decree on the moratorium on the creation of entities with 50% of shares/stakes in the quasi-state sector until 31 December 2021 (Government of Kazakhstan, 2021[47]). A new similar moratorium will take force soon until 31 December 2025 according to the recent initiatives on reforms of the quasi-state sector of Kazakhstan in the framework of the Presidential Decree No. 654/ 2022.

The Kazakh President announced in his most recent address to the nation a need to reduce the share of the state in the economy and to reform the quasi-state sector, in line with the *2025 National Development Plan* and the *2030 Concept for the Development of Public Administration*. The President particularly noted the acceleration of the privatisation processes and public IPOs in order to enhance both transparency and efficiency in asset management. He directed the government to initiate the privatisation of all non-core assets and to start conducting public IPOs for companies under Samruk-Kazyna, beginning in 2024. For

2025, he requested the public IPO for Air Astana, to prepare QazaqGaz for market entry, and to divest state assets in major companies.

Against the background of the President's continuous call for reform and decree 654, the MNE developed an analytical report and action plan, which includes seven points due to be implemented by 2028. Since the action plan has not yet been implemented, it currently remains unclear what the exact scope and coverage of SOE reform in Kazakhstan will be.

1.6.2. Amendments to the law on state property

In early 2023, the MNE requested inputs from the OECD team to the law on State Property which describes and specifies some aspects of Kazakhstan's ownership arrangements over SOEs. Although the amendments are still in process, this note will briefly refer to the main changes therein:

- Firstly, it has been proposed to pilot 4 000 entities with a revision of their classification, and to divide them into two main groups: economic (including infrastructural, production, and financial organisations) and non-economic (such as schools, national development institutions, and fundamental research organisations). This categorisation is based on criteria like funding sources, whether budget or off-budget, and the organisations' goals and objectives. The organisational and legal forms are being aligned with the nature of the organisation, with the "state institution" form being introduced for non-economic entities. Additionally, certain organisational and legal forms, such as state enterprises, are being liquidated. Standardised criteria are being set for the creation and operation of state-affiliated commercial organisations as JSCs or LLCs.
- Currently there are no strict rules on selecting a legal form when the state creates a new SOE. To counter this revisions envision that SOEs in Kazakhstan will have the option to either adopt the legal form of a JSC or LLC, depending on their plans for placing securities on the stock exchange. JSC is required when securities will be listed on the stock exchange, while all other organisations with state participation are categorised as LLCs. If implemented the state enterprises will therefore cease to exist.
- In addition, and most importantly, the MNE, alongside the MF is planning on putting in place a so-called national report of the quasi-state sector, or a type of aggregate reporting. The plan is to have an annual report, with the MNE developing the type of reporting and the MF administering/ collecting the information. It will be published online with the aim to support with monitoring activities. Holding companies are also obliged to provide the requested information. In order to gather the information, amendments have been included within the Budget Code. The reporting is supposed to feed into the privatisation plans of the country, by providing clear indications on which companies are to be liquidated/ reformed.
- Another focus of the reforms is reducing the share of state participation in the economy. This is being achieved by adhering to the principle of competitive neutrality, which ensures equal conditions for both SOEs and private companies. Clearer criteria are being established to determine the participation of SOEs in economic activities, specifically entrepreneurial activities.
- Moreover, efforts are underway to improve the corporate governance in SOEs, by defining principles for managing JSCs and LLCs with state participation. BOD and supervisory boards are being empowered to effectively perform their functions. Additionally, a centralised and transparent process for nominating and appointing board members is being introduced as well as unified registry of candidates to be appointed as independent directors of BODs.
- It is noted that it is planned to exclude political civil servants from being elected to the BOD of JSCs and LLCs belonging to the quasi-state sector. Clarifying or defining the role of a political civil servant would allow to understand what this change entails.

The Ministry of Economy has noted that the State Property law is planned to be submitted to the government (office of the Prime Minister) by the end of December, and by the first quarter of 2024 to Parliament. The timeline may change though, and even if the reforms will be included within the updated legislations, it remains unclear how they will be executed.

References

AIFC (2023), *More than 2100 cases resolved and enforced by the AIFC Court and IAC*, https://court.aifc.kz/en/news/more-than-2-100-cases-resolved-and-enforced-by-the-aifc-court-and-iac. [7]

Akimov, A. (2008), *Financial System Reform in Kazakhstan from 1993 to 2006 and Its Socioeconomic Effects*, Emerging Markets Finance and Trade, https://doi.org/10.2753/REE1540-496X440306. [11]

Akorda (2022), *Official Website of the President of the Republic of Kazakhstan*, https://www.akorda.kz/en/official_documents/strategies_and_programs. [41]

Asian Development Bank (2020), *Banking Sector of Kazakhstan under COVID-19*, https://www.adb.org/sites/default/files/institutional-document/654971/banking-sector-kazakhstan-covid-19-crisis.pdf. [12]

Dixon, A. (2020), "The Strategic Logics of State Investment Funds in Asia: Beyond Financialisation.", *Journal of Contemporary Asia*, Vol. 52/2, pp. 127-151, https://doi.org/10.1080/00472336.2020.1841267. [17]

Dixon, A. (2014), "Financializing development: toward a sympathetic critique of sovereign development fund", *Journal of Sustainable Finance & Investment*, Vol. 4/4, pp. 357-371, https://doi.org/10.1080/20430795.2014.980717. [48]

Government of Kazakhstan (2021), *Summary of the analytical report "Reforms in Kazakhstan: from Intentions to Actions. New course of President of the Republic of Kazakhstan Kassym-Jomart Tokayev"*, https://www.gov.kz/memleket/entities/mfa-ottawa/press/news/details/188560?lang=en. [47]

IMF (2022), *IMF.org*, https://www.imf.org/en/News/Articles/2022/10/07/mcs101022-kazakhstan-staff-concluding-statement-of-the-2022-article-iv-mission. [14]

Investing.com (2022), *Investing.com*, https://www.investing.com/rates-bonds/kazakhstan-10-year. [13]

KMGZ (2023), *National Company "KazMunayGaz" JSC (KMGZ)*, https://kase.kz/en/issuers/KMGZ/. [16]

Knox, C. (2008), *Kazakhstan: modernizing government in the context of political inertia.*, International Review of Administrative Sciences, https://doi.org/10.1177/0020852308095314. [6]

Lazzarini, M. (2014), *Reinventing State Capitalism*, Harvard University Press. [50]

Mertens, T. (2018), "Market-based but state-led: The role of public development banks in shaping market-based finance in the European Union", *Competition & Change*, Vol. 22/2, https://doi.org/10.1177/102452941875847. [49]

Ministry of Justice (2023), *Adilat*, https://adilet.zan.kz/eng/docs/Z000000132_. [5]

Ministry of Justice (2020), *On approval of the register of public services*, https://adilet.zan.kz/rus/docs/V2000019982. [32]

Ministry of Justice (2017), *On approval of the State Planning System in the Republic of Kazakhstan*, https://adilet.zan.kz/rus/docs/P1700000790. [29]

Ministry of Justice (2015), *About public procurement*, https://adilet.zan.kz/rus/docs/Z1500000434. [30]

Ministry of Justice (2015), *Entrepreneur Code of the Republic of Kazakhstan*, https://adilet.zan.kz/eng/docs/K1500000375. [22]

Ministry of Justice (2015), *On combating corruption*, https://adilet.zan.kz/rus/docs/Z1500000410. [24]

Ministry of Justice (2015), *On governmental audit and financial control*, https://adilet.zan.kz/eng/docs/Z1500000392. [37]

Ministry of Justice (2014), *About rehabilitation and bankruptcy*, https://adilet.zan.kz/rus/docs/Z1400000176. [25]

Ministry of Justice (2013), *About public services*, https://adilet.zan.kz/rus/docs/Z1300000088#z15. [31]

Ministry of Justice (2012), *On national security of the Republic of Kazakhstan*, https://adilet.zan.kz/eng/docs/Z1200000527. [23]

Ministry of Justice (2012), *On Sovereign Wealth Fund*, https://online.zakon.kz/Document/?doc_id=33422982. [38]

Ministry of Justice (2012), *On the approval of the draft Agreement on cooperation between the Government of the Republic of Kazakhstan and the National Wealth Fund "Samruk-Kazyna" Joint-Stock Company and the invalidation of some decisions of the Government of the Republic of Kazakhs*, https://adilet.zan.kz/rus/docs/P1200001599. [36]

Ministry of Justice (2009), *О Программе разгосударствления и приватизации государственной собственности в Казахской ССР на 1991-1992 год (I-й этап) и Положении о купонном механизме приватизации государственной собственности в Казахской ССР*, https://adilet.zan.kz/rus/docs/K910000444_. [43]

Ministry of Justice (2008), *Budget Code of the Republic of Kazakhstan*, https://adilet.zan.kz/rus/docs/K080000095_. [28]

Ministry of Justice (2005), *О Программе приватизации и реструктуризации государственной собственности в Республике Казахстан на 1996-1998 годы*, https://adilet.zan.kz/rus/docs/P960000246_. [45]

Ministry of Justice (2003), *Law on Joint Stock Companies*, https://adilet.zan.kz/rus/docs/Z030000415_/z030415.htm. [26]

Ministry of Justice (2003), *On state monitoring of property in sectors of the economy of strategic importance*, https://adilet.zan.kz/rus/docs/Z030000490_. [33]

Ministry of Justice (1999), *Об утверждении Программы приватизации и повышения эффективности управления государственным имуществом на 1999-2000 годы*, https://adilet.zan.kz/rus/docs/P990000683_. [46]

Ministry of Justice (1998), *Adilet*, https://adilet.zan.kz/rus/docs/Z980000220_. [27]

Ministry of Justice (1993), *О Национальной программе разгосударствления и приватизации в Республике Казахстан на 1993-1995 годы (II-ой этап)*, https://adilet.zan.kz/rus/docs/U930001135_. [44]

Narziev, O. (2021), *Genesis And Development Of Capital Market In Cis Countries: Cases From Russia, Kazakhstan, And Uzbekistan*, Turkish Journal of Computer and Mathematics Education, https://doi.org/10.17762/turcomat.v12i4.623. [18]

OECD (2023), *Insights on the Business Climate in Kazakhstan*, OECD Publishing, Paris, https://doi.org/10.1787/bd780306-en. [8]

OECD (2022), *Weathering Economic Storms in Central Asia: Initial Impacts of the War in Ukraine*, OECD Publishing, Paris, https://doi.org/10.1787/83348924-en. [4]

OECD (2021), *Ownership and Governance of State-Owned Enterprises: A Compendium of National Practices*, OECD, Paris, https://www.oecd.org/corporate/ownership-and-governance-of-state-owned-enterprises-a-compendium-of-national-practices.htm. [35]

OECD (2020), *Implementing the OECD Guidelines on Corporate Governance of State-Owned Enterprises: Review of Recent Developments*, OECD Publishing, Paris, https://doi.org/10.1787/4caa0c3b-en. [21]

OECD (2019), *Istanbul Anti-Corruption Action Plan: Methodology for the 4th Monitoring Round*, OECD, Paris, https://www.oecd.org/corruption/acn/OECD-ACN-4th-Round-Monitoring-Methodology-Amendments-2017-ENG.pdf. [10]

OECD (2017), *Multi-dimensional Review of Kazakhstan: Volume 2. In-depth Analysis and Recommendations*, OECD Development Pathways, OECD Publishing, Paris, https://doi.org/10.1787/9789264269200-en. [19]

OECD (2017), *The Size and Sectoral Distribution of State-Owned Enterprises*, OECD Publishing, Paris, https://doi.org/10.1787/9789264280663-en. [15]

OECD (2015), *OECD Guidelines on Corporate Governance of State-Owned Enterprises, 2015 Edition*, OECD Publishing, Paris, https://doi.org/10.1787/9789264244160-en. [34]

Pomfret, R. (2012), "Central Asia after Two Decades of Independence", in *Economies in Transition*, Palgrave Macmillan UK, London, https://doi.org/10.1057/9780230361836_16. [20]

Presidential Administration (2007), *On measures of the modernization of the economy of the Republic of Kazakhstan*. [39]

Prime Minister's Office (2022), *В Миннацэкономики подвели итоги за 2021 год и поделились планами работы на предстоящий период*, https://primeminister.kz/ru/news/reviews/v-minnacekonomiki-podveli-itogi-za-2021-god-i-podelilis-planami-raboty-na-predstoyashchiy-period-42556. [40]

Prime Minister's Office (2021), *Расширенная коллегия МНЭ РК: итоги деятельности за 2020 год и планы на 2021-й*, https://www.primeminister.kz/ru/news/reviews/rasshirennaya-kollegiya-mne-rk-itogi-deyatelnosti-za-2020-god-i-plany-na-2021-y-192260. [42]

Smagulova, K. (2022), *Administrative and Territorial Division of Kazakhstan in 2022: Symbolism or Reforms?*, Central Asian Bureau for Analytical Reporting, https://cabar.asia/en/administrative-and-territorial-division-of-kazakhstan-in-2022-symbolism-or-reforms. [3]

U.S. Department of State (2022), *2022 Investment Climate Statements: Kazakhstan*, https://www.state.gov/reports/2022-investment-climate-statements/kazakhstan/. [9]

Wang (2015), "The rise of the 'shareholding state': financialization of economic management in China", *Socio-Economic Review*, Vol. 13/3, pp. 603–625, https://doi.org/10.1093/ser/mwv016. [51]

World Bank (2023), *World Bank in Central Asia*, https://www.worldbank.org/en/region/eca/brief/central-asia. [1]

World Bank (2021), *Rural population (% of total population) - Kazakhstan*, https://data.worldbank.org/indicator/SP.RUR.TOTL.ZS?locations=KZ. [2]

Notes

[1] United Nations, the World Trade Organisation, the Commonwealth of Independent States (CIS), the Shanghai Cooperation Organisation, the Eurasian Economic Union, the Collective Security Treaty Organisation, the Organisation for Security and Cooperation in Europe, the Organisation of Islamic Cooperation, the Organisation of Turkic States, and the International Organisation of Turkic Culture.

[2] The first tier refers to regions and cities of republican significance. The second level includes districts in regions and cities of republican significance, as well as cities of regional significance. Akimats of villages, rural and settlement districts, cities of district and regional significance belong to units of administrative-territorial division of the third level.

[3] Poverty headcount ratio at national poverty lines (% of population).

[4] https://aifc.kz/

[5] https://aix.kz/about-aix/shareholders/

[6] Or State Property law

[7] According to paragraph 31, article 3 of the Budget Code, paragraph 7 article 1 of the JSC law and article 166 of the Entrepreneurial Code SOEs are divided into fully state-owned enterprises (100% state participation), legal entities in which more than fifty percent of shares belong to the state, and legal entities in which more than fifty percent of shares directly or indirectly belong to legal entities, more than fifty percent of the shares of which belong to the state.

[8] The term "quasi-public/state sector" typically refers to organisations or entities that have some characteristics of both public and private sectors. These entities are not fully government-owned or government-controlled, but they often operate in sectors that are traditionally associated with public services or have a significant impact on the public interest.

[9] Kazakhstan's laws refer to LLCs and Limited Liability Partnerships (LLPs). However, for ease of comparison, this report refers to Limited Liability Partnerships as Limited Liability Companies.

[10] Samruk-Kazyna and Baiterek

[11] QazBioPharm

[12] KazMunayGas, KEGOC, KazPost, Food Contract Corporation, Kazatomprom, National Information Technologies, Kazakhstan Temir Zholy, Kazakhtelecom, Kazakhstan Engineering, Kazakhstan Garysh Sapary, Tau-Ken Samruk, Aktau Trade Sea Port, QazExpoCongress, QazAutoZhol, Kazakh Invest, KazakhExport, Kazakh Tourism, QazaqGas, National Geological Service.

[13] OECD team observed that the State Registry has discrepancies with the data provided by the holding companies. Samruk-Kazyna has 282 companies on 6 levels, Baiterek has 58 enterprises on 5 levels, Kazakhstan Engineering has 22 on 2 levels, while the State Registry counts only 178, 12 and 17 enterprises of these holdings correspondingly.

[14] The remaining enterprises are under communal property.

[15] Excluding Akimats

[16] Article 22 of the Securities Market law carves out the conditions and procedure for issuing securities in the territory of a foreign state, which do encompass expectations on the value of the issued securities. According to the law, an organisation that is resident to Kazakhstan which intends to issue securities or derivative securities must offer them for purchase either through KASE and (or) stock exchange AIX on the same conditions of placement as in the territory of a foreign state, in the amount of at least 20% of the total volume planned for placement.

[17] This figure stems from the KASE and Samruk-Kazyna website, and collides with Kazakh government data received in Table 1.2.

[18] https://www.kmg.kz/en/sustainable-development/corporate-governance/shareholders/

[19] State financialisation describes a process in which the state pursues development policies through creating state-led financial investment institutions. (Dixon, 2020[17]) bases the definition of state financialisation on the research of (Dixon, 2014[48]) (Mertens, 2018[49]), (Lazzarini, 2014[50]), (Wang, 2015[51]), which identify an active role of the state in emulating market-based financial actors.

[20] This report refers to LLPs as LLCs throughout.

[21] State property law establishes that such supervisory boards should consist of at least 5 members, that have no relationship with the SE, 30% of which should be independent directors. MNE develops rules on selection process and criteria for board members.

[22] "financial organisations, joint-stock companies (with the exception of non-profit ones), state enterprises based on the right of economic management, subjects of state monopoly, special law, as well as organisations in the authorised capital of which there is a state share, and subsidiaries, dependent and other legal entities that are affiliated with them in accordance with the laws of the Republic of Kazakhstan."

[23] www.gosreestr.kz

[24] According to the MF as of 10 March 2023, out of 669 assets of the Comprehensive Privatization Plan for 2021-2025, 367 objects were sold for the amount of KZT 307.5 billion, while the electronic database indicates the sale of 306 assets for KZT 74.7 billion.

[25] The "strategic investor" could be an incumbent manager, hence this category encompasses management buy-outs.

[26] https://primeminister.kz/en/news/2025-zhylga-karay-memlekettin-ekonomikaga-katysu-ulesi-14-ga-deyin-kyskarady-a-smaylov-23828

[27] https://primeminister.kz/en/news/esep-komiteti-zhogary-auditorlyk-palata-bolyp-kayta-kuryladу-e-zhamaubaev-1825840

[28] 372 assets sold also includes 96 assets of KazMunayGas those 3% of shares were floated in local stock markets, however MNE and MF classify these 96 assets as sold. Other 58 assets of Kazakhstan Temir Zholy, Samruk-Energy, QazaqGas, Air Astana also included in the perimeter of IPO and accounts in total number of assets for privatisation, but in fact will not be sold.

[29] There is no data available on actual implementation data of the privatisation plan for 2014-2016.

[30] More than 280 assets were excluded from the plan starting from the end of 2021.

2 Assessment of Kazakhstan relative to the SOE Guidelines

This chapter outlines the corporate governance framework of Kazakh SOEs – notably, how policies and practices align with the recommendations of the OECD Guidelines of Corporate Governance of State-Owned Enterprises. Specifically, it assesses national practices relative to the seven areas covered by the Guidelines, covering: (i) rationales for state ownership; (ii) the state's role as an owner; (iii) SOEs in the marketplace; (iv) the equitable treatment of shareholders and other investors; (v) stakeholder relations and responsible business conduct; (vi) transparency and disclosure; and (vii) the responsibilities of the boards of directors of SOEs.

2.1. Rationales for state ownership

> ***The state exercises the ownership of SOEs in the interest of the general public. It should carefully evaluate and disclose the objectives that justify state ownership and subject these to a recurrent review.***

2.1.1. Articulating the rationales for state ownership

> ***A. The ultimate purpose of state ownership of enterprises should be to maximise value for society, through an efficient allocation of resources.***

Currently, Kazakhstan does not possess one single high-level ownership policy. Kazakh enterprises that belong to the quasi-state sector are regulated by a variety of documents which reflect in part the legal provisions outlining how state ownership is practiced and the conditions it is practiced under. Therefore, parts of these legal documents represent important aspects of what an ownership policy would ideally cover and can be said to constitute an "implicit ownership policy". As mentioned earlier, the legal framework surrounding state ownership is constituted from, *inter alia*:

- the law of the Republic of Kazakhstan "On State Property"
- the Entrepreneurial Code
- the law No. 415-II "On Joint Stock Companies"
- the law No. 220-I "On Limited Liability Companies"
- Budget Code of the Republic of Kazakhstan
- Civil Code of the Republic of Kazakhstan
- the law of the Republic of Kazakhstan "On the National Bank of the Republic of Kazakhstan".
- the law of the Republic of Kazakhstan "On the Sovereign Wealth Fund".

Outlining rationales for state ownership allows the state to clearly position itself as an owner, and provide SOEs, the market, and the public with predictability and understanding of its objectives. Presently, the law on State Property, which is the core document governing state property, does not provide a clear rationale for state ownership of enterprises. However, recent efforts to reform the quasi-state sector have been motivated in part by a privatisation agenda and hence clarifying Kazakhstan's rationales for state ownership has thus figured prominently. At this point in time, however, decisions on privatisation are taken on an ad hoc basis.

According to the law on State Property, a property of the state, including SOEs, may be subject to privatisation by auction or tender, bidding at a stock exchange, a two-stage procedure or direct sale. In the case of strategic assets owned by the state, the decision to privatise is subject to a special approval by the state authority. However, there are exceptions to which type of state property may be a subject to privatisation. The list of SOEs and other organisations part of the quasi-state sector which are not subject to alienation shall be approved by the government in co-ordination with the President. While the law on State Property does not include said list, it is stipulated that exempt quasi-state entities tend to be strategic in nature. There are also further caveats to alienating state property that is partially or wholly-owned by the National Bank of Kazakhstan.

Besides strategic and fiscal policy reasons for owning state property, the entrepreneurial Code positions further why the state may participate in entrepreneurial activities in the economy. Article 192 stipulates that such will be case when the following circumstances apply:

- national security, the defence capability of the state or society interests' protection
- use and maintenance of strategic facilities under state ownership
- legal or natural monopoly by the state

- the absence or low level of competition in the relevant product market
- the state can participate in entrepreneurial activities through SOEs that have already been established.

Hence, while rationales of state ownership can be gleaned from various legal documents, their dispersion across different instruments of policy renders their application to the quasi-state sector vague. Furthermore, several exemptions to either the scope of the law itself, or the relevant legal provision that details the applicability of a given rationale, may result in inconsistencies and shift the ultimate decision-making power to the Presidential administration.

The lack of a high-level and holistic document which describes state ownership arrangements on the state level makes it difficult to establish an all-encompassing rationale for state ownership. Efforts to formulate a rationale for the existence of the quasi-state sector should ideally remain applicable to the entire pool of commercially driven SOEs in Kazakhstan, rather than to specific sectors or types of SOEs.

2.1.2. Ownership policy

> ***B. The government should develop an ownership policy. The policy should inter alia define the overall rationales for state ownership, the state's role in the governance of SOEs, how the state will implement its ownership policy, and the respective roles and responsibilities of those government offices involved in its implementation.***

Various factors, such as the legal form of a SOE and its position in the ownership hierarchy as part of the portfolio of the sovereign wealth fund Samruk-Kazyna, influence how ownership is exercised in practice. The multitude of entities directly and indirectly involved in the ownership of SOEs poses a challenge to summarising expectations and defining an overall rationale for owning any given SOE.

The law on State Property determines the legal regime of state property and thus how state ownership is practiced. An enterprise owned by the state, any of its entities, or an enterprise owned by a regional administration classifies as state property and will therefore fall under the scope of the law. It defines the legal basis for the management of state property, and the legal grounds for acquiring and terminating rights to state property. A key specification of the document is to detail the roles across the various state entities involved in the management of SOEs. Other important areas cover:

- The definition of state property, which is divided into republican property owned by the state treasury – directly or via funds of the republican budget, the National Fund of Kazakhstan (Samruk-Kazyna) and other legal entities – and communal property.
- Procedures for exercising property rights, which includes outlining the competence of the central authorised body for state planning (MNE), authorised bodies for state property (MF), as well as the authorised body of the relevant industry (line ministry).
- Procedures for nationalisation and privatisation of state property. Nationalisation may be carried out in exceptional circumstances. According to the law, nationalisation is an exceptional case (exceptional form) of alienation of property owned by individuals and non-state legal entities, and is carried out only after the complete exhaustion of all other possible forms of alienation of property provided for by the civil Code of Kazakhstan. Nationalised property is to be included in the register of state property, for which three entries of nationalised LLCs are found.

As noted in chapter 1 of this report, the prospective changes of the law on State Property are envisioning the standardisation of the legal form of SOEs with state participation as JSC or LLC. Newly classified SOEs are further set to be monitored by the MF, which will also hold responsibility over tracking KPIs and data collection of SOEs' economic activity.

Standardising the legal forms of SOEs and formalising board nomination processes would align the law on State Property better with internationally accepted good practices. However, in practice there is a lack of procedural guidance on how to implement new amendments to the law in a timely manner. Prior to the current round of amendments, the law had been updated several times, most notably in January 2022, March 2022, and December 2022. Recent amendments further deepen structural challenges brought by multiple levels of ownership across the SWF, other holding companies and line ministries. To what extent the revised law on State Property can be instrumentalised for more structural reform of the quasi-state sector is unclear.

Overall, the size of the quasi-state sector, which encompasses a variety of commercial and non-commercial entities, poses a difficulty in organising the imposition of legal amendments to the law on State Property. Classifying all existing entities under a holistic system according to their economic activity requires a dedicated workstream and roll-out. Moreover, organising SOEs in line with legal provisions may further pose difficulties connected to establishing new procedures that are currently left unaddressed. There is a lack of a holistic plan of the roll out for the legal changes made.

2.1.3. Ownership policy accountability, disclosure and review

> ***C. The ownership policy should be subject to appropriate procedures of political accountability and disclosed to the general public. The government should review at regular intervals its ownership policy.***

As previously mentioned, the main policy document laying out state ownership, which is the law on State Property, is revised frequently. Although this could perhaps be said to provide regular opportunities to review the implicit ownership policy, it is hardly in itself a good practice. An excessive number of legal changes may hamper the ability of the public sector to keep abreast with regulatory expectations. It creates unreliable conditions and increases legal risks for enterprises. Introducing unexpected obligations might also lead to passivity and lower engagement in the reform process.

The ownership entity should have clearly defined relationships with relevant public bodies, including the state supreme audit institutions. Yet, in Kazakhstan, the ownership of SOEs is dispersed across multiple state entities involved in the management, oversight, and monitoring of SOEs. Each of these entities, which are the MNE, MF and respective line ministries, hold clearly identifiable functions which are laid out in the law on State Property.

Yet, some of the duties and responsibilities delegated to a given state entity have interdependencies with each other. For example, while the MF monitors and tracks key performance indicators regarding corporate governance of the quasi-state sector, the responsibility to inform and create new legal expectations lies within the MNE. Furthermore, industry-relevant line ministries might be involved in liaison and data collection and monitoring of a given SOE. This creates a complex communication pipeline that flows not only between ministries and SOEs, but also across ministries.

Furthermore, the exact role of national holdings and national management holdings, which often create an additional layer between the SOE and the state ownership entity, is left undefined in the law on State Property. This creates ambiguity, especially since national (management) holdings are responsible for delegating state owner objectives to the SOEs in their portfolio.

2.1.4. Defining SOE Objectives

> ***D. The state should define the rationales for owning individual SOEs and subject these to recurrent review. Any public policy objectives that individual SOEs, or groups of SOEs, are required to achieve should be clearly mandated by the relevant authorities and disclosed.***

State enterprises, including state-owned national holding companies, JSCs and LLCs of which a controlling stake in the authorised capital belongs to the state, are expected to implement five-year action plans, which define the main areas of activ ty and indicators of financial and economic activities.

These action plans are constructed based on 10-year development plans. Development plans are aligned with strategic policy documents issued by the Republic of Kazakhstan, and thus represent the objectives delegated by the state owner. Development plans are approved by the government of Kazakhstan, and their implementation is monitored based on the achievement of pre-set KPIs.

Action and development plans are specific to the SOE, SWF and SOHC that is expected to implement them. They outline key strategic and financial indicators that the enterprise is expected to meet within a given time frame. The action plan for Samruk-Kazyna additionally mentions indicators that apply to the fund group at large, such as the net asset value growth of its portfolio of SOEs, labour productivity, and the gross inflow of foreign direct investment. It also includes an indicator which tracks the share of electricity produced from renewable sources.

However, broad and high-level state-set objectives and motivations of state ownership are not articulated clearly. Furthermore, among the indicators that SOEs are monitored against, it is unclear which ones align with state-owner delegated objectives, and which ones are purely commercial in nature. In the Concept of State Property Management and Privatisation,[1] it is mentioned that a list of objectives of the state for the management of various types of state property should be determined by relevant legal acts. Yet, other legal documents surrounding state ownership lack a pronounced rationale for state ownership, and it remains unclear which legal acts may be deemed as relevant to include such information.

2.1.5. Summary

Unless Kazakhstan defines a holistic and high-level ownership policy which clarifies the rationales for state ownership, the applicable scope of other legal documents which cover certain aspects of ownership arrangements will remain constrained to specific sample of SOEs. In the larger oversight of the quasi-state sector and the legal provisions that surround it, there thus are differences between how certain SOEs may be held accountable towards the state owner, as well as how the state itself is accountable as an owner.

Ownership arrangements in Kazakhstan are carried by a plethora of laws which are frequently revised and amended. The expectations and objectives communicated by the ownership entity to the SOE are often implicit and KPIs that stem from state-set five- and 10-year development and action plans are often not directly accessible to the public. All this, in combination with the breadth of the legal framework surrounding state ownership, further amplifies the role of the President as the ultimate decision-making power where unclear ownership arrangements are called to be addressed and resolved. The current system relies on a high degree of discretionary power vested in the President to create and change rationales for state involvement in the corporate economy.

When directly comparing Kazakhstan's practices with respect to the recommended outcomes detailed in the SOE Guidelines, Kazakhstan appears to deviate in certain areas. Most notably, in the SOE Guidelines, it is recommended to clearly state the objectives that underpin state ownership and to disclose the overall rationale for ownership ideally in the context of an ownership policy. Such rationales should underscore how state ownership provides value to society. While the state details rationales for ownership in various legal documents, such justifications fail to cover the SOE sector as a whole, and often only apply to certain sub-sections of enterprises. Kazakhstan misses an ownership policy that comprehensively covers the entire quasi-state sector, and further work to scope and outline said sector to ensure all SOEs are considered in any legal provision that it is subject to.

2.2. The state's role as an owner

> ***The state should act as an informed and active owner, ensuring that the governance of SOEs is carried out in a transparent and accountable manner, with a high degree of professionalism and effectiveness.***

2.2.1. Simplification of operational practices and legal form

> ***A. Governments should simplify and standardise the legal forms under which SOEs operate. Their operational practices should follow commonly accepted corporate norms.***

As noted in chapter 1.3, the state, directly and via state-owned holding companies, currently holds 700 enterprises at the central level of government. The majority of these SOEs (46%) operate as LLCs, followed by JSC (32%), with differing corporate governance practices, which were noted throughout the paper (LLCs often being bound to less stringent rules). Each company type is governed by its own law which apply equally to JSCs and LLCs in the private sector. A third type of SOEs are the so-called state enterprises which have a separate legal form mandated by the State Property law.

Recent efforts have been made to align certain corporate governance practices, including the establishment of supervisory boards (with independent members) and committees, as well as disclosure requirements. Nevertheless, corporate governance standards and practices in LLCs and state enterprises, particularly related to board practices and internal controls, are typically weaker compared to JSCs, often lacking effective enforcement.

The planned reforms noted in chapter 1.6 - aimed at aligning the laws for state-owned enterprises - do not automatically equate to adherence to the same corporate governance norms as comparable privately-owned entities. Distinctions still exist in areas such as public procurement practices, bankruptcy or insolvency proceedings, access to financing and state guarantees, criteria for BODs, and the nomination and appointment practices of governing bodies. These will be clarified in the upcoming chapter.

2.2.2. Political intervention and operational autonomy

> ***B. The government should allow SOEs full operational autonomy to achieve their defined objectives and refrain from intervening in SOE management. The government as a shareholder should avoid redefining SOE objectives in a non-transparent manner.***

In Kazakhstan, the legal and regulatory framework for SOEs notes minor provisions related to governance and potential political interference. On the one hand, the model Corporate Governance Code for instance outlines the powers vested in the governing bodies of SOEs, aiming to limit direct involvement in day-to-day matters by the ownership entity. On the other hand, the state and ownership entities (including the holding company Samruk-Kazyna) retains authority to approve vital corporate documents, such as strategic plans and financial decisions, often resulting in competing objectives for SOEs.

In practice therefore the state – as a sole or dominant shareholder in most SOEs - may control a number of corporate decisions and thus limit SOEs' operational autonomy, including with regards to hiring decisions. In addition, SOEs' boards and executive management seem to be subject to a high degree of political intervention, as revealed by frequent dismissals of CEOs following announcements of the President. The Prime Minister is also sitting on the boards of Baiterek and Samruk-Kazyna.

Unlike most other countries, in Kazakhstan the President communicates clear guidance to state-owned enterprises, that are subsequently coined into implementable objectives by the relevant national authorities. Government ownership entities thus translate the President's strategic guidance for SOEs into action plans, with each point subsequently overseen by a responsible executor. The boards of the concerned SOEs are usually not consulted in the process, which is not in line with good practices. In addition, some state-owned enterprises are also assigned a special operator status. Here the government has the ongoing opportunity to intervene in their day-to-day operations, if this is considered as "strategic and needed for society".

> ***C. The state should let SOE boards exercise their responsibilities and should respect their independence.***

As mentioned above, Kazakh SOEs have historically been subject to political interference, which has also been the case through political appointees on boards and in executive positions. Board members are generally required to act "in the interest of the company" and to apply a duty of care in their activities as given in the model Corporate Governance Code for SOEs. Despite this, there is currently no clear definition of the respective personal and state liability when civil servants (not to mention, state officials) are on SOE boards. There are also generally no guidelines nor Codes of ethics for members of the ownership entity and other state representatives serving as SOE board member in Kazakhstan.

In JSC and LLCs, boards are required to have a number of independent members appointed according to clearly set criteria of professional qualifications and independence. However, the widespread practice notes differently. Apart from boards not including the number of independent directors they should, they do not tend to be truly independent in addition. Even if there are independent directors, the OECD noted that they are still recommended to vote with the majority, are held responsible for SOE operations, and generally receive little to no renumeration.

The situation in SOEs overseen by holding companies is more mixed. Starting in 2013, Samruk-Kazyna undertook significant efforts to professionalise boards and improve their performance management framework, in the aim of enhancing their autonomy and independence. They also removed all politicians from the boards. At the same time, most of the BODs of subsidiaries remain composed of 7 members, in most cases with the majority stemming from Samruk-Kazyna.

As recognised by this report SK subsidiaries have undergone substantial corporate governance reforms, and notable progress has been achieved to mitigate the risk of undue political interference. However, there have been cases where BOD apparently faced pressures, often in the form of direct or indirect political influence on decisions reserved for SOEs' governing bodies, leading to resignations of board members. The mission team was told of several recent cases where, in particular, foreign independent directors chose to leave the boards of SOEs.

2.2.3. Centralisation of the ownership function

> ***D. The exercise of ownership rights should be clearly identified within the state administration. The exercise of ownership rights should be centralised in a single ownership entity, or, if this is not possible, carried out by a co-ordinating body. This "ownership entity" should have the capacity and competencies to effectively carry out its duties.***

Kazakhstan has not established a centralised ownership entity to exercise state ownership. As mentioned in earlier sections, ownership in Kazakhstan is de-facto practiced by various line ministries. Decision-making authority as attributed by the law on State Property is vested in the MNE, which acts as a state planning organ. It exercises its powers as foreseen by the law, acts of the President and the government of Kazakhstan. Next to the MNE, the MF takes responsibility of the monitoring and oversight of operational results of enterprises part of the quasi-governmental sector. Furthermore, the NBK and other ministries, such as the MIID, as well as national (management) holdings, further hold stake in practicing ownership on behalf of the state next to the planning and monitoring functions implemented by the MNE and MF. The following sections specifically shine light on the two most important state ownership bodies – the MNE and MF, as well as the de-facto state owner of the largest share of state assets: Samruk-Kazyna.

Additionally, national management holding companies and national holding companies also further add fragmentation and dispersion to the existing model. There is no single entity responsible and accountable for execution of the state ownership function (or for co-ordination). This also leads to the lack of an aggregate report and an overview on state ownership.

Legislation, policymaking and planning in the hands of the Ministry of National Economy

The main policy and planning body part of the ownership function of the state is the MNE. According to the law on State Property, the MNE shall be responsible for drafting and forming policies in the sphere of state property management and develop and approve normative legal acts that relate to the management of state property. Together with other authorised bodies for state property management, the MNE develops and approves strategic development plans and the model Corporate Governance Code for JSCs, which also is applicable to Baiterek, but not to Samruk-Kazyna.

However, SOE governance in Kazakhstan lacks a broadly applicable, holistic ownership policy that clarifies the degree of involvement of the MNE insofar as the ownership rationales and objective of state ownership of certain companies is concerned. The overall magnitude and powers of the MNE are thus not comprehensively recognised and are likely to be understated in the overall implied ownership function of the state. Despite its far-reaching activities in SOE oversight, as *inter alia*, the state body organising the selection of members of SOE supervisory boards or early termination of the term of a given board member, its role as policymaker adds an important additional feature highlighting the MNE's authority. As the ministry overseeing the state budget, as well as being intricately involved in the policymaking process, the MNE is in a key position to conduct strategic fiscal planning.

Overall, the degree with which the MNE practices its law- and policy making powers appears to intersect with duties to supervise the management of the SOEs owned by it. Further to its role as fiscal planner of the state budget, its ability to influence strategic management of SOEs appears to create an imbalance between the powers of the MNE and other line ministries involved in the ownership of SOEs. This is additionally magnified by its role to act as the main contractor for public-private partnerships undergone in Kazakhstan, whereby it is part of the process in selecting suitable companies to carry out state-funded projects.

Monitoring of performance exercised by the Ministry of Finance

The MF complements the MNE's role in practicing oversight of the quasi-state sector by monitoring operational performance and financial results of SOEs. On top of this, it is in charge of executing the process of privatisation or alienation of SOEs. As part of its monitoring function for the sake of maintaining an overview of strategically important assets, the MF also assesses the effectiveness of management of SOEs. As part of the Ministry of Finance and in accordance with Law No. 490/2003, the State Property and Privatisation Committee monitors SOEs in sectors of the economy of strategic importance.

As laid out in the law On State Monitoring of Property in Sectors of Economy Having Strategic Significance, No. 490/2003 one of the main mandates of the MF's monitoring activities is to ensure economic security. This is defined as condition to protect national economics of Kazakhstan from internal and external conditions, processes and factors threatening its stable development and economic independence. The law identifies the extraction and processing of fuel and energy mineral resources (coal, oil, gas, uranium and metallic ores), machine industry, space activity, agro-industrial complex, water industry, chemical industry, transport and communication, production and electric energy distribution, as well as branches producing products of military-industrial purpose as economic areas of strategic importance.

In addition to monitoring the quasi-state sector's financial performance and KPI achievement, the MF also upkeeps the register for state property. The register offers a centralised repository of information of SOEs, and includes financial results for some of them. The state register, as was observed by the OECD team, is not complete and have registered on its accounts only part of the information on properties of holding companies and communal properties. Thus, the MF is tasked with the monitoring of SOEs that are of strategic importance among others, and to organise this information to provide advice on privatisation, liquidation, or alienation of state property. It lacks enforcement powers that allow for the maintenance of economic security, but rather appears to influence decision-making by other line ministries ownership, as well as the government.

Samruk-Kazyna as de-facto owner of state-owned shares of SOEs

While the law on State Property lays out the responsibilities and authorities of the MNE, MF, NBK, and other line ministries involved in state ownership, its applicability does not cover Samruk-Kazyna and the portfolio companies owned by it. Samruk-Kazyna is regulated by its own law No. 550-IV/2012 and sets the strategic plans for itself and its portfolio companies independently from the oversight of MNE.

According to information received by the Kazakh authorities, as well as to computations made by the OECD Secretariat, Samruk-Kazyna manages 61% of the state-owned sector in terms of asset size. Thus, it effectively plays an oversized role in the state-ownership function and its share of total state ownership is comparable to the central ownership agencies (or holding companies) by some OECD countries claiming to practice "largely centralised ownership models".

The special legal status of Samruk-Kazyna can to some extent be said to conflict with the competing objective vesting powers in a small number of responsible line ministries. While recent reform efforts made to the law on State Property increase the duties of responsibilities for the MNE and MF in a more centralised ownership model, Samruk-Kazyna's largely autonomous position in the state ownership hierarchy is a source of inconsistencies. As a result, Kazakhstan's overall ownership model is effectively a hybrid that involves elements of both centralised and decentralised structures.

2.2.4. Accountability of the ownership entity

> ***E. The ownership entity should be held accountable to the relevant representative bodies and have clearly defined relationships with relevant public bodies, including the state supreme audit institutions.***

In the absence of a centralised ownership entity practicing oversight of the state-owned sector, the main responsibility of managing and overseeing SOEs is vested in line ministries, with the Presidential administration retaining the highest decision-making authority. Despite the lack of such a centralised body in the Kazakh ownership system, the law on State Property includes a rather detailed description of the respective responsibilities of the MNE and the MF. This ensures a certain degree of transparency and accountability within the existent state ownership model and improves oversight of allocated duties across the different ministries and could be argued to provide elements of an ownership co-ordination model.

The supreme audit chamber of Kazakhstan is the supreme institution of public audit that implements external public audit and financial control and is directly accountable and subordinated to the President of Kazakhstan. It is the highest body of state audit and is primarily responsible for selecting independent external auditors and for managing the state budget, though may conduct ad-hoc state audits of state-owned enterprises at the request of the Presidential administration. In 2021, the national gas company QazaqGaz was instructed to improve the transparency surrounding its procurement system, as well as to conduct changes in its internal employee policy. A full-scale audit was ordered to shine light on the company's activities.

2.2.5. The state's exercise of ownership rights

> ***F. The state should act as an informed and active owner and should exercise its ownership rights according to the legal structure of each enterprise. Its prime responsibilities include:***
>
> ***F.1. Being represented at the general shareholders meetings and effectively exercising voting rights.***

The law on State Property differentiates between state controlled JSCs or limited LLPs, and JSCs and LLPs which do not have a dominating stake of state participation. In the case of dominant state control, the controlling block of stock or controlling stakes of participating in charter capital is more than 50% of the voting shares of JSCs or more than 50% of stakes of the LLP. According to Article 166, the authorised state body that is exercising rights of ownership and use of state block of shares, shall represent the interests of the state as the shareholder on issues referred to the competence of the general meeting of shareholders in accordance with the relevant legislation of Kazakhstan.

As elaborated in the prior chapter, the exact ownership interests are pooled from a variety of legal sources spanning areas of national security, the maintenance of oversight of national monopolies and markets with low level of competition, as well as strategic facilities. Given the low number of companies in the quasi-state sector that are not majority-owned, the state's representation of interests as an owner plays a prominent part in annual shareholder meetings. This particularly applies to large and significant companies owned by the state, which typically are more than 90% owned by the state. Conducive to Kazakhstan's dispersed ownership model, there may be different types of the state involved in maintaining state shares of a given company. This may create one-sided shareholder meetings dominated by majority owners of shares.

> ***F.2. [The state's prime responsibilities include:] Establishing well-structured, merit-based and transparent board nomination processes in fully- or majority-owned SOEs, actively participating in the nomination of all SOEs' boards and contributing to board diversity.***

Further to voting rights outlined above, state ownership bodies may also appoint representatives in SOE BOD of JSCs and LLPs in which the only shareholder is the state. As stated in the law on State Property, state ownership bodies may also suggest a candidate who, upon approval, is elected to the BOD in SOEs that are not wholly-owned.

A similar representative board member nomination system applies to portfolio companies managed under Samruk-Kazyna and Baiterek, which also position representatives on the boards of its portfolio SOEs. While each member of the BOD holds equal voting rights, there are special legal provisions on the liability of board members regarding voting decisions of strategic importance. If the board makes a decision that results in an economic loss, those board members that voted against the implemented strategic decision or who did not participate in the voting, are not held liable by law.

In a planned amendment to the law on State Property, the overall board nomination process is sought to be further refined. The planned amendment details that the MNE must approve a procedure for open recruitment of board members that have been nominated by state authorities as representative members. One aspect that is designed to make the procedure more transparent is the publication of a list of candidates, specifically of independent directors, that is maintained by the MNE. Such changes, while yet to be implemented, are welcomed to improve the effectiveness and overall balance of perspectives of boardroom discussions.

> ***F.3. [The state's prime responsibilities include:] Setting and monitoring the implementation of broad mandates and objectives for SOEs, including financial targets, capital structure objectives and risk tolerance levels.***

SOEs in Kazakhstan organise their 5- and 10-year strategy based on respective action and development plans. As mentioned in prior chapters of the report, development plans are aligned with strategic policy documents issued by the Republic of Kazakhstan, and thus represent the objectives delegated by the state owner. Development plans are approved by the government of Kazakhstan, and their implementation is monitored based on the achievement of pre-set KPIs.

Action and development plans are specific to the SOE, and SOHC that is expected to implement them. They outline key strategic and financial indicators that the enterprise is expected to meet within a given time frame. The action plan of Samruk-Kazyna mentions indicators that apply to the fund group at large and is largely self-decided. It includes a variety of KPIs that can be grouped to be commercial and non-commercial in nature.

The MF is tasked with the monitoring of financial and non-financial performance of SOEs overseen by state authorities. Overall, the top-down setting of large-scale targets for SOEs appears to leave little adaptability for SOE boards to overcome and foresee long-term strategic risks as they dawn. Although the monitoring function of the MF allows to effectively maintain an overview of SOEs and their achievements, there appears little autonomy and flexibility for boards in engaging in defining strategies to attain the detailed 5- and 10- year strategic roadmaps.

> ***F.4. [The state's prime responsibilities include:] Setting up reporting systems that allow the ownership entity to regularly monitor, audit and assess SOE performance, and oversee and monitor their compliance with applicable corporate governance standards.***

While there is no single centralised ownership entity in Kazakhstan and SOE monitoring, auditing, and assessment tasks are split across various responsible ministries and state audit institutions, the MF takes the lead in carrying out and overseeing most of them and publishing their results.

Reporting expectations on SOEs are found in various laws. The law on State Monitoring of Property in Sectors of the Economy of Strategic Importance No. 490/2003 requires state monitoring, including the observation, collection and analysis of information, for a small pool of SOEs. Currently, there are 133 enterprises which are considered to be of strategic importance and thus fall into the scope of the law. The results of the monitoring of strategic SOEs are to be shared on the electronic database of the state monitoring of state property, which is maintained by the MF.

State-controlled JSCs and LLPs, including national management holdings, national holdings, national companies of which the state is a shareholder, state bodies, individuals and legal entities that shall be parties to trust agreements, apart from Samruk-Kazyna, which has its own monitoring and assessment systems, are subject to the Resolution On approval of the Rules of conducting monitoring of management efficiency of state property No. 1546/ 2012. The main tasks of monitoring include:

- a comprehensive analysis of the effectiveness of management of monitoring facilities in production, technical, technological, financial, economic, legal, environmental and other parameters and a holistic assessment of the state property in terms of the predictability of its development in accordance with the interests of the state;
- analysis of fulfilment of obligations and conditions of concession agreements or public-private partnership agreements, trust management, property hiring (lease) of state property;
- identification of problems and development of recommendations for further development of state enterprises and legal entities with the participation of the state (hereinafter referred to as the monitoring facility);
- expert assessment of the prospects for the development of equipment, technology of monitoring facilities and their impact on the state of the regions;
- creation and maintenance of an electronic database for monitoring objects;
- creation of favourable conditions for ensuring economic growth of the state, maximum reduction of the degree of vulnerability of the economy from possible negative factors, promotion of investment inflow into the national economy.

When monitoring facilities, the above law foresees the monitoring data to be collected by independent experts who conduct on-site surveys. This data shall be drawn up in a report and primary materials that shall be stored in the form of an electronic report and then uploaded to an online register.

Once the monitoring procedure is drawn up, the respective state body or ministry tasked with the management of a given SOE must take monitoring results and recommendations issued by the MF into account for its own state property management results. It must then decide whether, in certain cases, to impose a disciplinary sanction on the head of the SOE in accordance with the law.

While there are assessment and monitoring systems in place, the dispersion of responsibilities cannot be undertaken at a central level, given the dispersed nature of ownership. Furthermore, Samruk-Kazyna and portfolio companies, again, are exempt from this procedure and instead follow their own protocol. As a result of this, there is a large stake of SOEs for which the state does not have a monitoring system in place.

> ***F.5. [The state's prime responsibilities include:] Developing a disclosure policy for SOEs that identifies what information should be publicly disclosed, the appropriate channels for disclosure, and mechanisms for ensuring quality of information.***

The state bodies involved in practicing ownership of SOEs do not detail precise SOE disclosure requirements that apply consistently across the quasi-state sector. Instead, the disclosure and reporting expectations are found in various laws that apply to commercial companies in general. The main legal document which outlines disclosure requirements is the law On Accounting and Financial Reporting No. 234/2007, which establishes the system of accounting and financial reporting in Kazakhstan for domestic companies. It details a set of minimum requirements to be included in the financial reporting of companies, including those (partially) owned by the state.

Furthermore, all domestic listed companies, financial institutions, large unlisted companies, as well as "organisations of public interest" shall prepare their financial statements and annual reports in accordance with a single set of international standards. These standards are the IFRS (international financial reporting standards). Whether SOEs comply with these rules is analysed in detail in later sections.

However, Kazakh authorities have shared plans to implement aggregate reporting on entities owned by the state. Aggregate reports can serve as a useful tool to conduct comparative analysis by the state owner. For this reason, publishing aggregate reports may serve as a useful exercise in identifying needs or gaps in the current reporting obligations for SOEs, and to adequately fill them in the future.

> ***F.6. [The state's prime responsibilities include:] When appropriate and permitted by the legal system and the state's level of ownership, maintaining continuous dialogue with external auditors and specific state control organs.***

State ownership bodies are not put in a position to maintain dialogue with the supreme audit chamber, which acts as Kazakhstan's supreme audit institution (SAI), responsible for conducting state audits. As detailed in the law on Governmental Audit and Financial Control No. 393/ 2025, regulation regarding state audits and financial control are carried out by the President, the government, and the supreme audit chamber itself. The applicable principle of independence of the chamber's work, which is the prevention of interference in governmental audit and financial control activities, may prevent this.

The extent to which the external auditor and state owner bodies exchange is unknown and not accounted for in the law surrounding external audits of enterprises belonging to the quasi-state sector.

> ***F.7. [The state's prime responsibilities include:] Establishing a clear remuneration policy for SOE boards that fosters the long- and medium-term interest of the enterprise and can attract and motivate qualified professionals.***

As described in the JSC law and the model Corporate Governance Code, it is the exclusive competence of the remuneration committee of the SOE boards to set the remuneration level for the CEO and executive body members. As also mentioned in the relevant board sections, in practice, remuneration is usually established between the CEO and the state ownership entities. General remuneration policies foresee that the size of the remuneration depends on the complexity of SOE operations, personal competence and the candidate's competitiveness in the market and the SOE's economic situation. Yet, whether this is consistent with long- and medium-term interests of the enterprise, and thus based on performance outcomes, is unclear.

The ownership entities can impose salary caps depending on the country's economic situation, as was the case during the COVID-19 pandemic. Remuneration does not appear to follow a standardised procedure delivering predictable and consistent remuneration outcomes across the quasi-state sector.

Samruk-Kazyna imposes holding-internal remuneration rules that apply to its portfolio companies in line with the Corporate HR Management Standard of the Samruk-Kazyna Group. Representatives of Samruk-Kazyna on the BOD of its state-owned enterprises that belong to its portfolio are subjected to a separate resolution of Samruk-Kazyna's management board, and appear to be decided in the context of opaque internal discussions and negotiations.

Samruk-Kazyna's large portfolio companies implement transparent procedures for non-representative board members, in line with the resolution and standard. Its largest portfolio asset, KazMunayGas, determines the remuneration policy alongside the performance of members of the board. Remuneration paid to members of the management board also include performance-related part to encourage such board members towards the strategic and priority goals outlined in measurable KPI scorecards.

2.2.6. Summary

The various legal forms and categories of SOEs in Kazakhstan result in the absence of standardised practices concerning corporate governance and law applicability. Kazakhstan has not established a centralised ownership entity to exercise state ownership (hybrid of twin-track and decentralised ownership), and is de-facto practiced by various line ministries. Holding companies constitute a de-facto (partial) centralisation of the ownership rights. As a result, the state in Kazakhstan cannot act as an informed and active owner.

Kazakh SOEs have also been historically subject to political interference, which has also been the case through political appointees on boards and in executive positions. Though increased transparency on the nomination and selection procedure would be welcomed to bring practices in Kazakhstan in closer alignment with international standards, the realisation of these planned amendments is still ongoing and presently an aim rather than a kickstarted reform effort. Another difficulty is that the state's role as an owner is dispersed across a multitude of different state bodies, as well as national (management) holding companies which tend to be out of reach of legal requirements that apply to other parts of the ownership function. These inconsistencies counter efforts to centralise ownership in the MNE and MF, while undermining the importance of Samruk-Kazyna as a de-facto owner of the majority of SOEs. There is currently no entity which assesses the performance of Samruk-Kazyna and other SOHC, rendering oversight difficult.

2.3. State-owned enterprises in the marketplace

> ***Consistent with the rationale for state ownership, the legal and regulatory framework for SOEs should ensure a level playing field when SOEs undertake economic activities.***

2.3.1. Separation of functions

> ***A. There should be a clear separation between the state's ownership function and other state functions that may influence the conditions for state-owned enterprises, particularly with regard to market regulation.***

While existent laws provide some clarity regarding the exercise of ownership by those state institutions that have a portfolio of SOEs, they provide little guidance as to how ownership is to be exercised on a whole-of-government basis. The main priority of the existent legal framework on state property management is to practice and enable effective state entrepreneurship. Utilising property, production, sale of goods, and provision of services provided by SOEs, Kazakhstan seeks to obtain income to finance the capability of the state to protect the interests of society. Comparatively little attention is given to securing the separation of the state's role as an enterprise owner from its roles as regulator and policy maker, which must be characterised as problematic given the complex and dispersed ownership structures that prevail.

Thus, the responsibility for industrial/sectorial policies is intricate to discern from the state's ownership function, with line ministries simultaneously performing ownership and regulatory functions. Additionally, line ministries participate in strategic decision making such as SOEs' development plans, investment projects, and senior management appointment.

Ministries and their subsidiary bodies play a vital role in overseeing and regulating various industries in Kazakhstan, including those relevant to SOEs. They enforce industry-specific laws and rules, issue licenses and permits, monitor compliance, and promote fair competition within their respective sectors (alongside the competition agency).

Table 2.1 shows the overseeing and regulatory bodies of the selected 20 SOEs. A number of SOEs note the same overseeing and regulatory government body, rendering it difficult to separate the two functions. OECD interviews have also hinted at the fact that the functions are carried out within the same departments, for instance the *Committee of State Property and Privatisation* within the MF carries out all functions related to SOEs. When analysing the 700 SOEs in Kazakhstan, the OECD team noted that some ministries oversee up to 30 SOEs each, with the SOEs operating exactly in the sector which is regulated by these particular ministries.

As for Samruk-Kazyna, it aims to differentiate its powers as a shareholder of the SOE and the powers related to the performance of government functions. Within 9 SOEs directly owned and overseen by holding companies, there is the aim for a clear separation between the ownership and regulative function. Different government bodies and structures are responsible for regulating the activities of these SOEs and executing ownership rights, which reduces the risk of creating a conflict of interest. KEGOC – the electric power company – is for instance regulated by the Ministry of Energy, alongside the Committee for Regulating National Monopolies. The Committee approves their tariffs, and sits within the MNE.

Table 2.1. Information of selected 20 SOEs on owner, overseeing and regulatory bodies

Full title of entity	Ownership form	Ownership share, %	Owner government body/SOHC	Line ministry/SOHC	Regulatory government body
National Company "QazaqGaz" JSC	SOHC	100	Samruk-Kazyna	Samruk-Kazyna	Ministry of Energy
KazTransGaz Aymak JSC	SOHC	100	Qazaq Gas	Qazaq Gas	MNE, Ministry of Energy, Agency for Protection & Development of Competition
National Company Kazakhstan Temir Zholy JSC	SOHC	100	Samruk-Kazyna	Samruk-Kazyna	Ministry of Industry and Infrastructure Development
Kazakhstan Railcars Building Company LLC	SOHC	78.47	Kaztemirtrans NC	Kazakhstan Temir Zholy NC	Ministry of Industry and Infrastructure Development
Kuryk Port LLC	SOHC	100	Kazakhstan Temir Zholy NC	Kazakhstan Temir Zholy NC	Ministry of Industry and Infrastructure Development
Fund on Entrepreneurship Development Damu JSC	SOHC	100	Baiterek	Baiterek	Ministry of National Economy
Authority AIFC JSC	State	100	National Bank	Ministry of Finance	Management Council and AIFC Governor
Banking Servicing Bureau of the National Bank JSC	State	100	National Bank	National Bank	National Bank
Kazakhavtodor LLC	State	100	KazAutoZhol NC	Ministry of Industry and	Ministry of Industry and

Full title of entity	Ownership form	Ownership share, %	Owner government body/SOHC	Line ministry/SOHC	Regulatory government body
			JSC	Infrastructure Development	Infrastructure Development
International Airport Nursultan Nazarbayev JSC	State	100	Ministry of Finance	Ministry of Industry and Infrastructure Development	Ministry of Industry and Infrastructure Development
Institute of Economic Research JSC	State	100	Ministry of Finance	Ministry of National Economy	Ministry of National Economy
National Center for Neirosurgery JSC	State	100	Ministry of Finance	Ministry of Healthcare	Ministry of Healthcare
SK-Pharmacy LLC	State	100	Ministry of Finance	Ministry of Healthcare	Ministry of Healthcare
National Geological Exploration Company "KazGeology" JSC	State	100	Ministry of Finance	Ministry of Ecology, Geology and Natural Resources	Ministry of Ecology, Geology and Natural Resources
Khabar Agency JSC	State	100	Ministry of Finance	Ministry of Information and Public Development	Ministry of Information and Public Development
Special Economic zone "Ontustyc" Management Company JSC	SOHC	100	Social Entrepreneurial Corporation Shymkent	Social Entrepreneurial Corporation Shymkent	State Enterprise Entrepreneurialship and Industrial-Innovational Development Shymkent city
Plant after name of Kirov S. JSC	SOHC	99.57	Kazakhstan Engineering	Kazakhstan Engineering	Ministry of Industry and Infrastructure Development
Machine Building Plant named after Kirov S. JSC	SOHC	97.71	Kazakhstan Engineering	Kazakhstan Engineering	Ministry of Industry and Infrastructure Development
Republican Center for Space Communication JSC	State	100	Ministry of Finance	Ministry of Digital Development, Innovation and Aerospace Industry	Ministry of Digital Development, Innovation and Aerospace Industry
QAZEXPOCONGRESS National Company JSC	State	100	Ministry of Finance	Ministry of Trade and Integration	Ministry of Trade and Integration

Source: Information as of March 2023 provided by the government of Kazakhstan to the OECD team.

2.3.2. Stakeholder rights

> ***B. Stakeholders and other interested parties, including creditors and competitors, should have access to efficient redress through unbiased legal or arbitration processes when they consider that their rights have been violated.***

According to the Kazakh authorities, SOE stakeholders, including creditors and competitors, have access to the same means of redress, including legal or arbitration processes, as the stakeholders of private companies. Commercial disputes between SOEs are to be settled through the court system or, if established via contract between the parties, arbitration. The law on state property management notes that all subjects are equal before the law.

Overall, the rights of creditors, consumers and business partners are regulated by applicable laws and regulations, including the Civil Code, Bankruptcy law, Consumer Protection law, Competition law, Commercial Code, Foreign Investment law, Contract law, Intellectual Property law, and Labor law. Contentious procedures carried out before competent courts, as well as arbitral procedures, are regulated by the dispute resolution law.

The legal framework for contract disputes is set out in Article 27 of the civil Code noting the process of dispute settlements either in Kazakhstan's courts or at international arbitration. Kazakhstan is a signatory to the 1958 *New York Convention on the Recognition* and *Enforcement of Foreign Arbitral Awards*. The Astana City Court and the Supreme Court both consider investment dispute cases, and the government has established a Specialised Judicial Board to resolve cases on investment contracts between large investors and government bodies. In some cases, the International Arbitration Centre and Court of the AIFC can also be made use of. In addition, the legality of a wide range of ADR mechanisms for disputes between two private parties has been codified in the Entrepreneurial Code and the law on Mediation (OECD, 2023[1]).

Kazakhstan put in place the law on Arbitration,[2] which governs dispute settlement for both domestic and international businesses. For now, investors still note shortcomings in the legal regulation of arbitration procedures, in terms of the lacking impartiality and transparency. As a result, there have been cases of arbitration processes being instigated where there was a serious risk of conflict of interest due to undisclosed connections between the arbitration institution and one of the parties. These risks being particularly troublesome where one of the parties is a public body, whether an agency or an SOE.

2.3.3. Identifying the costs of public policy objectives

> ***C. Where SOEs combine economic activities and public policy objectives, high standards of transparency and disclosure regarding their cost and revenue structures must be maintained, allowing for an attribution to main activity areas.***

So far, Kazakhstan has not undertaken a comprehensive review of the SOEs that simultaneously undertake economic and publ c policy objectives, which would be needed to comprehend how the costs of public policy objectives are identified and disclosed across the entire SOE sector.

According to the State Property law, some SOEs operate within key sectors of the economy, which require SOEs to implement public policies. These include, for example, public service obligations placed on the national railway company or electricity provider. The list of national managing holdings, national holdings, and national companies that pursue public policy objectives is approved by the Kazakh government. The oil and gas sector is a good example which showcases the social burden on selected SOEs in Kazakhstan: for instance, KazMunayGas has a lost profit due the sale of artificially cheap oil to the domestic market in 2021.

According to some estimates, about three-quarters of all electricity generated in Kazakhstan is distributed at lower prices within financial and industrial groups. The remaining quarter goes to the regional retail markets, that is, the population, SMEs and budgetary organisations. Based on the information available, there appears to be limited transparency regarding the costs of these public service obligations.

Public policy activities (or so-called state objectives) are usually prioritised over the commercial interests of the SOE. Instructions on social obligations like one-off expenses or execution of social investment projects, and other additional obligations related to the core operations of the SOE, may come directly from the government body or its representatives in the SOEs' boards in the form of action plans. Due to the absence of a separate accounting system in place that can separate state social expenses from commercial ones, it makes it difficult to attribute the exact costs and revenue structures behind economic activities and public policy objectives carried out by SOEs.

Recent sources note that the government is planning on acquiring shares of KazMunayGas through its National Fund at a non-market value. This can help to finance budget, social and infrastructure projects and add additional financing sources for state budget. Despite the fact that this change in the budget rules is mentioned in the republican budget, it violates fiscal policy. This type of transfer may motivate transfers from the National Fund to the republican budget, rendering it difficult to separate expenditure. Especially as changes to the *Public Financial Management Concept* in December 2022, now allow the National Fund to directly (and not through the budget, as it was earlier) lend to the Samruk-Kazyna.

An additional point relates to the low financial performance by some SOEs, which could hint at the existence of "informal" expectations from the state that are not purely commercial, for example maintaining employment levels or contributing to local communities (for instance in the case of KazMunayGas). In such a large and geographically fragmented country such as Kazakhstan, these type of objectives are often on the President's agenda.

Samruk-Kazyna tends to receive requirements from the government to construct social projects. For this, SK has introduced a special type of dividend payment to the sole shareholder, allowing for expenses spent on social objects to appear on financial statements.

> ***D. Costs related to public policy objectives should be funded by the state and disclosed.***

The competition agency finds that there currently is a lack of a unified system for monitoring public policy obligations (or 'state tasks' as called in Kazakhstan). Government entities themselves have therefore raised the need to create a monitoring system which prevents hiding the double counting of subsidies.

The renewed Budget Code is planning on including so-*called state tasks*, disclosing information on national projects and thereby determining funding limits for specific areas of support.

Listed SOEs already disclose expenditures incurred in their financial statements, including costs associated with non-core activity, such as the construction of social assets and other activities. KazMunayGas disclosed in its *2022 annual report*, that in accordance with the Government decree on the construction of a medical centre in Zhana-ozen town, the KazMunayGas croup accrued liabilities and paid KZT 12 597 mn (USD 26 322), classifying the expense as "distributions to Samruk-Kazyna". However, we observe that expenses are classified differently across reports, rendering it difficult to assess the entirety of public policy costs – let alone attribute main activity areas.

Potential shareholders can access information regarding the implementation of public policies and the roles of national companies and operators in the stock emission prospectus while existing shareholders can receive information on public policy execution in the SOE annual reports and audited consolidated financial statements. However, it is essential to clarify that SOEs do not have separate accounting or management systems that allow for clear and transparent classification of all public policy execution results from the regular commercial operations. For instance, the costs for maintaining certain employment levels in selected regions of KazMunayGas are not reflected in its financial statements.

From 2021 to 2022, the amount of funds allocated for the implementation of state tasks/ special operators nearly doubled, with a total number of approved applications of 157 and 119, respectively. The anti-monopoly agency has been observing a lack of state control in these cases, with little monitoring of these cases. Also, today there is no specific criteria provided within the legislation to classify services as a state task: this can be used by state bodies for the non-competitive purchase of goods (works, services) from subordinate organisations.

2.3.4. General application of laws and regulations

> ***E. As a guiding principle, SOEs undertaking economic activities should not be exempt from the application of general laws, tax codes and regulations. Laws and regulations should not unduly favour SOEs over their market competitors. SOEs' legal form should allow creditors to press their claims and to initiate insolvency procedures.***

Kazakh SOEs incorporated as LLC or JSC are not formally exempt from the application of general laws, tax Codes and regulations. Furthermore, in practice, both central and municipal SOEs have been the subject of several proceedings initiated by the Agency for the Protection and Development of Competition for the potential infringement of the Entrepreneurship Code and Yellow Pages rules. This indicates that SOEs are not systematically "protected" from competition law by virtue of their state ownership.

At the same time, Kazakhstan has legally created privileged conditions for SOEs, including granting special status and mandates, access to infrastructure, opportunities and financing. There are also many cases when national holding companies were excluded from selected legislation requirements. For instance, the security market law exempts SOHC from prudential requirements. Samruk-Kazyna is noted multiple times as an exception in the JSC law, and is additionally bound by its own law. It also has pre-emptive right to buy strategic facilities and bankrupt assets and the exclusion from some government procurement procedures.

Fully corporatised SOEs are subject to the same general laws and regulations applicable to private companies, but some SOEs established as state enterprises may benefit from some exemptions. Importantly, SOEs are not exempt from income tax.

Certain sectors are reportedly subject to particular attention by the competition agency, including the mining, electricity and telecom sectors, where SOEs have in the past been identified and sanctioned for engaging in anti-competitive behaviours and abuses of dominance – notably leading to the issuance in sanctions against firms. The agency has even identified a further concentration of market power across these sectors. Examples for distorting competition have been setting monopolistically high prices for needed inputs (transport/ oil), conflicts of interest and related party transactions, or cartel agreements. Another interesting development is the rise of anti-competitive actions of state bodies themselves.

In order to counter these trends, the agency is co-operating with the government and putting in place an action plan, focusing more on prevention in the following sectors:

1. Oil: The Action Plan provides for a number of measures to ensure equal access to oil, by adapting the cost of fuel and lubricants to the 2025 EAEU standard.
2. Coal: Work is planned to eliminate "unproductive" intermediaries.
3. Civil aviation: The roadmap aims at eliminating key barriers to the development of competition in the field of civil aviation (excessive state participation, limited access to infrastructure) and including, the sale of the state block of shares of QazaqAir and AirAstana, and extending the "open skies" regime until 2028, as well as securing non-discriminatory access for jet fuel retailers to airport refuelling complexes.
4. Construction: Until the end of 2023, the agency aims to curb the uncompetitive allocation of land plots through special economic zones and social and entrepreneurial corporations, and to toughen the responsibility of akimats in ensuring a transparent land sale/ market. The aim is to digitalise the process of purchasing property, and to enforce more scrutiny of the activities of a single operator (Kazakhstan Housing Company) when selecting engineering companies.
5. Healthcare: The plans include reducing excessive price regulation for medicine in the commercial segment and to reduce the level of state participation in the health sector. It also provides for a reduction in the share of non-competitive purchases for the storage and transportation of medicines and medical devices (Competition Agency, 2023[2]).
6. Telecommunications: The roadmap aims to demonopolise Kazakhtelecom and to ensure equal access to infrastructure between telecom operators, by introducing mandatory joint use of RFS and infrastructure (sharing).

2.3.5. Market consistent financing conditions

> ***F. SOEs' economic activities should face market consistent conditions regarding access to debt and equity finance.***
>
> ***In particular:***
>
> ***F.1. SOEs' relations with all financial institutions, as well as non-financial SOEs, should be based on purely commercial grounds.***

There have been several cases of interference by the state in market relations in the banking system and in the financial market more widely. After the financial crisis in 2008 in particular, the state began to actively offer state funding with low interest rates. This trend remains until today, with SOEs being among those corporate entities having facilitated access to loans. In 2021, the National Bank, the ARRFR and the government signed the *Agreement on the coordination of macroeconomic policy measures for 2021-2023*, in order to counter this trend – however, the plan has not come to fruit yet (Halyk Research, 2023[3]). In addition to offering cheaper loans, the state has also been increasing its ownership of commercial banks. The state recently became the owner of Bereke Bank and is increasing its ownership in the stock exchange, securities depository, and payment systems (Halyk Research, 2023[3]).

The Kazakh government's decision to increase state participation in commercial banks, particularly through the acquisition and subsequent activities of Bereke Bank, is apparently driven by the reported recognition of the bank's systemic importance, as well as the strategic intent to prepare it for a seamless transition to private ownership through effective restoration and rebranding measures.

Direct loans from the state to SOEs are not uncommon in Kazakhstan, and in addition SOEs can receive financial assistance from the government. This support may take the form of cash injections or other financial instruments. Kazakhstan's government has extended budget loans to SOEs at close-to-zero rates and preferential treatment of certain SOEs when issuing government guarantees for SOE loans. These special treatments have also been outlined in the Entrepreneurship Code.

SOEs generally have three options for obtaining funding, not all of which can be said to offer access market consistent conditions regarding access to debt and equity finance. The main sources of finance for Kazakhs SOEs are:

- equity capital through capital injections by its state-owner, including the form of government bonds, and fixed assets revaluation reserves
- bond issuances
- borrowing primarily through state-owned financial institutions (similar to Baiterek).

Moreover, for a number of SOEs raising capital in local and international financial markets proves to be difficult, since many find themselves at the early stages of establishing internationally-accepted corporate governance practices and standards of reporting and disclosure. Financially sound SOEs like KazMunayGas attract a significant portion of external debt from international bond markets. Majority of smaller SOE lending occurs within Kazakhstan.

This leaves many SOEs depending on state lending, which in many cases is provided on concessional terms. Concessional state lending has apparently contributed to the creation of a number of state monopolies in certain sectors of the economy financial market. Today, market lending has been almost completely replaced by the state in the markets: 1) mortgages; 2) leasing; and 3) agriculture (Halyk Research, 2023[3]).

> ***F.2. [SOEs' economic activities should face market consistent conditions regarding access to debt and equity finance. In particular:] SOEs' economic activities should not benefit from any indirect financial support that confers an advantage over private competitors, such as preferential financing, tax arrears or preferential trade credits from other SOEs. SOEs' economic activities should not receive inputs (such as energy, water or land) at prices or conditions more favourable than those available to private competitors.***

The state is a major provider of finance for a number of sectors either as a purchaser of their services or through subsidies and direct transfers. As of 2020, the state budget directed 32% of its expenditures to the quasi-state sector. In some sectors (social, construction, mass media in particular), the state acts as the main purchaser of their services. "This type of intra-budgetary circulation of service purchasing may distort competition" (Competition Agency, 2023[2]). For instance in 2020, 96% of Zerde National Infocommunication Holding JSC's revenues were received through the provision of IT services to various ministries.

The Kazakh government provides support to SOEs in various forms, including financial assistance, equity capital injections, or state property grants. SOEs gain privileged conditions compared to the private sector; they regularly receive support from the national budget, whether injections to equity (USD 1.25 bn 2020), subsidies (USD 1.25 bn in 2020), contracts awarded without competition, or market privileges; and have access to subsidised credit and direct links to government decision-makers. The holding companies also benefit from this situation: Samruk-Kazyna received USD 14 bn to finance its operations between 2008 to 2016.

The subsidiaries of Kazakhstan's holding companies have particularly experienced preferential treatment. For example, the "Damu" entrepreneurship fund's primary role is to function as a lending institution for Kazakh SMEs. Similarly, it is among the main objectives of KazAgroFinance to issue preferential leasing programs to modernise Kazakhstan's agricultural complex. Many of the companies managed under Baiterek's portfolio act as financing vehicles for the local community and have a strong social component in their mission statements. It is not their sole goal to attain revenues, but rather to help Kazakhstan achieve its national development plans. As a natural consequence, parts of the portfolio of both Baiterek and Samruk-Kazyna continue to underperform, while other firms are pulling their weight. The agency for competition further conducted an analysis of Baiterek's preferential measures, detecting:

- better lending rates for larger infrastructure projects
- priority treatment and accelerated consideration of applications when applying for support measures
- setting monopolistically high prices (Competition Agency, 2023[2]).

The Baiterek group is set up with the purpose of providing preferential finance to preferred economic activities in consistence with the national development plans. However, considering the number of preferential treatments subsidiaries receive, this is being found to distort the competitive landscape in Kazakhstan. The competition agency finds that the favoritism and the creation of unequal conditions for doing business by the state causes significant damage to entrepreneurship and the investment climate (Competition Agency, 2023[2]).

In 2022, a total of penalties in the amount of KZT 2.1 bl were imposed following detected violations of the competition law, of which KZT 1.9 bl or 90.5% were recovered (in 2017 - 3.2 billion tenge). Most penalties result from cartel formations or the abuse of monopoly positions.

> ***F.3. [SOEs' economic activities should face market consistent conditions regarding access to debt and equity finance. In particular:] SOEs' economic activities should be required to earn rates of return that are, taking into account their operational conditions, consistent with those obtained by competing private enterprises.***

Among the main providers of equity and financing for the SOEs, the largest national 'funds' (Samruk-Kazyna, Baiterek, and former KazAgro) show decreasing returns on equity and productivity over time, despite receiving capital injections from the government.

2.3.6. Public procurement procedures

> ***G. When SOEs engage in public procurement, whether as bidder or procurer, the procedures involved should be competitive, non-discriminatory and safeguarded by appropriate standards of transparency.***

There have been numerous legal reforms of the public procurement system in Kazakhstan, which has created difficulties for public procurers adapting to the new laws. An excessive use of direct procurement from one single supplier, a high number of failed bids, as well as a lack of integration of the market conditions depict the current procurement system. The national e-procurement system has been expanded, making it technically possible for nearly all procedures to be conducted electronically now.

While integrity measures exist, Kazakhstan has not yet developed a procurement-specific strategy. It has introduced a complaints management system, but could enhance the direct involvement of relevant external stakeholders. Public procurement in Kazakhstan remains administrative rather than a strategic function. Many issues which are prevalent in the public procurement system of Kazakhstan also apply to SOEs, including the extensive use of single source procurement and the low level of competition in procurement procedures. Previously, there were important differences in the legal and regulatory frameworks of SOEs and the government procurement sector. The most recent reform eliminated some discrepancies, but potential for further alignment remains (OECD, 2019[4]).

The primary legislation governing public procurement in Kazakhstan is the law on public procurement 530-V/ 2008, which applies to all public procurement entities, including SOEs, as both bidders and procurers. The government has further committed to improving procedures, also mentioned in the President's most recent state of the Nation address, raising the need for electronic procedures. This is important as the quasi-state sector remains a key player in the public procurement system, estimated at about 13% of GDP, slightly higher than the OECD average (12.6% in 2019).

Despite the legal provisions and political commitment, challenges related to transparency, fairness, and competition may still arise in practice. Certain practices – such as the separate public procurement system of SK - render it difficult to create an entirely transparent procurement system.

The state is a major provider of finance for a number of sectors either as a purchaser of their services or through subsidies and direct transfers. As of 2020, the state budget directed 32% of its expenditures to the quasi-state sector. In some sectors (social, construction, mass media in particular), the state acts as the main purchaser of their services. This type of intra-budgetary "circulation" of service purchasing may distort competition. For instance, in 2020, 96% of Zerde National Infocommunication Holding JSC's revenues were received through the provision of IT services to various ministries. The competition agency thus launched 133 investigations in 2022, with regard to public procurement and granting projects to related parties (Competition Agency, 2023[2]).

The state task or special operator status further justifies the provision of certain services aimed at ensuring socio-economic stability and (or) socio-cultural development of the state. The presence of this mechanism of public procurement simplifies the implementation of particularly urgent, important and complex projects (for example, seismic monitoring, ensuring financing of a guaranteed volume of free medical care, monitoring of territories affected by rocket and space activities) by SOEs. The status as special operator provides certain entities with exclusive rights, which allows the opportunity to purchase goods from one single entity. For example, in 2022, more than a third of all government purchases stemmed from a single entity (about USD 5 bn) (Competition Agency, 2023[2]).

2.3.7. Summary

Under the current state ownership arrangements in Kazakhstan, there is no particular separation between the government's ownership and regulatory functions. Line ministries undertake both regulatory and monitoring functions, as well as sectoral regulatory functions. Additionally, in terms of access to efficient redress through unbiased legal or arbitration processes, investors remain concerned about the reliability of domestic courts to adjudicate on disputes between private parties and the state or SOEs. Judicial corruption and integrity may dissuade foreign investors from entering Kazakhstan, and may discourage shareholders from pursuing dispute resolution through formal avenues.

Kazakhstan's SOEs are currently accounted for in a fragmented manner and there is no ongoing monitoring of the cost and revenue structures behind public policy objectives. On top of the difficulty of accounting, there is a lack of planning in distributing funds to specific areas which are considered as national projects. SOEs currently do not separate commercial and non-commercial activities and accounts, and the state does not develop adequate and transparent compensation for public service obligations.

Kazakh SOEs incorporated as LLC or JSC are not formally exempt from the application of general laws, tax Codes and regulations. At the same time, Kazakhstan has legally created privileged conditions for SOEs, including granting special status and mandates, access to infrastructure, opportunities and financing – which has proven to distort competition in the country. The number of SMEs and their contribution to GDP in Kazakhstan is markedly lower than in OECD countries.[3]

2.4. Equitable treatment of shareholders and other investors

> ***Where SOEs are listed or otherwise include non-state investors among their owners, the state and the enterprises should recognise the rights of all shareholders and ensure shareholders' equitable treatment and equal access to corporate information.***

2.4.1. Ensuring equitable treatment of shareholders

According to the MF, out of 700 SOEs, 174 enterprises have other shareholders apart from the state and holding companies. In 139 other companies the state and holding companies have holdings equal to or lower than 50%, i.e., non-controlling shares. This section covers SOEs in which the state or holding companies own controlling or majority shares. Minority shareholders of non-listed SOEs are dispersed and unorganised, rendering it difficult to monitor and assess the quality of interaction between minority shareholders and the SOE management. The minority shareholders of the six SOEs listed in the stock exchange usually individually co-ordinate and/ or via the *Qazaq Association of Minority Shareholders.*[4]

> ***The state should strive toward full implementation of the OECD Principles of Corporate Governance when it is not the sole owner of SOEs, and of all relevant sections when it is the sole owner of SOEs. Concerning shareholder protection this includes:***
>
> ***A.1. The state and SOEs should ensure that all shareholders are treated equitably.***

In an SOE where all voting shares are owned by one single shareholder, there is no requirement for general shareholder meetings. If other shareholders exist, the rules of convening and holding a general meeting, which are provided under the charter and JSC law, come into play.

Provisions regarding the equitable treatment of shareholders outlined in the JSC and LLC laws and applicable to corporatised SOEs with minority shareholders in the form of joint stock companies and limited liability companies. The state enterprises do not have shareholders but 100% state founders and thus minority shareholding is not applicable for this type of legal entities. In the non–listed 168 SOEs with minority/majority (private) shareholders, information regarding the shareholders' composition can be found in the audited financial statements placed on the financial statements' depository. The remaining six SOEs are listed on the Kazakhstan and foreign stock exchanges with generally low free floats in the range of 3% to 25% of shares.

The JSC law and SOE charter, broadly equivalent with applicable rules in most OECD countries, give the shareholders (as a whole) the rights to:

- participate in SOE management (via voting in general meetings, and by using all other rights that are reflected in the JSC law and in the SOE charter);
- the ability to access information on the SOE with written inquiries;
- request the confirmation that he/she is the owner/nominal owner of the stock;
- nominate candidates to the BOD;
- challenge SOE executive body decisions in court;
- receive a portion of SOE property upon liquidation;
- participate in preferential share purchases or changes in shares;

- propose agenda items for the general meeting of shareholders and obtaining information on the remuneration of BOD or executive body members (for shareholders with >5% ownership); and
- demand the convening of an extraordinary general meeting of shareholders or go to court if the BOD refuses, as well as convene a BOD meeting and request an audit of the SOE at the expense of the shareholder (majority shareholders with 10% and more shares).

Shareholders usually utilise their rights without limitations and in case of disagreement have an avenue to court appeals.

If an SOE conducts a general shareholder meeting, it adheres to the equitable treatment of all shareholders by ensuring that all shareholders have to be notified about the meeting at least 30 days in advance via simultaneous dissemination of information in the media and on the financial statements' depository website. During general shareholder meeting shareholders can cast votes in person or through an authorised representative. The JSC allows the general meeting of shareholders, including minority investors, to:

- amend and approve the charter and Corporate Governance Code
- approve the general meeting agenda and transactions related to issuing/delisting stocks, bonds and convertibles
- reorganise/ liquidate the SOE
- compose and renumerate the BOD
- select an audit company and approve audited financial statements
- distribute dividends and determine the share value for unorganised market redemption
- introduce or cancel the "golden share"
- approve major transactions.

The model Corporate Governance Code notes SOEs that with multiple shareholders, have to ensure fair and equitable treatment for all and "safeguard minority shareholders from potential exploitation by individuals who possess the capacity to directly, indirectly, or otherwise influence the SOEs' decisions".

However, since the model Code is not uniformly implemented there is often in practice a low level, or absence, of communication between majority and minority shareholders, and with the SOE. The disagreement between them usually relate to the situation where public policy objectives or SOE corporate decisions impact on minorities' financial interests, forcing minorities actively engage with majority shareholder, regulatory agencies and use social media platform to attract public attention to protect their interests.

To balance the interests of all shareholders or provide more rights to minority shareholders, some SOEs may assign additional rights to them and reflect this in their corporate charters. For instance, additional rights of parties to nominate the BOD/supervisory boards and executive bodies members, specifics of items for voting and others. Usually, such arrangements take place in non-listed SOEs that have several major shareholders in the ownership structure.[5] Usually disputes among major shareholders are resolved through negotiations between shareholders and the SOEs, with the option to appeal in court.

The general shareholder meeting may also overturn the executive body decisions, unless the SOE charter specifies otherwise. Decisions on the Corporate Governance Code, stock emission conditions, reorganisation and liquidation of the SOE, and the methodology to calculate the share value for buy-back must be taken by qualified majority voting (a majority of at least three quarters). The law does not impose restrictions or disclosure requirements on directors' dealings with the company's shares (EBRD, 2017[5]).

Shareholders may request a share buyback and use judicial mechanisms to enforce their rights if voted against in the general shareholders meeting. They can further request the:

- reorganisation of the SOE

- SOE's stock delisting
- major transactions
- changes to the charter which may limit shareholder rights and modifies the buyback methodology.

Box 2.1. Disputes related to Kazakhtelecom minority shareholders rights

End of 2018, the BOD of Kazakhtelecom approved an acquisition of 75% of the voting shares in Kcell, whose shares listed on the London Stock Exchange and KASE. Kcell is registered and provides mobile communication services in Kazakhstan. Close to 16 000 minority shareholders approved the deal, while in December 2018, Kazakhtelecom received 13 applications with demands from individual minority shareholders to buy-back their shares due to their disagreement with the BOD on the acquisition. As a result, Kazakhtelecom conducted negotiations with minorities and purchased the shares from 6 shareholders at a price determined by the BOD, while 3 applications were withdrawn by the shareholders with no explanation. Shareholders who acquired the shares after the deal date and requested buyback were denied. Four minorities appealed to court as they disagreed with the price of the buyback, but without avail. Kazakhtelecom initiated a criminal prosecution against some minority shareholders (for insider trading), but ultimately the allegations were not confirmed, and the prosecutor's office refused to open a case.

In the meantime, Kazakhtelecom's general shareholders meeting changed the rules for calculating the value of shares during a buyback, which was initially approved by the shareholders in 2006. The case showcases that minority shareholders have access to legal mechanisms to protect their rights, while the JSC legislation needs to incorporate more clear provisions regarding the procedures of interaction between shareholders and the SOE in case of disagreements.

Source: information generated by OECD team from different sources, including Kazakhtelecom JSC, www.kz.kursiv.media/2020-06-22/kazakhtelekom-protiv-minoritariya-pochemu-sud-dvazhdy-prinyal-storonu/; https://news.bloomberglaw.com/esg/kazakhtelecom-insider-trading-probe-triggered-by-buyout-attempt-1

Another intricate legal provision in Kazakhstan is that the state can exercise a "golden share" right, which gives the right to veto decisions of the general meeting of shareholders, the BOD and the executive body on issues specified by the company's charter. The right to veto, certified by a golden share, is non-transferable. However, in practice, according to the MNE information there are no cases when the state or holding companies were certified as an owner of the golden share.

> ***A.2. [Concerning shareholder protection this includes:] SOEs should observe a high degree of transparency, including as a general rule equal and simultaneous disclosure of information, towards all shareholders.***

All SOEs are required to publish its financial statements on the financial statements depositary's and stock exchange's website according to the regulations outlined in the State Property law, securities market law and the relevant regulatory directive.[6] Details regarding the SOE's affiliated individuals should also be available to the public. Shareholders have the right to access corporate documentation, and most companies provide a fair amount of information on KASE's website.

The JSC law ensures that the general meeting agenda should be prepared and accessible at the SOE's office for shareholder review at least ten days before the meeting date. Upon a shareholder's request, the documents must be provided within three working days. Shareholders have the right to access the minutes of the general meeting at any time and can receive a copy thereof. The OECD team could not find any information on cases in which minority shareholders were not granted information on shareholder meetings. In LLCs, participants are to be notified 30 days in advance about the meeting by "a body or an individual who calls the general meeting", which can be a corporate secretary in practice.

Certain documents (such as financial statements; share issuances) require prior approval by the BOD, and then approved on the general shareholders meeting. Thus, shareholders with representatives on the BOD have access to information earlier than minority investors, whose representatives may not be represented on the BOD.

In listed SOEs, the model Corporate Governance Code notes that an investor relations department should be established to handle shareholder and investor relations. It is also responsible for gathering, analysing, and preparing information for disclosure on the SOE's website. All six listed SOEs have investor relations departments that act as a communication channel between the SOE and shareholders.

To ensure the objectivity of the information on SOE websites, they are all requested to provide the same information:

- SOE charter
- development plans and strategic goals
- internal regulatory documents
- dividend policy and payment details
- profiles of BOD and executive body members
- financial statements and annual reports
- procurement details
- asset structure
- related party transactions and significant transactions details.

The selected 20 SOEs and 6 listed SOEs showcase different levels of information on their websites, with the highest degree observed for listed SOEs. The state and holding companies do not have appropriate control mechanisms to ensure placement of required by law information on SOEs' websites.

> ***A.3. [Concerning shareholder protection this includes:] SOEs should develop an active policy of communication and consultation with all shareholders.***

To ensure transparency and openness of decisions, the model Corporate Governance Code recommends communicating with fellow shareholders and representatives of SOEs on fundamental shareholder rights and corporate governance policy. The guidelines set by AA 1000 Shareholder Engagement Standard 12011[7] and details in the appendix of the Code enable minority shareholders to take part in the company's management. The Code outlines various methods for engaging with stakeholders, including questionnaires, focus groups, stakeholder meetings, public gatherings, seminars, feedback tools, and advisory councils. However, in practice these proceedings were not followed in pre-trail means, at least by listed SOEs.

Based on information provided by the *Qazaq Association of Minority Shareholders*, in SOEs that are publicly listed, the communication with the minority shareholders usually take place via exchange of the written correspondence. Additionally, based on legal rights a minority shareholder or his/her representative can participate and discuss the issues in the general shareholders' meetings. However, it is worth noting that in practice, open discussions or consultations between publicly listed SOEs and minority shareholders on significant operational and investment matters have reportedly been lacking in many cases. Typically, minority shareholders that have concerns about corporate transactions write to the CEO or his/her deputy (any deputy depending on the functionalities and case) of the company, majority shareholders of the listed company, the "investment ombudsman", or launch legal proceedings. The case below indicates poor communication and consultation between majority and minority shareholders and creates concerns regarding the ability of the BOD to conduct independent judgement and treat all shareholder interests equally.

Box 2.2. Disputes related to Kaztransoil minority shareholders rights

Kaztransoil (KTO) is a listed company those 10% of shares are floated on KASE. The President of Kazakhstan in his Address to the Nation on 1 September 2021 instructed to provide drinking water in the Atyrau and Mangistau regions. Based on this, KTO's subsidiary instructed to conduct a reconstruction and modernisation of the main water pipeline "Astrakhan - Mangyshlak".

At the end of 2022, minority shareholders of KTO repeatedly appealed to the investment ombudsman, Samruk-Kazyna, Ministry of Energy and KTO and raised concerns that the implementation of the project costing KZT 110 bn using corporate loans may harm the interests of shareholders. As a result, during 2022-2023 KTO improved the financing conditions by attracting KZT 70 bn from the National Fund at lower interest rates, decreasing the project costs down to KZT 100 bn.

Source: information provided to OECD team by KTO and Qazaq Association of Minority Shareholders.

Kazakhstan has also established an investment ombudsman, designated by the Kazakh government to assist with safeguarding the rights and lawful interests of investors. The primary functions are to address investor concerns through non-judicial and pre-trial means, and to submit recommendations to improve Kazakhstan's legislation on investment activities. Thus, minority shareholders have access to the investment ombudsman as an alternative and additional avenue to resolve disputes related to SOEs. However, important concerns arise as the role of the investment ombudsman is carried out by the Prime Minister. In addition to his general role in the oversight of state ownership practices he also holds the position of the Chairman of Samruk-Kazyna's BOD. This would seem to represent a conflict of interest, since all listed companies in Kazakhstan fall under the Samruk-Kazyna umbrella.

Depending on the ownership structure and percentage of shares of non-state shareholders of non-listed SOEs (in most cases this relates to private major shareholder), SOEs usually conduct preliminary consultations and communications with all shareholders on key transactions or decisions that should be taken by the BOD or general shareholders meetings. Such regular consultations allow to balance and preliminarily agree the positions of all shareholders, including term sheets before item will be included into agenda of governing bodies, leaving only critical unresolved issues for discussion at BOD or general shareholders meeting before their final decisions.

> ***A.4. [Concerning shareholder protection this includes:] The participation of minority shareholders in shareholder meetings should be facilitated so they can take part in fundamental corporate decisions such as board election.***

The JSC law provides some protections for minority shareholders, providing them with the right to vote at general meetings of shareholders. However, the extent of their influence on the management of the company may be limited, as the state often holds a controlling stake in these enterprises.

Shareholders owning, independently or together with other shareholders, 5% or more of the voting shares of the company, have the right to propose additional agenda items to the general shareholder meeting agenda, and demand compensation for losses caused by the company's authorities. Shareholders representing 10% of shares may convene a shareholder meeting. Meanwhile, the JSC law in detail notes that major corporate changes require a supermajority at the general shareholders' meeting. Conversely, there is no special provision in the JSC law to ensure minority shareholders (a) seat(s) on the BOD. The JSC law simply establishes that all shareholders have the right to propose their candidates to the BOD (whether majority or minority shareholder), after which the general meeting decides on the candidate.

Annex B on the composition of BOD of listed SOEs demonstrates that representatives of minority shareholders are infrequently present on the BOD of listed SOEs. Consequently, the ability of minority shareholders to take part in "fundamental corporate decisions" would seem to be in practice somewhat curtailed.

Although cumulative voting is in place, it does not apply in the case of a single director's resignation. When several members of the BOD are to be replaced, cumulative voting is used, however, the insignificant number of holding shares does not allow minorities to make an impact on general shareholders meeting voting results nor are minority representatives obliged to be elected as board members.

2.4.2. Adherence to the Corporate Governance Code

> ***B. National Corporate Governance Codes should be adhered to by all listed and, where practical, unlisted SOEs.***

A so-called *national Corporate Governance Code* applicable to all JSCs irrespective of state or private ownership structure has been developed by the National Entrepreneurial Chamber "Atameken" in 2021. The Corporate Governance Code of Samruk-Kazyna and the Model Corporate Governance Code were developed and approved years before in 2012 and 2018 respectively. Listed SOEs follow Samruk-Kazyna's Code, which generally have greater provisions related to corporate governance practices. Irrespective to the application of these two Codes, it does not appear that there is much monitoring being carried out by the SOEs, BOD and ownership entities on execution of the Codes' requirements and the quality of non-financial disclosure. There is no reference to the National Corporate Governance Code in the MNE's and Samruk-Kazyna's Codes and in the State Property Law.

Corporatised SOEs in Kazakhstan are obliged to adhere to corporate governance mandates in alignment with the JSC legislation, along with other relevant laws and provisions, such as the State Property law, SWF law and other government resolutions as applicable. Figure 2.1 indicates that several Corporate Governance Codes exist in Kazakhstan for SOEs, one that is applicable to controlled subsidiaries of the Samruk-Kazyna group of companies, and the other to the remaining SOEs in Kazakhstan.

Based on paragraph 182 of the State Property law, the MNE develops the model Corporate Governance Code for state-owned JSCs, which is in turn approved and applied by each individual SOE. The model Corporate Governance Code is obliged for JSCs and recommended for LLCs, the model Code does not cover corporate governance of state enterprises with the supervisory boards. Samruk-Kazyna and its group of companies applies its own Code. Every SOE should conduct an independent assessment of corporate governance at least once every three years, the results of which are publicly available on the website of each SOE. Kazakhstan's model Corporate Governance Code, with its most recent update in September 2022, outlines corporate governance principles and encompasses various aspects, including:

- defining objectives
- shareholders' rights
- stakeholder engagement
- board responsibilities
- management interaction
- transparency and disclosure
- internal controls
- ethical standards
- evaluations of corporate governance practices.

Samruk-Kazyna's Corporate Governance Code is approved by the sole shareholder and applicable to all JSC and LLC controlled by Samruk-Kazyna. The executive body of Samruk-Kazyna approves the same

Corporate Governance Code for its controlled subsidiaries, while for subsidiaries with several shareholders the Code is recommended for approval by the general shareholders meeting. Samruk-Kazyna's Code is based on similar principles and provisions as the model Corporate Governance Code however includes greater details and exceptions.[8] Among them is that Samruk-Kazyna's subsidiaries do not have government members on the BOD of subsidiaries. In addition, Samruk-Kazyna's Corporate Governance Code requires listed SOEs to publish in their annual reports on their adherence to the Corporate Governance Code. Currently, all listed SOEs are under the Samruk-Kazyna umbrella, thus adhering to the Samruk-Kazyna's Corporate Governance Code.

Figure 2.1. Corporate Governance Codes in Kazakhstan

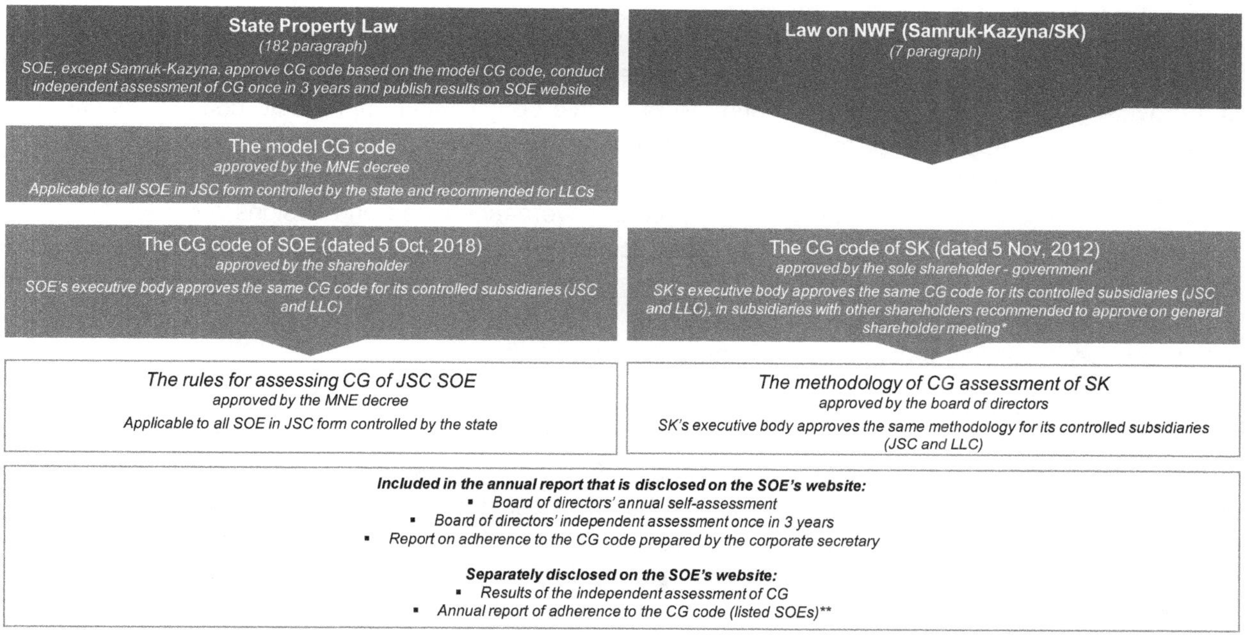

Note: * SOEs with other shareholders may deviate from Samruk-Kazyna's Code upon approval by the general shareholders meeting.
** applicable to the Samruk-Kazyna's listed companies.
Source: legislation and relevant rules and internal documents reflected in the infographic.

Some of SK's subsidiaries - with other shareholders - may choose to apply other regulatory norms in their Codes – if approved by the general shareholders meeting. Out of the 6 listed SOEs, only 4 companies (Kazatomprom, KazMunayGas, KEGOC and KazTransOil) follow Samruk-Kazyna' Code, while the remaining 2 (Kazakhtelecom and Kcell) have developed their own Corporate Governance Codes approved by the general shareholders meeting. While the Corporate Governance Code of the Air Astana JSC is approved by the general shareholders meeting and aligns with the principles, standards reflected in the AIFC Rule #FR0003 dated 2017.

To ensure the adherence to the model Corporate Governance Code provisions, the MNE developed the *Rules for Assessing Corporate Governance of JSC SOEs Controlled by the State*. The rules note that a corporate secretary can make an annual assessment and/ or independent consultant can do the same every 3 years. The assessments are based on the OECD guidelines on corporate governance of SOEs and other international recommendations on corporate governance adopted in Kazakhstan. The methodology for conducting a corporate governance assessment is very opaque and general, rendering it difficult to conduct a high-quality evaluation. The rules provide only five general elements for assessment:

- corporate ratings
- the negative influence of the shareholders on corporate governance practices

- key positive aspects
- disadvantages/shortcomings
- recommendations for elimination/further improvement of identified inconsistencies.

The methodologies of the assessment of Samruk-Kazyna and its subsidiaries are developed by PWC and approved by the BOD and executive body of Samruk-Kazyna respectively. The methodology itself is more comprehensive than those of the MNE, and contains details, mechanisms, descriptions and assessment criteria to assign a corporate governance rating. The document covers the assessment of the effectiveness of the BOD and executive body, risk management, internal control and audit, sustainable development, shareholder rights, transparency, and contains additional requirements for the assessment of listed companies.

For both types of Codes, on top of the BOD self- and independent assessment, the BOD are given the responsibility to assess the adherence to the Corporate Governance Code. Corporate secretaries monitor and provide guidance to both the BOD and the executive body on the appropriate compliance with the Code's principles. They are also responsible for generating an annual report that outlines the compliance or non-compliance with the Code's principles and provisions. Once every 3 years, an independent consultant assesses the adherence to the Corporate Governance Code and assigns a corporate rating. These reports subsequently undergo regular assessment by the BOD committees, are approved by the BOD, integrated into the company's annual report and disclosed on the website. Instances where non-compliance with this Code's provisions arises are deliberated during committee and BOD meetings, resulting in decisions to improve the corporate governance within the SOE.

According to the 20 selected SOEs' responses to the OECD questionnaire, 35% of the 20 selected SOEs do not undergo an independent assessment of their corporate governance practices, which is not in line with the Corporate Governance Codes. Among 35% of the selected SOEs (including SK-Pharmacy LLC), regular independent assessments are conducted, but their results are not publicly available. Only 3 SOEs, which represent 15% of the selected entities (Damu Fund, International Airport Nazarbayev N., QazExpoCongress), conduct independent assessments and publicly disclose their results. The remaining 15% of SOEs are LLC which are not required to conduct such independent assessments.

Listed SOEs consistently perform evaluations to ensure compliance with the applicable Corporate Governance Codes and make the results publicly available. Out of six listed SOEs four of them (Kazatomprom, KazMunayGas, KEGOC and KazTransOil) publish separate reports, while two (Kazakhtelecom and Kcell) integrated results into annual reports. Based on 2021 results of the independent assessment of the corporate governance of KazMunayGas, Kazakhtelecom and KEGOC improved their ratings from "BB" to "BBB", Kazatomprom improved from "BBB" to "A",[9] while KazTransOil and Kcell did not conduct independent assessments.[10]

2.4.3. Disclosure of public policy objectives

> ***C. Where SOEs are required to pursue public policy objectives, adequate information about these should be available to non-state shareholders at all times.***

According to the model Corporate Governance Code, business transactions and associations involving the SOE, shareholders, and related parties are conducted in accordance with commercial principles defined by existing Kazakh laws (such as the Entrepreneurial Code). This is valid unless one of the principal objectives of the SOE pertains to executing or supporting the execution of public policies targeting the advancement of specific industries within Kazakhstan.

In practice, transparency about public policy objectives can be ensured in two different ways: (I) by categorising SOEs according to the nature of their operations; and (ii) by disclosing information about the PPOs of individual SOEs. Further to the first point, according to the State Property law, some SOEs operate within key sectors of the economy, that require SOEs to implement state/public policies. The list of national managing holdings, national holdings, and national companies that pursue public policy objectives is approved by the Kazakh government.

Table 2.2. Information on status of national companies and national operators

SOE	National Company (Y/N)?	Status of National Operator
National Company "QazaqGaz" JSC	Y	National operator in the field of gas and gas supply
KazTransGaz Aymak JSC	N	Qazaq Gas executes National operator functions through this enterprise
National Company Kazakhstan Temir Zholy JSC	Y	National Operator of Infrastructure operates, maintains, modernises, builds the main railway network and provides services to the main railway network, as well as providing priority support for military transportation
SK-Pharmacy LLC	N	A single national operator for the purchase of medicines and medical devices for the implementation of a guaranteed volume of free medical care (GOBMP) and in the system of compulsory social health insurance (OSMI) and a single operator for receiving humanitarian assistance
Republican Center for Space Communication JSC	N	National operator of the space communication system
QAZEXPOCONGRESS National Company JSC	Y	A single operator for holding important state and quasi-state international trade and economic events
Kazatomprom NC JSC	Y	National operator for the export and import of uranium and its compounds, nuclear fuel for nuclear power plants, special equipment and technologies, dual-use materials
KEGOC JSC	Y	National (system) operator of electrical distribution networks
KazMunayGas NC JSC	Y	Represents government commercial interests in contracts for offshore oil operations and other oil operations through equity participation in the contract
Kazakhtelecom JSC	Y	National telecom operator
KazTransOil JSC	N	National operator for the main oil pipeline

Source: SOEs websites, annual reports, relevant laws

Under Decree No. 376/ 2011, Kazakhstan has two national managing holdings, one national holding, and 20 national companies. In addition to the mentioned "national" statuses of SOEs, the government also assigns some SOEs with a "national operator" status and provides them with an exclusive right to act on behalf of the government in specific areas of selected industries. For instance, QazaqGaz, being a national gas operator, supplies gas to the domestic market by providing more than half of the country's population with gas at low prices and cross-subsidises this loss-making business with gas exports. The law on Gas and Gas Supply No. 532-IV/ 2012 clearly lists all obligations and functions that have to be conducted by the national gas operator to ensure implementation of the public policy on gas and gas supply. Similar to QazaqGas, the roles and supplementary responsibilities that national companies and operators have (see Table 2.2) are outlined in relevant laws and governmental directives – openly accessible to the public. Listed SOEs provide comprehensive information about their status as national companies and operators that available to all shareholders (see examples below).

However, national companies and operators may not be limited only by the mentioned above specific law provisions. On top of the listed in the legislation key functions, national companies and operators may be forced by the government or major state shareholders to engage in activities outside of their core businesses. For instance, they may be engaged in acquiring assets other than on an arm's length basis or involved in different types of transactions that goes beyond national operator legislation such as construction of a hospital/school/cultural object etc., that may impact on commercial interests of shareholders. Two cases can be found below in Box 2.3 and Box 2.4. showcasing that the functions of national companies and operators are not precise and clear.

In the case of Samruk-Kazyna and its subsidiaries, the Corporate Governance Code requires to disclose in the annual report if a *socially significant project* is undertaken. However, such disclosures usually take place post factum and are decided by the BOD, not the general shareholders meeting. This does not allow minority shareholders to oppose such decisions, forcing them to use other avenues to communicate their position (see example of such case in Box 2.3).

Box 2.3. Disclosure of public policy objectives and associated risks in Kazatomprom's stock emission prospects

The details about the national company and national operator status of Kazatomprom and the execution of public policy objectives are outlined in the stock emission prospect, providing details of benefits and risks associated with its implementation. This information is accessible to all shareholders, including minority shareholders, during IPO:

> *The Company is the national atomic company of Kazakhstan and, among other things, is responsible for, and has a preferential right to perform and coordinate, mining uranium in Kazakhstan and exporting uranium and its compounds from Kazakhstan pursuant to the Decree of the President of Republic of Kazakhstan No. 3593 dated 14 July 1997.*
>
> *The respective status of a national company in Kazakhstan allows the Group to benefit from certain privileges, including, among other things, obtaining subsoil use agreements through direct negotiation with the government rather than through a tender process which would otherwise be required. This effectively grants the Group priority access to such opportunities, including the high-quality and ISR-conducive deposits of natural uranium, which are abundant in the Republic of Kazakhstan.*
>
> *If the Company were to lose its national operator or national company status as a result of a change in the government's policy, due to the government's loss of indirect control over the Company, or for any other reason, this could result in the loss of the Group's priority access to new resources, such as uranium deposits, and otherwise have a material adverse effect on the Group's business, prospects, financial condition, cash flows, results of operations and or the price of the Securities.*
>
> *There can be no assurance that the government will not, through Samruk-Kazyna, cause the Group to engage in business practices that may materially adversely affect the Group's ability to operate on a commercial basis or in a way that is inconsistent with the best interests of the Company's other shareholders. In addition, the Group may be forced by the gGovernment, through Samruk-Kazyna, to engage in activities outside of its core businesses and/ or acquire assets other than on an arm's length basis.*
>
> *Additionally, the Company, as national operator, has certain functions including the following: (i) controlling Kazakhstan's performance of the Agreement Suspending the Antidumping Investigation of Uranium from Kazakhstan, and usage of quotes for supply of Kazakhstan uranium to the U.S. market; (ii) assisting in implementing Kazakhstan's policy on preventing of dumping processes on the uranium market within and outside of Kazakhstan; (iii) securing strict observance of quotas on export and import of uranium-bearing materials and equipment for producers operating within Kazakhstan;(iv) securing export, import and manufacturing of special equipment and technologies and materials of dual application pursuant to IAEA rules;(v) maintaining records on sales of atomic energy industry products; (vi) determining transportation routes and supply schedules of uranium-bearing raw materials to reprocessing facilities within Kazakhstan; and (vii) participating in the resolution of issues related to transit of foreign export production through Kazakhstan.*

Source: (Kazatomprom, 2018[6])

Box 2.4. Disclosure of public policy details in the KazMunayGas NC JSC annual report

The Commission for Demonopolisation of the Economy is an advisory body operating under the Kazakh government. The primary role of the Commission is to formulate suggestions on demonopolisation in sectors such as telecommunications, railway infrastructure, media assets, and similar areas.

The disclosure of the acquisition of a 49% stake for the nominal value of 1 tenge, in accordance with the decision of the *Commission for Demonopolisation of the Economy*, was presented in the annual report and consolidated financial statements of KazMunayGas. This information was accessible to all shareholders.

Excerpts from the KazMunayGas annual report:

> *On July 1, 2022, in accordance with the minutes of the meeting of the Commission under the chairmanship of the Prime Minister of RK for the demonopolization of the economy, namely the market of fuels and lubricants, the Company acquired 49% interest in PetroSun, that specializes in the sale of liquefied petroleum gas and petroleum products. The acquisition price was 1 tenge. The difference between the consideration paid and the fair value of identifiable assets and liabilities of PetroSun at the date of acquisition was recognized as a contribution from Samruk-Kazyna based on instruction in minutes above and presented in the line "Acquisition of joint ventures" in consolidated statement of changes in equity in the amount of 10,989 million tenge (Note 26).*
>
> *The difference between the consideration paid for the acquisition of 49% interest in PetroSun for 1 tenge and the fair value of identifiable assets and liabilities of PetroSun at the date of acquisition in the amount of 10,989 million tenge was recognized as a contribution from Samruk-Kazyna and presented in the line "Acquisition of joint ventures" in consolidated statement of changes in equity in the amount of 10,989 million tenge.*

Source: (KMG, 2022[7])

2.4.4. Joint ventures and public private partnerships

> ***D. When SOEs engage in co-operative projects such as joint ventures and public private partnerships, the contracting party should ensure that contractual rights are upheld and that disputes are addressed in a timely and objective manner.***

The State Property law and JSC laws do not impose limitations on SOEs regarding the establishment and engagement in joint ventures, a decision lying with the BOD of the SOE. The resolution of contractual rights and disputes is governed by the Civil Code, JSC laws, and other legislative regulatory documents of Kazakhstan.

The law on Public-Private Partnerships (PPPs) No. 379-V LRK/2015 notes that SOEs can engage in public-private partnerships through various means, such as participating in legal entities, transferring property rights, attracting investments, and providing supportive services. SOEs can also contribute to the construction, operation, and modernisation of public-private partnership facilities, while exploring other compliant forms as per the laws of Kazakhstan.

In addition to outlining the partnership terms, the PPP agreement also encompasses provisions on the resolution of disputes through both judicial and non-judicial means, as well as procedures for handling corporate disputes. Disputes arising from the execution and termination of the agreement are settled according to the laws of Kazakhstan and the stipulations within the PPP agreement. However, as far as the mission team has been able to establish, no cases have so far had to be resolved. Moreover, out of

1,312 public private partnership projects implemented as of August 2023, merely four have been executed with the participation of SOEs in the form of social-entrepreneurial corporations.

2.4.5. Summary

It appears that – apart from the special case of golden shares – minority investors in Kazakhstan's SOEs have broadly the same rights and the same level of protection as is the case in privately owned companies. However, this level of protection is not internationally very high. The right to vote one's shares does not confer much influence when the state is a majority shareholder, and safeguards that exist in some other countries (e.g. majority-of-the-minority provisions) are not in place in Kazakhstan. This problem is highlighted by the fact that many Kazakh SOEs are subject to public policy objectives that, if implemented or changed with scant regard to the interests of non-state shareholders could lower rates of return and dividends to the detriment of the latter.

SOEs usually provide and disclose publicly information that is required by the legal framework, however it's not a general practice to disclose more information on top of required ones, limiting it to minimum required level. Majority shareholders get access to the general shareholder meeting agenda items quicker than minority shareholders who do not have representatives at BOD level.

Despite having related provisions in the regulatory documents, SOEs are not keen to use an active policy of communication and consultation with the minority shareholders of the listed SOEs, mostly preferring to exchange written correspondence and court filings. While communication with the majority shareholders of the non-listed SOEs is usually conducted more regularly by the SOEs based on agreements reflected in the SOEs' charters and using other avenues.

Although the public policy objectives and functions that SOEs are expected to fulfill as part of their national company and operator status are available in open sources, the phrasing and scope of these functions are often quite broad. This complexity makes it challenging to create a precise and comprehensive list of all the functions these entities should undertake. Clearly defining criteria and conditions that determine whether specific actions and functions of SOEs align with their status would enhance the transparency of decisions and directives for social functions from the Kazakh government. This would also improve predictability and expectations regarding the potential effects of these decisions on all shareholders, including non-state and minority shareholders.

Overall, despite having comprehensive regulatory norms that co-ordinates the processes and requirements of the general shareholder meetings, BOD and executive bodies, the practical implication of the Corporate Governance Codes remains challenging. Lack of controlling and monitoring of SOEs compliance to Codes impacts on independent judgement of members of SOEs' governing bodies and may negatively affect to treating all shareholders equitably.

Thus, in relation to the SOE guidelines, there are challenges to ensure the equitable treatment of all shareholders, resulting from a non-transparent nomination of BOD members which may affect their ability to make independent judgements. SOEs and ownership entities do not actively involve minority shareholders of listed companies for consultations. The small floating size of shares does not allow minority shareholders' representatives to sit at the SOE BODs, despite the legal rights to do so.

2.5. Stakeholder relations and responsible business

> ***The state ownership policy should fully recognise SOEs' responsibilities towards stakeholders and request that SOEs report on their relations with stakeholders. It should make clear any expectations the state has in respect of responsible business conduct by SOEs.***

2.5.1. Recognising and respecting stakeholders' rights

> ***A. Governments, the state ownership entities and SOEs themselves should recognise and respect stakeholders' rights established by law or through mutual agreements.***

In Kazakhstan, the different legal forms of SOEs do not provide for the different treatment of employees (e.g. regarding remuneration, pension rights and job protection). The rights and obligations of employees are the same across all company types, although civil servants may enjoy additional privileges. In particular, employment relationships in Kazakh companies are regulated by the Labour Code No. 414-V KRZ/ 2015, which establishes employees' fundamental rights. It notes for instance that employees have the right to authorise representatives to negotiate on their behalf with the CEO or supervising department of the SOE.

Kazakhstan also established a mechanism like the Business Ombudsman to address business grievances and promote responsible business conduct. However, it seems as though employees of SOEs who had concerns related to their employment or labor rights typically reported such issues to relevant government labor or employment authorities, rather than the Business Ombudsman.

Since employees do not tend to own company shares, their ability to participate in shareholder meetings is limited. The quasi-state sector does not use stock options as a way to compensate employees, although some companies had tried to introduce this method previously.

Kazakhstan has implemented internationally recognised human rights instruments, including those stated in the *International Bill of Human Rights* and ILO conventions. An office of the Human Rights Commissioner oversees constitutional human rights and handles citizen appeals in case of violations. The country has not yet introduced a human rights strategy however and human rights challenges can exist in certain SOEs, particularly in sectors like mining or extraction.

In Kazakhstan, there are no specific policies or practices in place for providing stakeholders with timely and adequate information about SOEs, other than those outlined in chapter 2 of this report. The dissemination of information typically covers aspects of SOEs' legal structure, capital, management bodies, and more. In more detail:

- The Commercial Register and relevant government registries provide information on the legal structure, capital, and management bodies of SOEs in Kazakhstan.
- Certain SOEs publish additional information about their operations, financial performance, and corporate governance practices on their official websites. Listed SOEs have additional obligations to publish information, such as the compliance with the Corporate Governance Code.
- The law on access to information (401-V/ 2015) allows interested parties to request specific information from SOEs in writing, to obtain information beyond what is publicly available.

In order to protect (foreign) investors, Kazakhstan has also signed a number of international investment agreements: These treaties typically protect existing investments against expropriation, and provide investors access to investor-state dispute settlement mechanisms. In addition to 47 bilateral investment treaties, Kazakhstan also adheres to a plethora of multilateral investment treaties. In total, around half of Kazakhstan's investment treaties are concluded with adherents to the OECD *Declaration on International Investment and Multinational Enterprises*. Due to relatively broad provisions in most of Kazakhstan's investment treaties, arbitrators are left with a lot of leeway: "vague standards that fail to clearly reflect government intent may undermine the right balance between investor protection and the power to regulate" (OECD, 2019[8]).

The Entrepreneurial Code which entered into force in 2016 replaced the previous Investment law, and other laws regulating and protecting investment activity. It aims to increase the consistency and transparency of the applicable legal rules for businesses, and investors specifically, and to thereby strengthen investor confidence. The government has further lifted foreign equity restrictions in air transport and fixed-line telecommunications, allowing for complete foreign ownership.

The government has made notable efforts over the last decade to modernise environmental legislation and address the legacy of the Soviet period, as reflected in an increase in the position in international rankings on environmental performance. The government has introduced environmental regulations to ensure stakeholder protection, although these are all rather recent endeavours and focused on ensuring equal access to public goods. These encompass broader legislations like the Environmental Code No. 212/ 2007, along with specific Codes related to subsoil and water, which also apply to SOEs in their operations. Companies, including SOEs, are required to prepare EIA reports before certain activities, outlining activities, potential risks, and socio-economic development prospects. After assessment, companies engage in consultations with communities and the government before making decisions.

However, challenges such as non-standardised EIA reporting, corruption and limited civil society participation may persist. Complex reporting and sometimes discretionary decision-making have impeded the correct assessment of the true extent of possible environmental impacts of business/ SOE activities. Some enterprises have complained about the lack of transparency of environmental regulations, and expressed concerns about irregular and inexplicable fines (OECD, 2019[8]).

Particular ownership entities have also taken on the responsibility for the well-being of stakeholders. For instance, SK has been undertaking environmental audits, and notable SOEs such as KazMunayGas and KEGOC have taken proactive steps in embracing social and environmental preservation initiatives. In addition, the Ministry of Labor and Social Protection of the Population has emphasised the significance of fostering social responsibility within enterprises, although without extensive details.

> ***B. Listed or large SOEs should report on stakeholder relations, including where relevant and feasible with regard to labour, creditors and affected communities.***

Kazakhstan's model Corporate Governance Code and Samruk-Kazyna's Corporate Governance Code provide guidelines on disclosure and reporting requirements for listed companies on aspects related to ESG. In theory, these are applicable to SOEs therefore.

- In paragraph 167, the Samruk-Kazyna Code further notes that "in organisations whose shares are listed on the stock exchange, as well as participating in ESG ratings, reporting indicators undergo independent certification (verification) by a third party".
- The Kazakhstan Stock Exchange (KASE) has listing requirements that encourage or mandate ESG reporting by listed companies. These requirements include disclosures related to sustainability practices, social responsibility, and governance.
- Listed SOEs follow international reporting frameworks such as the Global Reporting Initiative (GRI) or the United Nations Global Compact (UNGC) to report on ESG factors. Samruk-Kazyna for instance issues consolidated sustainable development reports based on GRI standards, which every subsidiary is now requested to do.
- Companies engaged in activities with potential environmental impacts may be subject to specific environmental reporting requirements and regulations.
- Kazakhstan has anti-corruption laws and regulations that apply to businesses, and companies may be expected to report on their anti-corruption efforts and measures as part of their corporate governance and compliance practices.
- Some companies in Kazakhstan, including listed ones, issue separate sustainability or CSR (Corporate Social Responsibility) reports that provide detailed information on their ESG performance, social initiatives, and sustainability efforts.

Subsidiaries under Samruk-Kazyna are encouraged to incorporate non-financial KPIs to monitor the impacts of their operations, encompassing social, environmental, and anti-corruption dimensions. Overall, non-financial reporting in Kazakhstan is in its beginning stages and can vary among companies. Key SOEs have shown improvements in their reporting practices recently. For instance, entities like KazMunayGas, KEGOC, and Kazatomprom have consistently published non-financial reports. There are instances of enhanced disclosure practices as seen with companies like Samruk-Energy and Tau-Ken Samruk. While certain enterprises, such as Astana International Airport and Kazakhstan Temir Zholy (Kazakhstan Railways), express commitment to corporate social responsibility and international responsible conduct standards, their issuance of non-financial reports might not be explicitly documented.

While requirements on non-financial reporting have been partially expanded as recommended by the OECD in 2012, they remain weak in practice. However, some promising initiatives to promote transparency have emerged, such as the inclusion of a specific chapter on transparency in SK's Corporate Governance Code. Additionally, KASE participates in the *Sustainable Stock Exchanges Initiative* has been declared compliant with the Extractive Industries Transparency Initiative, which is particularly notable due to the importance of the extractives sector. There are also clear intentions that suggest a greater alignment with various ESG reporting items for the large and/ or listed entities. This may come as a result of aiming to comply with foreign stock exchange listing rules, or to perform well in ESG ratings.

2.5.2. Internal controls, ethics and compliance programmes

> ***C. The boards of SOEs should develop, implement, monitor and communicate internal controls, ethics and compliance programmes or measures, including those which contribute to preventing fraud and corruption. They should be based on country norms, in conformity with international commitments and apply to the SOE and its subsidiaries.***

Kazakhstan has comprehensive anti-corruption laws that apply to all entities, including SOEs. The key piece of legislation is the law on Combating Corruption No. 410-V/2015 which establishes the legal framework for anti-corruption measures, defines corrupt practices, and outlines penalties for corruption offenses. It specifically notes that it also applies to the quasi-state and its members.

The criminal Code of Kazakhstan also includes provisions related to corruption and bribery offenses. It sets out criminal liability for individuals engaged in corrupt practices, including those within SOEs. Kazakhstan is also a signatory to international agreements and conventions aimed at combating corruption, including the United Nations Convention against Corruption (UNCAC), which also addresses SOEs.[11]

The model Corporate Governance Code obliges all SOEs to establish and implement internal controls, ethics, and compliance provisions. It stipulates that the Code of conduct and ethics should address conflicts of interest, confidentiality, fair business practices, and the protection and proper use of company assets. Based on the feedback provided by the 20 chosen SOEs, each one has formulated and ratified a Code of conduct and ethics. The State Property law further mandates that BODs, where established, create "anti-corruption policies" applicable to SOEs of all legal forms.

SOEs have initiated anti-corruption programs and communication channels, yet their effectiveness may vary. The model Code has also recommended for SOEs to put in place an ombudsman and compliance officers, but it remains questionable how many SOEs follow this rule and whether they are useful.

Despite the development of laws and Codes of conducts, Kazakhstan's SOEs, in sectors like oil and gas, continue to grapple with significant corruption challenges. The effectiveness of anti-corruption programmes remains questionable, partly lacking political will and the dispersed ownership which limits the capacity to oversee the entire portfolio of SOEs. It is also unclear to what extent the different ownership entities are involved in ensuring the effectiveness of anti-corruption programs and assessing their alignment with state expectations regarding integrity and anti-corruption efforts.

While a few SOEs in Kazakhstan have established comprehensive internal controls, ethics, compliance measures, and whistle-blower protection mechanisms, the functionality of these internal controls and programs might be inadequate. Monitoring generally seems to be an issue.

2.5.3. Responsible business conduct

> ***D. SOEs should observe high standards of responsible business conduct. Expectations established by the government in this regard should be publicly disclosed and mechanisms for their implementation be clearly established.***

In Kazakhstan, SOEs are expected to proactively mitigate risks and uphold high standards of responsible business conduct across various domains, including the environment, employees, public health and safety, and human rights. While the concept of RBC is still developing, Kazakhstan has introduced relevant regulations and policies to promote such practices.

As part of its commitment to the OECD *Guidelines on Multinational Enterprises,*[12] Kazakhstan has established a National Contact Point (NCP) charged with promoting responsible business principles, handling related inquiries in the national context and providing a mediation and conciliation platform for resolving practical issues that may arise. The NCP sits within the MNE.

In general, awareness of RBC has increased in Kazakhstan in recent years. Numerous public and private initiatives have been established, with notable efforts to promote RBC by Samruk-Kazyna; the National Chamber of Entrepreneurs, Kazakhstan's umbrella business organisation; and several civil society organisations. On a policy level, the Entrepreneurial Code includes a legal definition of social responsibility and commits the state to creating the conditions and not interfering with business activities in this area, a welcome development in light of previously reported practices that social responsibility projects amounted to a charity tax.

Although the government has yet to develop a coherent government strategy on RBC, individual Ministries have put in place RBC-related initiatives, albeit fragmented and on an ad hoc basis.

Samruk-Kazyna's Corporate Governance Code is another notable effort, as it calls for transparency and accountability, respect for human rights, and environmental protection and envisions the development of action plans on sustainable development. Resulting from the Code, several SOEs have implemented RBC-related principles and standards, incorporating due diligence mechanisms at the supervisory and management board levels. For instance, entities like KazMunayGas have established committees responsible for health, safety, environment, and reserves, which formulate strategies, policies, plans, and risk assessments in these domains. Integrated management units have been instituted to monitor RBC-related risks, and the adoption of pertinent environmental, social (including health and safety), and anti-corruption policies is evident (OECD, 2017[9]).

Similar standards, due diligence practices, and disclosure mechanisms are noticeable in other SOEs, including KEGOC. Moreover, various SOEs have set up dedicated corporate social responsibility units tasked with implementing sustainability initiatives. Notably, some companies contribute to local communities in their operational areas, while other enterprises engage in cross-border co-operation to ensure the sustainability of shared resources, such as water reservoirs.

However, many SOEs are yet to adopt comprehensive RBC policies and institute due diligence mechanisms. A lack of clarity surrounding RBC, coupled with limited application beyond company operations and supply chains, remains a challenge. Additionally, certain sectors experience pronounced RBC-related issues. For instance, state-owned mines create significant emissions and contribute to environmental degradation, which is difficult in a country which is already experiencing the effects of climate change (OECD, 2017[9]).

2.5.4. Financing political activities

> ***E. SOEs should not be used as vehicles for financing political activities. SOEs themselves should not make political campaign contributions.***

The law on Political Parties in Kazakhstan prohibits state and municipal enterprises, institutions, organisations, and legal entities where the state and local governments hold at least 10% of authorised capital or voting rights, either directly or indirectly, from making contributions to support political parties. However, it is important to note that there might exist indirect methods of financing or supporting political activities, particularly at the municipal level. At the same time, the political regime in Kazakhstan may render political financing uninteresting in any case.

2.5.5. Summary

There are a number of laws/ regulations to ensure the protection of employees, creditors, consumers, and stakeholders in Kazakhstan. The country has ratified most relevant international conventions, yet issues with the protection of human and labour rights persist, also related to SOE activities. The issues result from 1) the discrepancy between the written law and its actual implementation; 2) the need for a more centralised and co-ordinated effort from the government to ensure SOEs' responsible behaviour and stakeholder protection; and 3) the limited effectiveness of these provisions for SOEs in particular.

ESG reporting has been developing in Kazakhstan, albeit being in its beginning stages. For the time being, however, there remain divergences in the individual SOE efforts (and dependent on the ownership structure), and dependent on the voluntary efforts of the SOE themselves.

SOEs have initiated anti-corruption programs and communication channels, yet their effectiveness may vary. The model Code has also recommended for SOEs to put in place an ombudsman and compliance officers, but it remains questionable how many SOEs follow this rule and whether they are useful. Thus, despite the development of laws and Codes of conducts on anti-corruption, Kazakhstan's SOEs, in sectors like oil and gas, continue to grapple with significant corruption challenges. The effectiveness of anti-corruption programmes remains questionable, partly due to resource limitations and the dispersed ownership structure which limits the capacity to oversee the entire portfolio of SOEs. It is also unclear to what extent the different ownership entities are involved in ensuring the effectiveness of anti-corruption programs and assessing their alignment with state expectations regarding integrity and anti-corruption efforts.

While a few SOEs in Kazakhstan have established comprehensive internal controls, ethics, compliance measures, and whistle-blower protection mechanisms, the functionality of these internal controls and programs might be inadequate. Monitoring generally seems to be an issue.

Overall, while steps have been taken by some SOEs to embrace RBC, a comprehensive and uniform approach is needed to address RBC challenges effectively across all state-owned enterprises in Kazakhstan. It is important to note that the promotion of RBC in SOEs is an ongoing process, and Kazakhstan may continue to refine its policies and practices in this regard.

2.6. Disclosure and transparency

> ***State-owned enterprises should observe high standards of transparency and be subject to the same high-quality accounting, disclosure, compliance and auditing standards as listed companies.***

2.6.1. Applicable disclosure standards and practices

The law On Accounting and Financial Reporting No. 234/2007 establishes the system of accounting and financial reporting in Kazakhstan. It is the main law outlining the reporting and disclosure obligations for the state-owned sector and domestic companies. In general, it foresees that financial reporting shall represent information on the financial position of a company, the results of the activity, and changes in the financial position of the company. The basic elements that are expected to be included in financial statements are the 1) accounting balance; 2) profit-and-loss report; 3) statement of cash receipts and disbursements; 4) statements on changes in the capital; and 5) an explanatory note.

According to the law, all domestic listed companies, financial institutions, large unlisted companies, as well as "*organisations of public interest*" shall prepare their financial statements and annual reports in accordance with a single set of international standards. These standards are the IFRS (international financial reporting standards), previously known as IAS (international accounting standards).

The legal definition of an organisation of public interest is not the same as what is considered a quasi-state enterprise. An organisation of public interest can be, *inter alia*, any JSC where the state holds a share in the authorised capital, a subsidiary of the former, a subject of state monopoly or special law and dependent legal entities.

There are exceptions to the definition which render the assessment of which state-owned entities qualify as organisations of public interest unclear. For instance, "non-commercial" JSCs, organisations extracting common minerals, and licensed legal entities working for exchange operations with foreign currency are exempt from the definition as organisation of public interest but may qualify as quasi-state enterprise.

If SOEs were to violate their reporting requirements of the law On Accounting and Financial Reporting, Art. 25 foresees that the company must take responsibility. Whether this entails the payment of fines, the liability of BOD for damages caused, or other penalties is not elaborated in the legal text. It is also not detailed which legislation will apply in such an instance.

Overall, the exact scope of the law which requires SOEs to comply with the IFRS is not comprehensively covering the public sector. Ambiguity in the legal definition of what is considered a "non-commercial" JSC, and reasons as to why a non-commercial public interest venture may be considered as a joint-stock company in the first place, reveals that SOEs in Kazakhstan do not strictly incur reporting obligations. Instead, the reporting standard applicable depends on the legal form a SOE may take, as well as how their individual operations and purpose may be interpreted (as either commercial or non-commercial in nature).

Table 2.3. Overview of disclosure practices of selected SOEs

	ChVI.RA1	ChVI.RA2	ChVI.RA3	ChVI.RA4	ChVI.RA5	ChVI.RA6	ChVI.RA7	ChVI.RA7	ChVI.RA8	ChVI.RA9
	Statement of SOE objectives and their fulfilment	Separation of accounts related to public policy and non-public policy	Governance, ownership and voting structure of the enterprise	Remuneration of board members and key executives	Board member qualifications, independence, selection process	Material risk factors and their risk management systems	Guarantees and/or subsidies received from the state	Public-private partnerships and disclosure	Disclosure requirements for transactions with related parties	Disclosure of issues related to employees and stakeholders
National Company "QazaqGaz"	✓	No	✓	Aggregate remuneration	✓	✓	✓	No	✓	✓
KazTransGaz Aymak	✓	No	✓	Aggregate remuneration	✓	✓	✓	No	✓	✓
National Company Kazakhstan Temir Zholy	✓	No	✓	Aggregate remuneration	✓	✓	✓	No	✓	✓
Kazakhstan Railcars Building Company	N/A	N/A	N/A	N/A	N/A	N/A	N/A	N/A	N/A	N/A
Kuryk Port	No	No	No	Aggregate remuneration	No	Yes	N/A	No	Yes	No
Fund on Entreprenuership Development Damu	✓	No	✓	Aggregate remuneration	✓	✓	✓	No	✓	✓
Authority AIFC	✓	Unclear	No	No	✓	Partial	No	No	No	No
Banking Servicing Bureau of the National Bank	Partial	No	No	Aggregate remuneration	No	✓	N/A	No	✓	No
Kazakhavtodor	Partial	No	No	No	No	✓	N/A	No	✓	No
International Airport	✓	No	✓	Aggregate remuneration	✓	Partial	✓	No	✓	✓
Institute of Economic Research	✓	No	✓	Aggregate remuneration	No	Partial	N/A	No	✓	No

	ChVI.RA1	ChVI.RA2	ChVI.RA3	ChVI.RA4	ChVI.RA5	ChVI.RA6	ChVI.RA7	ChVI.RA7	ChVI.RA8	ChVI.RA9
	Statement of SOE objectives and their fulfilment	Separation of accounts related to public policy and non-public policy	Governance, ownership and voting structure of the enterprise	Remuneration of board members and key executives	Board member qualifications, independence, selection process	Material risk factors and their risk management systems	Guarantees and/or subsidies received from the state	Public-private partnerships and disclosure	Disclosure requirements for transactions with related parties	Disclosure of issues related to employees and stakeholders
National Center for Neirosurgery	✓	No	✓	Aggregate remuneration	Partial	✓	✓	No	✓	Partial
SK-Pharmacy	✓	No	✓	Aggregate remuneration	✓	✓	N/A	No	✓	✓
National Geological Exploration Company "KazGeology"	✓	No	✓	Aggregate remuneration	Partial	✓	N/A	No	✓	✓
Khabar Agency	✓	No	✓	Aggregate remuneration	Partial	✓	N/A	No	✓	No
Special Economic zone "Ontustyc"	No	No	✓	Aggregate remuneration	No	✓	N/A	No	✓	No
Plant after name of Kirov S.	Partial	No	✓	Aggregate remuneration	No	✓	N/A	No	✓	No
Machine Building Plant named after Kirov S.	Partial	No	✓	Aggregate remuneration	No	✓	N/A	No	✓	No
Republican Center for Space Communication	✓	No	✓	Aggregate remuneration	Partial	✓	N/A	No	✓	No
QAZEXPOCONGRESS National Company	✓	No	✓	Aggregate remuneration	✓	✓	✓	No	✓	✓

2.6.2. Disclosure standards and practices of selected SOEs

> ***A. SOEs should report material financial and non-financial information on the enterprise in line with high quality internationally recognised standards of corporate disclosure, and including areas of significant concern for the state as an owner and the general public. This includes in particular SOE activities that are carried out in the public interest. With due regard to enterprise capacity and size, examples of such information include:***
>
> ***A1. A clear statement to the public of enterprise objectives and their fulfilment (for fully-owned SOEs this would include any mandate elaborated by the state ownership entity).***

There is no formal requirement in the law to compile periodic non-financial reports. Given that Kazakhstan lacks a holistic and high-level ownership policy outlining the mandate of SOEs, there is also no further description of how SOE mandates would be carried out under certain objectives in their annual reports.

Despite the lack of legal obligation to disclose SOE objectives, several large and listed SOEs include a description of their objectives in their management reports. This tends to cover the strategic goals as elaborated in the respective 10-year development plan which is agreed by the government shareholder. For instance, the sovereign wealth fund Samruk-Kazyna, as well as the national company Kazakhstan Temir Zholy, which is wholly-owned by Samruk-Kazyna, report on how their 10-year strategies relate to concrete objectives.

Many of the unlisted and small SOEs do not appear to report on non-financial objectives or achievements. Oftentimes, they do not publish annual management reports altogether, or only decide to disclose limited aspects of their strategic long-term goals. As a result, SOEs that are held as part of the portfolio of the national (management) holding companies tend to disclose more rigorously than those which are held under a different ownership structure. This also appears to hold true for to the analysed companies that are held on the subsidiary level of a portfolio SOE. For example, KazTransGaz Aymak, which is a subsidiary of QazaqGaz, details the same disclosure items as its parent company. QazaqGaz is fully owned by Samruk-Kazyna.

This divergence in disclosure practices reveals that the role of the national (management) holding companies is currently understated. While they elevate the overall standard of disclosure of objectives for their portfolio SOEs and their own economic activities, no clear line is drawn between the objectives set by the SOHCs independently, and which represents an interest from the state as a majority shareholder. This diminishes political accountability towards objective setters and creates a disconnect in how the state may mandate objectives to the SOE sector at large.

> ***A2. Enterprise financial and operating results, including where relevant the costs and funding arrangements pertaining to public policy objectives.***

The MF maintains a depository of financial statements made by public interest organisations. As mentioned before, public interest organisations are not the same as quasi-state sector entities, however, the overlap between the two categories of entities is estimated as large. The depository provides access to financial data stored in Russian language free of charge.

Most Kazakh SOEs that are JSCs and commercial in nature are required to report financial and operating results in their financial statements, in accordance with the IFRS. Nevertheless, there are legal exceptions to this rule that are difficult to interpret, given the ambiguous meaning of what a “commercial” or “non-commercial” JSC may be.

Among the analysed SOEs, it often remains unclear whether a given objective outlined in the annual report is delegated by the governmental body owning it. As such, it becomes almost impossible to report on the financial position of a given public objective.

A3. The governance, ownership and voting structure of the enterprise, including the content of any Corporate Governance Code or policy and implementation processes.

Many of the analysed SOEs lack transparency of their governance, ownership and voting structures. It is mostly large SOEs, JSCs, national (management) holding companies, or portfolio SOEs of a national (management) holding company that detail their shareholding arrangements clearly. Both Samruk-Kazyna and Baiterek lay out principles in their Corporate Governance Codes, which they also report in their respective annual reports. It appears that portfolio companies of the two holding companies are elevated to similar disclosure standards.

Out of the analysed SOEs, most are wholly-owned or majority-owned by the state or a national (management) holding company. Those quasi-state entities which do disclose their ownership arrangements will often include information on the powers of the sole or controlling shareholder. For the largest and most significant SOEs and SOHCs, this is typically accompanied by information on the internal dividend policy.

According to the JSC law, JSCs with state participation (except for Samruk-Kazyna) shall approve Corporate Governance Codes during the general meeting of the shareholders in accordance with the model Corporate Governance Code, which details a pre-set number of considerations.

Thus, the wide discrepancy between corporate governance disclosure standards across SOEs is likely to be a function of the model of state ownership. SOEs overseen as portfolio companies appear to benefit off greater reporting assistance from their respective parent holding. JSCs that are SOEs are held to certain standards of corporate governance by the law. Other SOEs, however, appear less likely to engage in corporate governance disclosure practices, and the exact number of SOEs which are affected by this is unknown.

A4. The remuneration of board members and key executives.

There is no legal requirement to disclose the remuneration of the BOD or key executives in SOE annual reports or financial statements. Nevertheless, the JSC law details that for JSCs, the Chairman of the BOD shall inform the shareholders of the company on the amount of remuneration and compensation paid to the members of the BOD and the executive body of the company. Any SOE that is also a JSC will therefore make remuneration information available to its shareholders.

Additionally, remuneration disclosure is dependent on whether an SOE falls under the scope of companies required to comply with listing requirements of KASE. KASE requires the total remuneration of and bonuses to the BOD, as well as the total remuneration to the executive body to be disclosed.

Thus, listed SOEs tend to include the aggregate remuneration of their key management personnel or board members. Not a single SOE among the ones analysed reports individual remuneration levels of board members. Typically, it is observed that SOEs share their remuneration policy instead of information on remuneration levels. Overall, wide discrepancies in practices can be identified, which are likely to arise from the incomprehensive applicability of the legal framework for disclosure across the quasi-state sector.

A5. Board member qualifications, selection process, including board diversity policies, roles on other company boards and whether they are considered as independent by the SOE board.

The JSC law provides that it is within the competence of the general meeting of the shareholders to determine the quantitative composition, terms of office, election and re-election and early termination, as well as the compensation of members for JSCs. There is no provision that asks for the disclosure of this information to the wider public.

For SOEs of which the state is the sole shareholder, the number of directors and the term of office of the BOD is determined by the state owner. In accordance with the finding above, the same remains true for SOEs that are JSCs and majority state-owned.

The selection of members of the BOD of JSCs is influenced by the requirement to have representatives of the shareholder as part of the board. Furthermore, executives are not able to become board members, and at least 30% or members should be independent. There are no qualification-related criteria pronounced in the law.

Disclosure on board composition, board member qualifications and whether they are considered as independent widely varies across the analysed SOEs. Despite the lack of legal requirements regarding the disclosure of SOE board member qualifications, boards of large and listed SOEs demonstrate a balanced mix of skills of board members as disclosed in their annual reports.

> ***A6. Any material foreseeable risk factors and measures taken to manage such risks.***

In Kazakhstan, there are no legal requirements for SOEs to disclose material foreseeable risk factors and the measures taken to manage such risk. As stated in the law "On Banks and Banking Activities in the Republic of Kazakhstan" No 2444/1995, the board of the National Bank of Kazakhstan requires banks and bank holdings to create and report on their risk management policy and to establish an internal control system. Therefore, this reporting item seems only applicable for few SOEs part of the financial sector.

Nonetheless, many non-financial state-owned entities include information on material risks in their financial statements, as covered by the IFRS. As part of the disclosure requirements described by IFRS 7, compliant entities are required to report on the nature and extent of exposure to risk arising from financial instruments. This entails qualitative disclosures on risk exposures for each type of financial instrument, management objectives and processes for managing such risks, and changes to these risks. Furthermore, it requires quantitative disclosures of the exposure to material risks, focussing specifically on credit risk, liquidity risk, and market risk.

> ***A7. Any financial assistance, including guarantees, received from the state and commitments made on behalf of the SOE, including contractual commitments and liabilities arising from public-private partnerships.***

In Kazakhstan, funding arrangements between the state and SOEs, as well as between SOEs on different levels of the ownership hierarchy, usually take the form of favourable borrowing arrangements, fixed interest rate borrowings and financial guarantees. While there is no national law that describes the obligation to report this information as part of the financial statements, these items usually fall into the scope of reporting requirements under the IFRS' related party disclosures.

Many of the analysed SOEs which are compliant with IFRS, thus include an explanation of these funding arrangements in the notes of their financial statements. Out of the selected SOEs, none appeared to be involved in any PPPs. Thus, contractual contingencies and liabilities of PPPs were not reported on.

The JSC *Kazakhstan Centre for Public-Private Partnership* was established to implement the mobilisation of financial, managerial, technological, physical and other resources for their use in PPPs. The centres work is based on the law On Public-Private Partnerships" which law does not foresee any disclosures in relation to PPPs on the part of the enterprise. Rather, the centre's work revolves around research activities surrounding PPPs and publishes hosts a database with ongoing projects. It is influenced by various Ministerial orders on the approval of several steps in the project pipeline, as well as issues relating to implementation of PPPs.

> ***A8. Any material transactions with the state and other related entities.***

As mentioned before, Kazakh SOEs, especially those belonging to the same holding company portfolio, tend to extend borrowing arrangements and financial guarantees to each other. The disclosure of these transactions is required under the IFRS for those SOEs compliant with it. These state funding arrangements are typically recognised as related party transaction with a shareholder, or other entity, or as government subsidy or loan.

While SOEs that comply with IFRS explain related party transactions as part of their notes of the financial statements, it appears that some of the assessed SOEs balance their financial positions under various types of reporting items. This may misrepresent some of the information reported in the financial statements.

For example, in the consolidated financial statements of the Damu Fund, it is mentioned that in 2014-2015, Damu received funds from Baiterek in the amount of KZT 200 bn at 0.15% per annum with a maturity of 20 years. This transaction was recognised as a government grant under below market rates in the profit and loss statement as per IAS 20.

In 2019, Damu further borrowed funds from Baiterek in the amount of KZT 16 bn at a rate of 0.1% per annum for a 15-year term. The main target of the loan was to pay off earlier issued securities. Damu concluded an absence of a connection to operational activities, which meant the difference between the fair value of the loan and received cash had not been recognised as a government subsidy, but as an operation with a shareholder. While this does not constitute wrongful reporting, practices such as the above may understate the extent of related party transactions between SOEs and the state.

> ***A9. Any relevant issues relating to employees and other stakeholders.***

There is no formal requirement to report on employees and other stakeholders for SOEs in Kazakhstan. Some large and listed SOEs will disclose this information as per internal Corporate Governance Codes and principles, however.

> ***B. SOEs' annual financial statements should be subject to an independent external audit based on high-quality standards. Specific state control procedures do not substitute for an independent external audit.***

As mentioned in previous sections, the law on State Audit and Financial Control 393-IV LRK/2015 sets out expectations and provisions on the state audit function. The supreme audit chamber of Kazakhstan, which acts as the state auditor, is the responsible entity for overseeing the selection of external auditors to ensure the lawful management of republican state budget. It may perform ad-hoc state audits of SOEs as part of an order of the President of Kazakhstan. Such may be the case in instances of suspected shortcomings and violations in the financial and economic activities of the SOE and takes the form of a full audit of activities and subsidiaries, as was the case for QazaqGaz in 2021.

External auditors are required to be independent from the audited SOE and appointed by the general meeting of shareholders or board of the SOE. The non-existence of a rotation requirement for selected auditors brings upon various weaknesses in the safeguarding for conflicts of interest. Out of the SOEs analysed, three have maintained the same external auditor for the period of 2012-2021 (Table 2.4). One of them, the *Institute of Economic Research*, has changed its external auditor every year in the analysed timespan.

Lacking the legal requirement to rotate auditors over a given timeframe severely compromises the independence requirement. Effectively, in those cases, external auditors are revisiting their work periodically, and thus cannot assure that their assessments remain unbiased. Yet, changing external auditors often, as it is the case for the *Institute of Economic Research*, which switches to a new external auditing service on a yearly basis throughout the analysed period, is also not considered good practice. The rotation requirement would ideally strike a balance – not requiring external auditors to change too often nor too seldomly. The ability to enforce the law which requires independence of auditors overall is likely to be weakened by excessive as well as never occurring rotations of external auditors.

Table 2.4. External audit of selected SOEs

Audited SOE	Number of audit companies during 2012-2021	Periods of analysis	External Auditor in 2021
National Company "QazaqGaz" JSC	1	2012-2021	Ernst & Young
KazTransGaz Aymak JSC	1	2012-2021	Ernst & Young
National Company Kazakhstan Temir Zholy JSC	1	2012-2021	Deloitte
Kazakhstan Railcars building company JSC	N/A	2012-2021	N/A
Kuryk Port LLC	1	2021	AR Group Audit LLP
Fund on Entreprenuership Development Damu JSC	2	2012-2021	PWC
Authority AIFC JSC	2	2020-2021, 2016-2017	Russel Bedford A+ Partners LLC
Banking servicing beaurau of the National Bank JSC	4	2012-2021	CenterAudit Kazakhstan LLC
Kazakhavtodor LLC	5	2014-2012	AuditBukhCenter LLC
International Airport Nursultan Nazarbayev JSC	7	2012-2021	Crowe Audit KZ LLC
Institute of Economic Research JSC	10	2012-2021	ARIP Consultng Group LLC
National Center for Neirosurgery JSC	4	2012-2021	BR Audit LLC
SK-Pharmacy LLC	5	2015-2021	ProgressAuditKZ LLC
National Geological exploration company "KazGeology" JSC	2	2012-2021	Ernst & Young
Khabar Agency JSC	7	2012-2021	StarAudit LLC
Special Economic zone "Ontustyc" Management Company JSC	5	2014-2021	AiSer Consulting and Aidut LLC
Plant after name of Kirov S. JSC	3	2012-2021	Moore Kazakhstan LLC
Machine Building Plant named after Kirov S. JSC	3	2012-2021	Moore Kazakhstan LLC
Republican Center for Space Communication JSC	3	2015-2021	Audit Company Asia KZT LLC
QAZEXPOCONGRESS National Company JSC	1	2013-2021	KPMG Audit

2.6.3. Aggregate annual reporting of SOEs

> ***C. The ownership entity should develop consistent reporting on SOEs and publish annually an aggregate report on SOEs. Good practice calls for the use of web-based communications to facilitate access by the general public.***

While the government of Kazakhstan does not yet publish an aggregate report on its SOEs, the MF maintains a repository of financial statements made by public interest organisations. The repository is accessible to the public online and allows to conduct searches for SOE audit reports for a given year. Among the downloadable PDF files of audit reports, financial information and the auditor's opinion is made available. The reports stored in the repository are drawn up in either Russian or Kazakh language, but are not available in English.

In practice, the repository allows to consult data on SOEs. Yet, the operation of the portal requires knowledge of firm-specific information to perform searches. It is not harmonised across companies and it lacks a comprehensive overview of the various SOEs and their comparable performance, hence generally does not enable an analytical assessment of the enterprises for which information is available. The plan of the government to put in place an aggregate report is thus welcomed.

2.6.4. Summary

Overall, SOEs in Kazakhstan do not incur a baseline set of disclosure and reporting requirements. Their disclosure and reporting standard is dependent on their legal form, whether they may be considered "non-commercial" in nature, their size, ownership entity, and listing status. As a result, there is a high degree of variability in disclosure practices observed across the state-owned sector.

SOEs that are also portfolio companies of national (management) holding companies tend to be held accountable to stricter rules on disclosure than SOEs which are comparably small and whose ownership responsibility lies in a given line ministry. Although disclosure standards for portfolio companies as expected by Samruk-Kazyna and Baiterek appear to be complied with more closely than disclosure requirements for other SOEs, elevated disclosure also reveals certain shortcomings in the corporate governance of SOEs in general.

Related party transactions between a portfolio company and its respective national (management) holding company, or among portfolio SOEs, tend to be large, and, in some cases understated by choosing to recognise them under different reporting items. It is further expected that for those SOEs that do not comply with IFRS, favourable borrowing arrangements, the issuance of financial guarantees and subsidies financed by the state budget may possible be not reported at all.

External independent audits of SOEs lack a rotation requirement that updates the external audit after an appropriate number of years. Currently, independent audits are conducted either too frequently or too seldomly, thus also weakening the independence of the external auditor for some of the SOEs.

When it comes to aggregate reporting on the state ownership level, the MF's repository of financial statements offers a useful centralised data storage on SOE's auditor's reports and financial statements. However, the auditor's reports are often only published in either Russian and Kazakh language, and thus the primary audience for the data storage remains constricted. The information included in auditor's reports is also often not fully comparable to the information provided as part of financial statements drawn up in line with IFRS. The data repository also lacks an analytical element which allows to meaningfully compare and assess SOE performance with the information that is shared.

2.7. Responsibilities of the boards of state-owned enterprises

> ***The boards of SOEs should have the necessary authority, competencies and objectivity to carry out their functions of strategic guidance and monitoring of management. They should act with integrity and be held accountable for their actions.***

2.7.1. Board mandate and responsibility for enterprise performance

> ***A. The boards of SOEs should be assigned a clear mandate and ultimate responsibility for the enterprise's performance. The role of SOE boards should be clearly defined in legislation, preferably according to company law. The board should be fully accountable to the owners, act in the best interest of the enterprise and treat all shareholders equitably.***

The mandates, rights, obligations and responsibilities of SOE BOD are generally outlined in the JSC and LLC laws, followed by regulatory documents developed by the MNE. As a general rule the boards of SOEs are granted rights and duties equivalent to those in private companies.

The JSC, State Property laws and the model Corporate Governance Code provide comprehensive provisions on BOD composition, terms, roles, responsibilities and accountabilities:

- A BOD must be established in all JSC, including members such as state representatives[13] and independent directors. Most of the SOEs' governing bodies are organised as two-tier boards with separate a BOD and executive body.[14] In rare cases, one-tier boards may be established.[15]
- Terms for elected members is 3 years, with the option of renewal for up to 9 years. Further exceptions allow renewals on an annual basis.
- The general shareholder meeting defines the board's size, which is 3 to 11 members depending on the enterprise size.
- The main duties of the board members are monitoring and eliminating potential conflicts of interest, protecting the interests of the SOE and shareholders, ensuring the integrity of the accounting and financial reporting system, conducting an independent audit, ensuring the disclosure of information, and treating all shareholders equally. The board has the authority[16] to 1) make decisions on issuing shares and giving the preliminary approval of the annual financial statements and payment for audit services; 2) approve the regulations of BOD committees and define the composition, term of office, election and remuneration (salaries, bonuses) of the executive body members, corporate secretary and internal audit; and 3) approve selected internal regulatory documents, amongst others. Board members can attract experts (external or internal) to support its decisions, and the general shareholders' meeting can reverse board decisions.
- Members have the fiduciary duties to carry out professional activities "with good faith and reasonability during conflicts of interest, when the members must act exclusively in the interests of the SOE". Governing bodies are liable to the SOE and its shareholders for damages caused by their actions (or inactions). Before court procedures, a shareholder with more than 5% shares can request a BOD to call a meeting and redeem the damages caused by the activities of boards. A member of the BOD who did not participate or voted against a decision that violated established laws and charter has the right to court appeal.
- Even though the executive body is obliged to execute all decisions of the general shareholder meeting and the BOD, the lack of clear division of control and management functions limits the ability of board members to check the executive body's activities or appeal its decisions in court. The responsibilities, liability, fiduciary duties, and conflict of interests are weakly monitored without any case law or judicial practice on these matters.

The LLC law provides an option to create a supervisory board or revision commission if this option is reflected in the company's charter, with no legal requirement to appoint independent directors. The general term of the board can be a maximum of 5 years. LLCs' – if they have one - usually have one-tier boards and the executive body may consist of either 1) a single person (general director or a CEO); or 2) a collegiate body (such as a management board) headed by a CEO. The main decision-making bodies of LLCs are the general participants meeting, while the supervisory board has basic rights to inspect activities of the executive body at any time and has unconditional access to all relevant documentation. The members of the supervisory boards are liable for losses caused to LLC and third parties due to their improper control over the activities of the executive body and may be held liable at the request of any of the partners of the LLC for compensation for losses caused by them.

In state enterprises without supervisory boards, the head of the enterprise is solely responsible for the activities of the enterprise. While state enterprises that operate in the healthcare and education sectors may create supervisory boards by the government approval. In such cases the supervisory board operates mostly as an intermediary body rather than a separate corporate governance body. The responsibilities of the board are established in the State Property law and are mostly related to the preliminary approval of key and strategic decisions before their final approval by the line ministry.[17] The following key responsibilities of the supervisory boards deviate from the general corporate governance practices observed in the JSC and LLC SOEs:

- agrees to the proposals of the line ministry on the appointment and dismissal of the head of the state enterprise
- proposes amendments to the charter to the line ministry
- develops proposals on key priority areas of operations to the line ministry.

Even though the legal framework and the model of Corporate Governance Code assigns the BOD with a clear mandate and responsibility for the SOE performance, in practice the boards face certain limitations that do not allow them to be fully accountable to the owners and treat all shareholders equitably:

- On an annual basis shareholders send the Chair of the BOD (supervisory boards) the shareholder expectations,[18] including strategic guidelines and KPIs for the upcoming years. To achieve these expectations the board prepares development and action plans, and at the general shareholders meeting the Chair reports on the execution of these expectations and adherence to the Corporate Governance Code. However, in fact, the results of the expectations merely impact the remuneration and decision on renewal or termination of terms of the executive body members. While the board members' performance evaluation is limited with qualitative assessment like organisational excellence, clarity of strategic objectives, effectiveness of interactions among board members and shareholders, quality of board discussions etc. Thus, the responsibility of the board to owners is limited and not directly linked with the SOE performance. Rather the board's self and independent assessment results are used by the general shareholders meeting to decide on term renewal and remuneration size for the board members.
- Usually, SOEs or entire boards are replaced without any official explanation, rendering it difficult to assess how this links to the company's performance. However, in most cases in which this occurred, there had been preceding criticism across the media and/or the President towards the CEO of the company.
- Board members and the Chair are predominantly nominated by the majority shareholders. In all observed SOEs (except for Kazatomprom and SK Pharmacy) the board Chairs usually have an employment relationship with the majority shareholders, which may compromise the board's independence in objective judgement and equitable treatment of all shareholders.

2.7.2. Setting strategy and supervising management

> ***B. SOE boards should effectively carry out their functions of setting strategy and supervising management, based on broad mandates and objectives set by the government. They should have the power to appoint and remove the CEO. They should set executive remuneration levels that are in the long-term interest of the enterprise.***

While SOE boards have been granted a number of powers, a number of apparent shortfalls remain. There is no legal definition of "undue influence" or "political interference" in BOD operations, and in practice SOE boards appear to have limited ability to carry out such key functions as setting strategy, supervising management and appointing and removing the CEO. Further, government bodies have the power to approve the final versions of strategic documents.

The BOD establishes a 10-year development plan based on strategic documents[19] and the President's addresses to the nation. The plan of national holdings and national companies is agreed on by the MNE (except for Samruk-Kazyna and its subsidiaries) and approved by the government, while the subsequent 5-year action plan approved by the BOD. Other SOEs require the approval of the development plan by their BOD or supervisory boards. State enterprises with supervisory boards approve their strategies by the decision of the line ministry, while the board serves as a preliminary approver of strategic documents with a right to make proposals. The numerous rules indicate that the dispersed ownership structure over SOEs in Kazakhstan renders it impossible to have clear/ aligned mandates and objectives.

Procedures for appointing management in SOEs are outlined in the JSC law and the SOEs' charters. According to the law, the BOD (supervisory board) should decide on the removal or appointment of CEOs and set terms of contract and remuneration. However, government decree No. 784/ 2002 – once again depending on the type of SOE - requires government oversight bodies to provide the final consent on CEO selection and appointment. This renders it difficult for the BOD to independently monitor and, if necessary, change the top management. Table 2.5 notes the diverse appointment/ nomination and approval procedures, while also showcasing that CEOs can be appointed or removed on the recommendation of the Prime Minister of Kazakhstan, the government and Presidential Administration. This reveals direct political influence, which is not in line with the SOE guidelines.

Table 2.5. CEO appointment/ nomination/ approval process of selected SOEs

Entity	Appointed by	Nominated by	Approved by
National Company "QazaqGaz" JSC	Executive Management Board of Samruk-Kazyna	Prime Minister	Chief of Staff of the Presidential Administration[1]
National Company Kazakhstan Temir Zholy JSC	Executive Management Board of Samruk-Kazyna	Prime Minister	Chief of Staff of the Presidential Administration[1]
Entrepreneurship Development Fund Damu JSC	BOD of Baiterek	Chairman of the Management Board of Baiterek JSC	Prime Minister or on his behalf with the Chief of Staff of the government
SK-Pharmacy LLC	Minister of Healthcare	N/A	Ministry of Finance
National Geological Exploration Company "KazGeology" JSC	BOD of KazGeology JSC	Ministers	Prime Minister or on his behalf with the Chief of Staff of the government
QazExpoCongress National Company JSC	BOD of QazExpoCongress JSC	Ministers	Prime Minister or on his behalf with the Chief of Staff of the government

Note: The table consists of only 6 SOEs out of selected 20 SOE that require CEO appointment additional procedures on top of the JSC law provisions. The word "Chairman of the Management Board" is used interchangeably with "CEO".

1. After expiration of President Decree #828 dated 29 March 2002, the new procedures of approval of the CEOs of national holdings and companies by the President Administration will not be disclosed publicly.

Source: Government Decree #784 dated 16 July 2002, President Decree #828 dated 29 March 2002 (expired on 31 July 2023) and President Decree #290 dated 31 July 2023.

In the case of Samruk-Kazyna, the appointment of CEOs in fully-owned subsidiaries requires preliminary approval by the parent company's executive body. As the CEO of SK is directly appointed by the government, this implies sharing the accountability and responsibility of the BOD for appointing and dismissing CEO with the state shareholder.

The overall process of CEO appointment is not particularly transparent and there have been allegations of undue political influence. The laws and regulations lack provisions of pre-established professional criteria for CEO selection, nomination and dismissal. The process rarely involves hiring an independent executive search company to assist with the selection. In most cases, the BOD considers only one candidate for the CEO position, and thus heavily relies on the proposals from ownership entities. This may be influenced by political connections rather than merit and professional qualifications. In practice:

1. the CEO nomination process starts with the ownership entity (line ministry, holding companies) selecting and preliminary approving candidates
2. hereinafter they aim to get the approval from required government structures, which is
3. transferred to the SOE's boards for final appointment.

Preliminary approval and selection of the CEO by representatives of the ownership entity creates a potential conflict for the CEO. In effect, it shifts the CEO's accountability for SOE performance from the BOD to the shareholder directly, thereby reducing the board's role to, at most, a compliance-checking function.

The BOD (supervisory boards) officially appoints a CEO, who signs a management contract with the Chair of the BOD on behalf of the SOE, while ownership entities are not involved in this stage of the process. Management contracts with other members of the executive body are signed by the CEO.

State enterprises' heads are appointed by the line ministry. The process of selection of the head and his/her performance measurement is conducted according to the rules developed and approved by the MNE.[20] In the case of state enterprises with the supervisory boards, the board is responsible for the preliminary approval of the candidate before final decision of the line ministry.

The exclusive competence of the BOD, in particular its remuneration committee, is to set the remuneration for the CEO and management team. The Chair of BOD signs a management contract with the CEO, however, remuneration is usually agreed between the CEO and the ownership entities. The size of the remuneration depends on economics, the complexity of SOE operations, personal competence and his/her competitiveness in the market. While the specific methodology of setting remuneration remains unclear, there is no evidence as to whether the current remuneration caps take market-based pricing in a given sector into consideration. The ownership entities can impose salary caps depending on the country's economic situation, for instance, amidst the COVID-19 pandemic. The BOD conducts an evaluation of the potential bonus size depending on the executive body's performance and achievement of preset KPIs. KPIs are offered by the CEO and approved by the BOD on an annual basis.

2.7.3. Board composition and exercise of objective and independent judgment

> ***C. SOE board composition should allow the exercise of objective and independent judgment. All board members, including any public officials, should be nominated based on qualifications and have equivalent legal responsibilities.***

To ensure independent, objective, and effective decisions in the best interest of the SOE and fair treatment of all shareholders, the BOD and its committees should maintain a balance of skills, experience, knowledge and gender diversity (30% women recommended, but not obligatory). The model Corporate Governance Code defines basic criteria for the BOD' member selection as work experience, education, special certificates (in specific industries), business reputation, absence of conflict of interest, and individual contribution to the board efficiency (if a term is renewed). However, the BOD composition faces several challenges:

- To prevent state authorities' intervention in the SOEs' operations and to increase the responsibility for BOD decisions, the model Code requests shareholders to avoid the election of state body representatives as members of the BOD. This in fact contradicts the state property law requirement to have the line ministry and MF representatives on the BOD. Some SOEs can even have representatives from the Prime Minister's office and the President's Administration on their boards. This and potential government pressure through direct shareholders can lead to their involvement in the management process, create a conflict of interest and limit the time available for board discussions due to the politicians' busy schedules.
- In some BODs of SOEs, the government bodies responsible for overseeing and regulating these enterprises are the same agencies,[21] which may hinder the separation of the state ownership function and other state functions.
- The Ministry of Finance appoints its representatives, who serve as either the Chairman or Deputy Chairman of the committee on state property and privatisation, to sit on the SOE boards. This may potentially lead to lacking expertise to effectively contribute to the decision-making process, as these SOEs may operate in diverse industries and require specialised expertise. For instance, one representative may simultaneously serve on the BOD of an SOE in airport logistics, neurosurgery, pharmacy, and TV media industries.

- The JSC law allows the CEO of the SOE to sit at the BOD, although he/ she has similar voting rights as other members. The selected 20 SOEs (Annex B) showcases that the majority have CEOs (15%), independent professionals (39%), and representatives of ownership entities (46%) sitting on their BODs. Ownership entities have at least two, and sometimes even up to four representatives on the boards of their subsidiaries – which can mean that they make up the majority of BOD members. This is the case for Samruk-Kazyna' subsidiaries, in which BODs are usually composed of seven members, out of which three represent the ownership entity, alongside the CEO. The BOD composition of the six listed SOEs consists of the holding companies (39%), CEOs (12%), independent directors (46%), and others (2%). Only Kcell has a minority shareholder representative from Freedom Finance JSC in its BOD. Although the law allows minority shareholders to have representative on the board, in reality, this does not occur.

The procedure for ownership entities nominating BOD candidates is not transparent. Usually, the ownership entity selects a candidate and proposes him/her to the general shareholders meeting for voting. Samruk-Kazyna, in co-operation with the Chair of the subsidiary BOD and two remuneration committees (subsidiary's and Samruk-Kazyna's) defines the qualification criteria for candidates, and evaluates and shortlists candidates. In most cases, a candidate's current position within an ownership entity relates to the function of managing the asset, which a candidate is being nominated for. However, it is not a rule of thumb, and employees from other functions as well as individuals not related to shareholders can be nominated to the BOD. Independent search companies are rarely made use of. For instance, Qazaq Gas, Kazakhstan Temir Zholy, and the *National Centre for Neurosurgery* have one representative of the shareholder on the BOD who has no direct link to the shareholder's organisation. In most cases, the general shareholder meeting considers only one candidate for one vacant position of the BOD member position, which limits the choice to select the best candidate among other possible candidates and eliminates the possibility to apply cumulative voting.

The supervisory boards of state enterprises are regulated by the separate rules developed by the MNE and covers the aspects of establishing the board, criteria of its members and members selection.[22] The line ministry creates a nomination committee from its employees, that develops contest conditions and places a public announcement in the media and website of the line ministry. The State Property law establishes that these supervisory boards should consist of at least five members, which have no relationship with the state enterprise, 30% of which should be independent directors.

The relations between the members of the BOD and the SOE's shareholders are formalised through contracts, specifying the rights, obligations, responsibilities to comply with the Corporate Governance Code, including devoting sufficient time to perform the functions, and nondisclosure of information. The model Corporate Governance Code requires BOD members to undertake an induction program. However, our survey noted that 60% of the SOEs do not provide training to prepare BOD members for their responsibilities. This may lead to challenges in effectively onboarding new members to the boards, resulting in a lack of preparedness to fulfil their responsibilities fully and efficiently.

Civil servants, politicians, and representatives (employees) of the holding companies are eligible to serve on the BOD or supervisory board of JSCs or LLPs with state participation, but they do not receive remuneration for these roles. While representatives of the shareholders who do not serve as their employees are eligible to receive remuneration from the SOE board membership.

The government bodies' and Baiterek representatives sitting on the subsidiary boards can vote on agenda items and take all decisions under their personal discretion. Samruk-Kazyna's representatives however need to conduct internal consultations through a so-called *strategic investment committee* before making final decisions on votes. Eventually, the responsibility for the final vote lies in the hands of Samruk-Kazyna's representative.

The duties of BOD members are usually terminated by the initiative of the ownership entity. During the termination process, the ownership entity does not provide a transparent or clear reasoning for the termination, more often referring to the expiration of contract terms or voluntary dismissal.

2.7.4. Independent board members

> ***D. Independent board members, where applicable, should be free of any interests or relationships with the enterprise, its management, other major shareholders and the ownership entity that could jeopardise their exercise of objective judgment.***

As noted in chapter 1 and in accordance with article 54 of JSC law, the number of independent directors (INEDs) should be sufficient to ensure the independence of the decisions made and the fair treatment of all shareholders, at least 30% of INEDs. The model Corporate Governance Code recommends increasing the number of independent directors up to 50% regardless of their listing status. LLCs have no legal obligation to have independent directors on their boards. According to the existing legal framework an independent member must meet the following criteria:

- Not be affiliated with the JSC or have been affiliated within the three years prior to their election (except for serving as an independent director of the same JSC).
- Not be affiliated with individuals or organisations that are connected by subordination to the JSC or have been so within the three years prior to their election.
- Not hold a position as a public servant.
- Not act as a representative of a shareholder in the JSC's body meetings within the three years preceding their election.
- Not be involved in auditing the JSC or having participated in such an audit within the three years preceding their election.
- Additionally, the independent member must fulfill any other requirements established by the laws of the Republic of Kazakhstan.
- Be free from any material interests or relations with the SOE, its management, its property or other interested parties.
- If an INED loses independence, this information needs to be brought to the attention of the shareholders to make appropriate decisions. INEDs are elected as Chairmen of board committees of strategic planning, HR and remuneration, internal audit, social and other issues.
- The JSC law also requires concluding transactions with interested parties by simple majority of votes of BOD members who are not interested in its completion. So, in most of the cases such transactions are voted only by the INEDs. INEDs are requested to participate in discussions with possible conflict of interest:
  - preparation of financial statements and non-financial reporting
  - transactions with interested/related parties
  - the nomination of candidates to the BOD
  - deciding on the remuneration for them.

Samruk-Kazyna's CG Code establishes additional requirements to assess the independence of a director as he/she 1) has been an employer of the company or its group within the last three years; 2) had during the last three years a material business relationship with the company directly or as a partner, shareholder, director or general manager of the body or maintains such a relationship with the company; 3) received or is receiving remuneration from the company in addition to the director's remuneration, participates in a share option of the company or in a performance-based payment scheme, or is a participant in the company's pension scheme; 4) has a membership in BOD or has connections with other directors through participation in other companies or bodies; 5) represents a major shareholder; and 6) has served on the BOD for more than nine years since their first appointment.

All 20 observed SOEs align with the legal requirements stipulated by the JSC law in terms of INED composition. Although the LLC law does not note a minimum number for INEDs nor a mandate for them, SK Pharmacy LLC, voluntarily allocated 60% of its board membership to INEDs. The remaining three SOEs in LLC form do not have INEDs on their supervisory boards.

The state enterprises supervisory boards' composition should contain 30% of INEDs, however the dedicated rule does not establish the criteria of independence. The general criteria for board member only stipulate that members should be free of any relationship with each other and with the state enterprise's head, should not have an outstanding criminal record and a corruption offense, and should not be a head of bankrupt legal entity one year before board nomination.

Table 2.6. INEDs in the BOD of selected 20 SOEs as of 1 August 2023

Number of SOEs	Percent of INEDs in the composition of the BOD and supervisory boards
3	0%
6	30-40%
9	41-50%
2	>50%

Source: Government of Kazakhstan & OECD team calculations

In the vast majority of JSCs in Kazakhstan, INEDs — as well as other board members — are appointed and dismissed by the decision of the sole or dominant shareholder that is common practice in almost all countries. However, the process of setting INEDs criteria, competitive and transparent selection process finally defines the level of independence of these members. In case of Kazakhstan, we observe that only in 20% of cases out of 20 selected SOEs, the INEDs were selected through open contests that were publicly available on company or government body websites. The lack of a standardised and regulated process on the nomination/ selection of INEDs, may cause a potential bias and favouritism in their selection. The absence of a centralised database for INED candidates, tailored to the SOE render it difficult to conduct a fair and transparent selection process for them. The state level regulations do not contain a requirement to create a government nomination committee that will ensure transparent and competitive bases for candidates' selection. The process of nomination of SOE BOD members rarely involves hiring an independent executive search company to assist with the selection of individuals who have no relationship with the shareholders and SOEs. In most cases, the general shareholder meetings or sole shareholder considers only one candidate for one vacant position of INED, which limits the choice to select the best candidate among other possible candidates.

Favouritism among INED candidates has led to special relationship between ownership entities and major shareholders of SOEs. Based on available information of selected 20 and the 6 listed SOEs, some INEDs tend to have strong relationships with holding companies that allowed some INEDs to be on the boards of at least 2 (subsidiary SOE) to 4 SOEs simultaneously within one holding group. For instance, one INED sits on the board of KazMunayGas, Kazatomprom, Samruk-Energy, Tau-Ken Samruk at the same time. The same case can be observed in the BODs of QazaqGas, KEGOC, SK Construction and Kazpost.

In such circumstances, it is difficult to evaluate the independence of a director, even if he/she meets the independence criteria set forth in the JSC law. With such direct dependence, independent directors are powerless to fulfil one of their central functions, namely "to ensure that the interests of all shareholders are respected".

2.7.5. Mechanisms to prevent conflicts of interest

> ***E. Mechanisms should be implemented to avoid conflicts of interest preventing board members from objectively carrying out their board duties and to limit political interference in board processes.***

The JSC law obliges BOD's to prevent conflicts of interest through 1) monitoring and, if possible, elimination of potential conflicts of interest at the level of officials and shareholders; and 2) monitoring the effectiveness of corporate governance practices in the company. BOD members must treat all shareholders fairly and make objective, independent judgments. The JSC law provides separate provisions on related party transactions, noting that the list of individuals and legal entities that are affiliated with the SOE must be made available to the public, and decided upon by the BOD simple majority voting by members who are not interested in its completion. The main mechanism to prevent conflicts of interest are enshrined in the Code of business ethics of the SOE.

High-level government officials and regulating/line ministry on SOE boards may perceive that they should decide according to their party line and the government's overall objectives, rather than the company's best interests. This remains as a significant risk, and effectively, there is no mechanism to eliminate this risk.

According to the latest amendments to State Property law, the MF is supposed to be given the authority to centralise the implementation of state ownership. Alongside the MNE, they are responsible for managing state property and monitoring the implementation of the line ministries of state policy on state property management. However, this setup has the potential to create a conflict of interest, particularly in SOEs where the MF has appointed its representatives as BOD members.

In general, despite having the legal framework in place and specific regulations in the Code of Corporate Governance to decrease the conflict of interests, implementation remains weak:

- BOD members and INEDs are still elected in an in transparent manner, affecting voting decisions
- the difficulty for government representatives in BODs to separate functions as a shareholder and other regulatory functions
- the presence of high-level politicians and regulatory government bodies on BODs.

2.7.6. Role and responsibilities of the Chair

> ***F. The Chair should assume responsibilities for boardroom efficiency, and when necessary in co-ordination with other board members, act as the liaison for communications with the state ownership entity. Good practice calls for the Chair to be separate from the CEO.***

The Chair's powers are elaborated in the JSC law, the model Corporate Governance Code, and further internal regulatory documents. Currently there are two-tier boards in Kazakhstan, which separates the roles of the Chair of the BOD and the CEO – head of the executive body. While the LLC law does not provide any provisions regarding the functions and roles of the Chair of the BOD, these provisions may be outlined within the SOE's charter.

According to the JSC law, any member of the BOD can be elected as Chair, except the CEO, by a majority of votes of BOD members by secret ballot and can be re-elected at any time, unless otherwise provided by the charter of the SOE.[23] In fully owned subsidiaries, the sole shareholder elects the Chair. State enterprises' supervisory board Chairs are also elected by the majority of board member votes.

The model Corporate Governance Code provides more details on Chair functions that include:

- planning meetings of the BOD, setting the agenda and ensuring timely receipt of information for decision making

- building proper communication and interaction with shareholders, and consulting with major shareholders in key strategic decisions
- ensuring monitoring and supervision of the proper execution of the BOD and general shareholders meeting decisions
- in the event of corporate conflicts, taking measures to resolve them and minimise the negative impact on the SOE's activities.

Each member of the BOD has one vote, and the decisions are made by a simple majority. The model Corporate Governance Code establishes that in case of equal distribution of votes, the Chair's vote becomes decisive in SOEs, though in non-SOE JSCs, provisions regarding a casting vote should be outlined in the charter. Out of the 20 selected and 6 listed SOE, only 3 BODs are chaired by INEDs (Kazatomprom JSC, Kcell JSC, SK Pharmacy LLC), the remaining 23 boards are chaired by the representatives of the ownership entities (overseeing, owner, regulatory bodies and holding companies). Thus, the Chairs' decisive voting in these 23 SOEs will predominantly represent the ownership entity – major shareholder interests in case of equal votes. Representation of the ownership entities in the SOE's BOD Chair position does not allow them to exercise objective, independent judgment and treat all shareholders equitably.

While according to the legal and regulatory framework, the Chair of the BOD acts as the main contact point between the ownership entity and the SOE, a lack of dialogue between the owner and the BOD has been observed. It is the CEO that, in practice, acts as the representative and main contact point with the ownership entity and then informs the BOD of progress. Considering that the Chairs in the observed SOEs are the representatives of the ownership entities, and they are directly employed by the ownership, the Chairs' independence is obviously compromised if his/her day-job is with the ownership entity.

2.7.7. Employee representation

> ***G. If employee representation on the board is mandated, mechanisms should be developed to guarantee that this representation is exercised effectively and contributes to the enhancement of the board skills, information and independence.***

The State Property law, JSC law and model Corporate Governance Code of Kazakhstan do not include any provisions, requirements, or directives concerning the inclusion of representatives from local self-government entities, trade unions, or other bodies authorised by labor collectives in the BOD meetings of SOEs.

2.7.8. Board committees

> ***H. SOE boards should consider setting up specialised committees, composed of independent and qualified members, to support the full board in performing its functions, particularly in respect to audit, risk management and remuneration. The establishment of specialised committees should improve boardroom efficiency and should not detract from the responsibility of the full board.***

The law governing JSCs requires all companies, regardless of size, business activity and whether or not they are publicly traded to have board committees. They are generally responsible for areas such as auditing; strategy and planning; nomination and remuneration; and ethics and integrity. These areas can be covered by one or several committees, except for audit issues that requires to be considered at a separate audit committee. Independent directors must chair these committees, but executives, the CEO, outsiders and external experts that are not members of the board, may also serve on board committees, except audit committee that should consist of exclusively of members of the BOD. The CEO cannot chair these committees.

The arrangement and functioning of the BOD committees, including their quantity and membership, are determined by the Committee's regulations, which are endorsed by the BOD, with a recommendation reflected in the model Corporate Governance Code to compose these committees with at least three members.

Among the observed 20 SOEs, 75% of them have committees under the BOD. Regardless of the legal requirements not all companies seem to have established committees. Out of 25% BOD without committees, 3 noted that this is due to the absence of such a requirement in the LLC law, and 2 of them face financial difficulties during their current stage of development, which has hindered the establishment of committees (see Annex B). 15% of the SOEs (Institute of Economic Research JSC, National Center of Neirosurgery JSC and NGEC KazGeology JSC) do not have separate audit committees, albeit mandated by the JSC law.

The JSC law and the Corporate Governance Code do not require listed companies to have a majority of independent directors on their committees. However, we observe that in most cases in which committees are established – particularly the audit committees - these are dominated by independent directors.

Committees should conduct a detailed analysis and develop recommendations on important agenda items before their consideration at the BOD meeting, while the final decision is made by the BOD:

- *The strategic planning committee* considers the items related to the development of priority areas and strategy for the SOE, including SOE activities, its long-term value and sustainable development. It should be chaired by the INED, except for Samruk-Kazyna's strategy committee, which is chaired by the MNE.
- *The audit committee* considers items related to external audit, financial reporting, effectiveness of the internal control and risk management systems, and compliance with the legislation. It also evaluates candidates for internal auditors and audit companies of the SOE. This committee should be chaired by an INED. In large and most significant SOEs, only independent directors are members of the audit committee and members are appointed by the BOD. The committee typically meets at least once a quarter, to review the results of the internal audits. The committee also reviews the SOE's financial statements and ensures that they comply with applicable accounting standards. The audit committee reports and gives recommendations to the BOD and communicates with the external auditor, if necessary. The committee is also responsible for ensuring that the internal audit function is adequately resourced and staffed with qualified personnel. They may also engage external consultants to assist with specific audit projects or to provide training to internal auditors.
- *The HR and remuneration committee* determines the criteria for selecting candidates for members of the BOD and executive body, considers internal regulatory documents related to remuneration, regularly evaluates the activities of board members and executive body. It also makes preliminary decisions on appointment, sets KPIs, performance assessment, remuneration and succession of the CEO and members of the executive body, appointment and remuneration of the corporate secretary and internal audit service employees, composition of the BOD itself. The Committee should consist of a majority of independent directors.

When committees exist, their mandates, composition and working procedures seem to be well-defined and disclosed. The establishment of a separate risk management committee is not required by legislation or Code, though functions of risk assessment and management may be integrated within other committees such as the audit committee. Based on the observations of the OECD team in terms of the effective ability of BOD's to exercise independent and objective judgement, it remains questionable how effective the work of the committees eventually is.

2.7.9. Annual performance evaluation

> ***I. SOE boards should, under the Chair's oversight, carry out an annual, well-structured evaluation to appraise their performance and efficiency.***

The process of an annual evaluation of BOD performance is regulated by the model Corporate Governance Code. To improve the professionalism of the BOD and its members, each SOE's BOD, its committees and members must conduct an annual self-assessment as well as an independent consultant's assessment at least once every three years. The assessment includes aspects, such as the board composition, vision and strategy, succession plans, board functioning, interaction with shareholders and management, individual director effectiveness, committee activities effectiveness, information quality, quality of discussions, corporate secretary performance, process clarity, risk identification and assessment, and engagement with stakeholders. The results of the assessment are reviewed by the HR and remuneration committee, affecting the BOD members re-election, termination, and/ or remuneration. The regulations do not mention the Chair's oversight role in this process. The results must be incorporated into the annual report of the SOE, which must be published on the website of the SOE.

Based on the results of the questionnaire of 20 SOEs, 45% of them do not conduct any self-assessments, while 35% carry out the self-assessment exercise without posting the results publicly. Among the observed SOEs, only the Damu Entrepreneurship Fund conducted a self-assessment and made the results public. Among the four observed LLCs, three of them (15%) do not conduct any self-assessments. However, SK Pharmacy LLC stands out as an exception and conducts both a self-assessment and an independent assessment. Nevertheless, the results of SK Pharmacy assessments are not publicly available.

In fact, some annual or sustainable development reports of the reviewed SOEs included the results of a self or independent assessment. Nonetheless, the annual reports are lacking crucial evaluation elements on succession plans, quality of discussions, engagement with stakeholders, shareholders, management, individual members effectiveness, misalignments, measures for improvement, etc. The information included in the reports rather appears as BOD's annual activities reports rather than self or independent assessment results.

2.7.10. Internal audit

> ***J. SOEs should develop efficient internal audit procedures and establish an internal audit function that is monitored by and reports directly to the board and to the audit committee or the equivalent corporate organ.***

Kazakhstan's SOEs can be audited in four different ways:

- *State audit and financial control bodies (supreme audit chamber)* that audit the use of budgetary funds, efficiency of the state assets and reports to Parliament and the President.
- *Audit committee under the BOD* that considers external audit, financial reporting, effectiveness of the internal control and risk management systems, compliance with the legislation and reports directly to the BOD.
- *External audit* conducted by the independent auditor to audit the SOE's financial statements and assesses internal control systems. External auditors collaborate with the audit committee and its results are approved by the general shareholders meeting.
- *internal audit functions* of SOEs which report their findings to the management and the BOD on financial and economic activities of the SOE, assessment of internal audit and control, risk management, compliance with legislation, and remain directly accountable to the BOD.

According to the JSC law, the SOE may establish an internal audit function in order to exercise control over financial and economic activities. It reports directly to BOD, and its employees cannot be elected to the BOD and executive body. Reporting to the BOD ensures that the internal audit findings and recommendations reach the highest level of oversight and decision-making authority within the SOE. The internal audit function collaborates with a professional audit council established according to the auditing legislation of the Republic of Kazakhstan. Article 53 of the JSC law outlines that one of the exclusive responsibilities of the BOD is to decide on various aspects concerning the internal audit service. This includes specifying the number of members, their tenure, selecting the head and members, and determining the conditions for their dismissal, as well as the remuneration and bonuses for its employees.

The model Corporate Governance Code establishes additional functions to the internal auditors on top of the general provisions provided by the legislation, such as:

- assistance and advice to the BODs and employees of the SOE, co-operation with external auditor and consultants in regard of improvement of risk management and internal control system, corporate governance
- conducting internal audits of subsidiaries
- verification of compliance of executive body members and SOE employees with the legislation requirements regarding insider information, prevention of corruption, and compliance with ethical requirements
- monitoring the implementation of the external auditor's recommendations.

According to the LLC law, a means of overseeing the financial and economic activities of the executive body of an LLC is through the establishment of a revision commission. This commission can be composed of LLC participants or their representatives and comprises up to five individuals, unless the LLC's charter permits a larger membership. The revision commission's responsibilities can be fulfilled by an individual from the LLC or their representative, acting as a sole auditor. The selection of the revision commission or sole auditor is made by the general meeting for a duration specified in the LLC's charter, which must not exceed five years. Members of the revision commission (auditor) cannot simultaneously hold positions within the LLC's executive body.

2.7.11. Summary

The BOD's approval of the CEO is rather considered as a formal approval stamp, than being given the right to nominate, appoint or remove the CEO, as provided by the SOE Guidelines. This makes it difficult for the BOD to fully exercise their monitoring function and assume responsibility for the SOE's performance. State objectives are prioritised over commercial interests resulting from rendering it difficult for the BOD to effectively carry out its functions to independently set the strategy and supervise management without political interference.

The absence of legal requirements regarding board members' qualifications, coupled with a lack of competitive base for selection, transparency, and accountability in their selection and appointment, can be subjectively used to select a "favorite" or a "comfortable" member. The appointments may be influenced by political or shareholder connections rather than merit. Board members might have personal or business ties to the SOE and its shareholders, potentially affecting decision-making to the detriment of the company and the state. Generally, the lack of transparency and competition surrounding board appointments in Kazakhstan may prevent SOE boards from effectively exercising objective, independent judgment and treatment of all shareholders equally.

The majority of SOE boards are populated either by government bodies or holding companies - which may effectively add pressure for them in prioritising state and social objectives beyond company interests. This situation could potentially lead to adverse consequences for minority shareholders and the commercial interests of the company. Ensuring transparency in INEDs' appointments can help mitigate these potential issues and promote fair decision-making in the best interests of all stakeholders.

The requirements on the BOD's self and independent assessment remain opaque rendering it difficult to make informed decisions on the re-election or termination of powers of board members. As the results of the selected SOEs' questionnaires show, some of them do not conduct such assessments which is not in line with the model Corporate Governance Code requirements.

Thus, despite having a comprehensive legal framework and provisions of the SOE Corporate Governance Code, the execution of these provisions remains opaque. The lack of monitoring and controlling functions from the ownership entities and lack of responsibility for non-compliance makes these frameworks rather formal requirements than practical guidance.

Despite the fact that Kazakh BODs formally have a relatively large array of rights stipulated across different laws and regulations, their role remains rather constrained: on CEO's nomination and dismissal, strategy setting, or being responsible for SOE performance. The current composition of most BODs – namely the majority being represented by majority shareholders - creates concerns on the objectivity of BOD decisions. On top of that, the lack of a transparent and competitive nomination of BOD members, including INEDs, may prevent SOE BODs from effectively exercising objective and independent judgement and treating all shareholders equally.

References

Competition Agency (2023), *ОТЧЕТ О СОСТОЯНИИ КОНКУРЕНЦИИ НА ОТДЕЛЬНЫХ ТОВАРНЫХ РЫНКАХ И ПРИНИМАЕМЫХ МЕРАХ ПО ОГРАНИЧЕНИЮ МОНОПОЛИСТИЧЕСКОЙ ДЕЯТЕЛЬНОСТИ ЗА 2022 ГОД*, https://www.gov.kz/memleket/entities/zk/documents/details/486951?lang=ru. [2]

EBRD (2017), *Corporate Governance in Transition Economies*, https://www.ebrd.com/documents/legal-reform/kazakhstan.pdf. [5]

Halyk Research (2023), *Проблемы государственного участия в экономике Казахстана*. [3]

Kazatomprom (2018), *Prospectus*, https://www.kazatomprom.kz/storage/b5/lse_prospectus.pdf. [6]

KMG (2022), *Annual Report*, https://www.kmg.kz/upload/iblock/9b5/oi2bn0en04rjbgb8s3m1706o3sl851lg/KMG_AR2022_ENG%20(1).pdf. [7]

OECD (2023), *Insights on the Business Climate in Kazakhstan*, OECD Publishing, Paris, https://doi.org/10.1787/bd780306-en. [1]

OECD (2019), *Istanbul Anti-Corruption Action Plan: Methodology for the 4th Monitoring Round*, OECD, Paris, https://www.oecd.org/corruption/acn/OECD-ACN-4th-Round-Monitoring-Methodology-Amendments-2017-ENG.pdf. [8]

OECD (2019), *Public Procurement in Kazakhstan: Reforming for Efficiency*, OECD Public Governance Reviews, OECD Publishing, Paris, https://doi.org/10.1787/c11183ae-en. [4]

OECD (2017), *OECD Investment Policy Reviews*, OECD Publishing, Paris, https://doi.org/10.1787/19900910. [9]

Notes

[1] This concept was developed in 2000, during which the state ownership function was centralised within the Ministry of National Economy's State Property and Privatisation Committee. Since then, the policy was transferred to the Ministry of National Economy, the Government established holding companies, and the State Property Law was developed.

[2] Aligning it with the United Nations Commission on International Trade law (UNCITRAL) Model on International Commercial Arbitration, the New York Convention on the Recognition and Enforcement of Foreign Arbitral Awards, and the European Convention on International Commercial Arbitration.

[3] As of the end of 2020, SMEs employed 3.4 mn in Kazakhstan, or 38.6% of the total employed. SMEs produced a total output of KZT 32.7 trillion in 2020 and contributed 31.6% to GDP. In OECD countries SMEs make up over 99% of firms, are the source of 40-80% of all employment, and provide between 30 and 70% of GDP.

[4] Since November 2022 the Association of Minority Shareholders also co-ordinates the non-listed companies' minority shareholders

[5] Air Astana JSC can be as an example of such case. Air Astana that has two shareholders in the ownership structure (Samruk-Kazyna JSC 51%, BAE Systems Kazakhstan Ltd 49%) based on paragraph 13.2. of the Charter defined that the board of directors consists of 8 or 9 members who are elected by the general meeting of shareholders by cumulative voting using voting ballots. The board of directors consists of 2 members proposed for election by Samruk-Kazyna, 2 members proposed for the election by BAE Systems, the President, 3 independent directors, and in the case where the board of directors consists of 9 members, 1 additional member determined by the shareholders. Paragraph 13.10 indicated that the Chairman of the board of directors is elected from among the candidates proposed by the Samruk-Kazyna.

[6] Every government body that somehow regulates the SOE has its own requirement what exactly documents should be publicly available and should be disclosed on the financial statements depository. The main requirements on disclosure of SOE information is outlined in the Rules on keeping the register of state property developed by the MF.

[7] https://www.accountability.org/standards/aa1000-stakeholder-engagement-standard/

[8] Samruk-Kazyna's Corporate Governance Code has greater details compared to the MNE's code. For instance, the process of agreeing the SK participation in the state programme documents, in government consulting bodies, requirement of disclosure the execution of the low return or socially important investment projects with funding sources, conditions under which SK can intervene into subsidiaries operations, disclosure of any forms and conditions of co-operation of listed subsidiaries with the government and state bodies, recommendation to have up to 50% of board composition as independent directors, election of the senior independent director, for 100% owned subsidiaries the Chair of the board of directors elected by the sole shareholder decision and description of the process of the board member election, the candidacy for the CEO is preliminarily agreed by the SK executive body, the government appoints the CEO of Samruk-Kazyna, etc.

[9] Based on the Methodology of the corporate governance assessment of controlling subsidiaries of Samruk-Kazyna the rating is assigned based on the following scale from the lowest to the highest: C –1, B – 2, BB – 3, BBB – 4, A – 5, AA – 6, AAA – 7.

[10] OECD team reviewed companies' websites and other publicly available sources and did not detect the independent assessment results for recent years.

[11] (1) Preventive Measures (Article 6): UNCAC's Article 6 emphasises the importance of implementing preventive measures to address corruption within both public and private sectors. It calls for measures to promote integrity, transparency, and accountability in the management of public affairs and in government-owned assets. (2) Management of Public Finances (Article 9): Article 9 of UNCAC focuses on the management of public finances, including the oversight of state enterprises and public procurement. It calls for measures to prevent corruption in the management of public assets, including SOEs. (3) Public Procurement (Article 9): UNCAC addresses corruption risks in public procurement, which often involves state enterprises. It promotes transparency, competition, and accountability in the procurement process to prevent corrupt practices. (4) Transparency and Reporting (Article 13): Article 13 encourages measures to promote transparency in the public administration, including the activities of SOEs. It calls for the development and maintenance of systems that facilitate public access to information. (5) Accountability of Public Officials (Article 15): UNCAC's Article 15 deals with the accountability of public officials. This includes officials in state enterprises, who are expected to be held accountable for any corrupt acts they engage in. (6) Criminalization of Corruption (Articles 15 and 16): UNCAC requires member states to criminalise various forms of corruption, including bribery, embezzlement, and abuse of functions. This applies to both public officials and individuals within state enterprises. (7) Recovery of Assets (Chapter V): UNCAC's Chapter V addresses the recovery of assets acquired through corrupt practices. This chapter can be relevant in cases where state enterprises are involved in corruption, and it provides a framework for recovering stolen assets.

[12] which provides recommendations on RBC in the areas of information disclosure, human rights, employment and industrial relations, environment, bribery and corruption, consumer interests, science and technology, competition, and taxation.

[13] except for Samruk-Kazyna's subsidiaries that are regulated by the separate NFW law.

[14] according to legal documents in Kazakhstan an executive body is titled the management board.

[15] according to the Air Astana JSC charter, the company has a one-tier board, and its executive body is represented by the CEO.

[16] Samruk-Kazyna's law considers the delegation of some mandates and responsibilities of the general shareholder meetings to the board of directors and mandates and responsibilities of the board of directors to the executive body level.

[17] https://adilet.zan.kz/rus/docs/V1500010503

[18] OECD team was not provided by an example of such shareholder expectations to assess the practical implication of the code. According to of the MNE, such expectations usually communicated orally during board meetings. Based on SWF law Samruk-Kazyna's BOD has a Strategy committee chaired by the MNE

that is used as a platform to communicate shareholder expectations to the Samruk-Kazyna and its subsidiaries and control their execution.

[19] (1) Development Strategy of Kazakhstan until 2050, (2) National priorities (with 1-2 measurable indicators), (3) National development Plan of Kazakhstan (with strategic indicators) and National Security Strategy of Kazakhstan, (4) Plan for territorial development of the country, (5) the concept of industry development, National Projects, (6) development plans of state bodies, regions, cities of republican significance, the capital, national management holdings, national holdings/companies.

[20] https://adilet.zan.kz/rus/docs/V1500010379

[21] For instance, from the legal perspective the operations of the National Geological Exploration Company "KazGeology" are regulated by the Ministry of ecology, geology and natural resources, while the representatives of this ministry are set in the BOD of the SOE.

[22] https://adilet.zan.kz/rus/docs/V1500010503

[23] In the case of having another majority shareholder, apart from the state and other governmental and holding entities, the authority to nominate the Chair can be fixed in the SOE charters. For instance, Air Astana JSC board of directors' Chair can be elected only from a candidate nominated by the Samruk-Kazyna.

3 Conclusions and recommendations for Kazakhstan's state-owned sector

The Kazakh Government has undertaken important reform efforts over the past decade to improve the governance and performance its state-owned enterprises. Yet, significant implementation shortcomings exist. This chapter provides some overarching conclusions emanating from the Review, and subsequent policy recommendations to help Kazakh authorities implement planned reforms and undertake further reforms to align Kazakhstan with the *OECD Guidelines on Corporate Governance of State-Owned Enterprises*.

The government of Kazakhstan has taken steps in recent years to improve the management and corporate governance of SOEs. As recounted in the President's various addresses to the nation, the government and holding companies have streamlined corporate governance practices for SOEs, improved reporting mechanisms and aimed to further reduce the state's substantial presence in the economy.

Despite stated aims and related progress, this report raises important and varied concerns. Kazakhstan's current ownership arrangements make it difficult to exercise state ownership rights on a whole-of-government basis. Line ministries and the two largest holding companies function alongside one another, seemingly with little to no co-ordination or communication. The situation is further complicated by a lack of clarity on roles and responsibilities between ownership entities and SOEs. The absence of a formal state ownership policy and thus of a clear rationale for ownership, and the presence of ambiguities regarding the extent of SOEs' commercial and non-commercial objectives, make it difficult for the state to monitor and encourage improvements in SOEs' sub-optimal performance.

The ownership arrangements in Kazakhstan are pieced together through a multitude of laws, Codes, decrees and regulations that are frequently revised and amended. The expectations and objectives – delegated by the state owner to the SOE – are often implicit, and KPIs that stem from development and action plans are often not directly accessible to the public.

In the current ownership landscape, there is no separation between the government's ownership, regulatory and other state functions. Line ministries undertake both regulatory and monitoring functions, as well as sectoral regulatory functions. While the model Corporate Governance Code outlines the powers vested in the governing bodies of SOEs, aiming to limit direct involvement in day-to-day matters by the ownership entity, the state retains the authority to approve vital corporate documents, such as strategic plans and financial decisions. This practice has many implications, including the issuance of competing objectives for SOEs.

In practice, the state – as a sole or dominant shareholder – may control directly or indirectly a number of corporate decisions and thus limit SOEs' operational autonomy, including with regards to hiring decisions. Perhaps relatedly, SOE boards and executive management seem to be subject to a high degree of political intervention, as revealed by frequent dismissals of CEOs following interventions by the President or the government. There are thus instances where state influence in SOEs goes beyond the strategic level and involves operational decisions. This risk seems higher where the government has a strong interest in a particular enterprise or sector, which likely stems from, inter alia, government policies and the importance of the enterprise to the national economy.

The risk of political interference in SOEs is, reportedly, a historical phenomenon, particularly regarding political appointees on boards and in executive positions. Board of Directors (BOD) currently have neither the independence nor the responsibilities to fulfil essential strategy setting and corporate oversight roles. Nomination procedures are not uniform across SOEs and do not sufficiently protect boards from political interference. In practice, therefore, many SOEs operate either as extensions of their ownership ministries or at the discretion of their executive management (whose representatives are appointed by the state rather than the BODs).

Access to unbiased legal or arbitration processes remains a concern frequently expressed by private businesses who expressed doubt about the domestic courts' reliability in resolving disputes between private parties and the state or SOEs. Kazakh SOEs have special privileges, distorting competition. Minority investors in SOEs have limited rights and protections, particularly in cases where state interests may conflict with commercial interests.

SOEs in Kazakhstan function within an incomplete accounting system, making it challenging to distinguish their financial activities and effectively allocate funds. Commercial and non-commercial activities are not separated, and compensation for public service obligations is not transparent. Although the public policy objectives and functions that SOEs are expected to fulfill as part of their national company and operator status are available in open sources, the phrasing and scope of these functions are often quite broad and lacking in specificity.

3.1. Recommendations

At the request of the Republic of Kazakhstan, this report reviewed Kazakhstan's SOE corporate governance framework against the *OECD Guidelines on Corporate Governance of State-Owned Enterprises*. The Guidelines were developed by the WPSOPP to help governments ensure that the enterprises they own or control are more competitive, efficient and transparent. The WPSOPP recognises that, by requesting this review, Kazakhstan has positively indicated a willingness to assess and improve the corporate governance laws, rules, and practices that determine how their SOEs do business. This is of paramount importance for Kazakhstan given the prominent role of SOEs in the Kazakh economy.

This report finds that Kazakhstan's SOE corporate framework, as it was at the time of writing, diverges from the Guidelines in certain fundamental respects. Effectively and promptly addressing these shortcomings could help ensure that SOEs contribute, to the fullest extent possible, to the Kazakh economy and citizens, and in line with state reform priorities. The Review has identified the following priority areas for reform:

- **Strengthening the state ownership function**. The government should issue an explicit ownership policy which specifies how the state exercises its ownership rights, setting out the rationales for state ownership of companies. The policy should apply to all commercially-oriented enterprises in the state-owned sector and be subject to periodic reviews.
- **Professionalising boards.** The government should develop, and ensure the enforcement of, transparent and competitive procedures for nominating directors, with particular attention placed on ensuring that members of boards have the requisite professional qualifications and are capable of and willing to exercise objective and independent judgement. It should further consider increasing the number of independent board members.
- **Enhancing transparency and disclosure.** In order to enhance transparency, the Kazakh authorities should implement their indicated action plan, which notes the development of an annual aggregate report on SOEs that covers all SOEs fully or majority-owned at the central level of government.
- **Equitable treatment of shareholders and other investors.** Ensure that the rights of non-state shareholders in SOEs are fully respected. They should have access to full information about the companies' non-commercial objectives and be shielded from subsequent ad-hoc interventions by the state.
- **Maintaining a level playing field.** To avoid distorting competition, public service obligation frameworks should be clarified and improved, with a clear compensation methodology established. SOEs should be required to maintain separate accounts for commercial and non-commercial activities to ensure competitively neutral compensation for carrying out public service obligations. The government should review the bankruptcy rules and moratoria applicable to SOEs, while eliminating the unconditional (in terms of duration and amount) use of state guarantees for SOEs to access finance. The government should require SOEs to access finance on commercial terms, which, among other things, means that they should be able to pledge their assets. In turn, boards and management should have the right incentives for sound financial management. To this end, the Ministry of Finance should strengthen its system for monitoring fiscal risks and ensure that all SOEs begin to have their annual financial statements audited by external independent auditors.

The following sections provide further details on the aforementioned priority areas for reform, and propose a number of additional areas for reform that the authorities are strongly encouraged to address when appropriate.

3.1.1. Strengthening the state ownership function

- **The Kazakh government is encouraged to develop an ownership policy**, which should *inter alia* define the overall rationales for state ownership, the state's role in the governance of SOEs, how the state will implement its ownership policy, and the respective roles and responsibilities of those government offices involved in its implementation. It may be considered good practice to include, in the ownership policy, objectives such as the creation of value, the provision of public services or strategic goals such as the maintenance of certain industries under national ownership.
- **The government should further consider transitioning from the existing separate track ownership model towards a more centralised model**. This could be done by collecting the ownership of all commercially oriented SOEs under the aegis of the existent holding company Samruk-Kazyna/Baiterek or by establishing a new holding company or ownership agency to replace it. If this is not politically or practically feasible, the government should consider establishing a co-ordinating body reporting directly to the government of Kazakhstan. Its tasks would include formulating and upholding the state's governance and transparency benchmarks for SOEs, monitoring SOE performance and ensuring regular public disclosure. Additionally, the body should actively contribute to the selection of board members for SOEs by proposing candidates to ownership ministries, thereby facilitating the establishment of proficient boards.

3.1.2. Professionalising boards

- **More professional boards with an adequate degree of independence are needed**. In line with the law, the boards of selected SOEs should be required to comprise a majority of independent directors, with clear criteria for their independence and selection (open contest for instance). The ownership entity should ensure that BODs are composed of majority independent directors to avoid undue political interference and have the necessary autonomy to carry out their work. No state representatives – civil servants or otherwise – should be considered as independent. Nomination procedures should ensure that BOD members of all majority- and fully-owned SOEs are selected based on their professional qualifications and subject to a transparent and competitive procedure. The state's board member remuneration policy and practices should ensure that it is able to attract and retain qualified professionals.
- **There is a need for clear criteria and processes for the selection, nomination and dismissal of SOE board members**. The government should develop clear instructions for nominating directors, with a special view to ensuring that members of boards have the requisite professional qualifications and are capable of and willing to exercise objective and independent judgement. It should further establish safeguards to ensure that the implementation of these instructions is continually and consistently enforced.
- **The state should empower boards to carry out functions of setting strategy and supervising management**. While the boards' role in this respect is already provided by law, the combination of weak boards and politically affiliated CEOs and board members leave much to be desired. The current role and responsibility of SOE boards in Kazakhstan should be strengthened to empower them to consistently oversee strategy, appoint the CEO and supervise management, free from political pressure and interference. To this end, the state could review procedures that require prior approval of corporate strategies by and establish an on-going and active dialogue of the ownership entity with the BOD on draft key strategic documents and corporate performance.

- **SOE boards should be expected to conduct comprehensive self and independent assessments of the BOD** – in line with what is already given in the law. Clear grounds for the early termination of powers of the BOD members should be established, which should be decoupled from the board evaluation process. Moreover, reliable monitoring and controlling functions should be established.

3.1.3. Enhancing transparency and disclosure

- **The government is encouraged to proceed with the planned reform and establish an annual procedure for aggregate reporting**. In order to enhance transparency, the Kazakh authorities should develop annual aggregate reports on SOEs that cover SOEs fully or majority-owned at the central level of government. SOEs' financial and non-financial objectives and related performance should be included on top of an assessment of SOEs' compliance with the state's applicable governance and disclosure rules. Ideally such a document would also disclose the costs and revenues resulting from costs on public policy objectives.
- Disclosure and reporting practices across Kazakh SOEs vary extensively and largely depend on the ownership entity (Ministry or holding company). It remains unclear to which companies the national legal framework (which requires IFRS compliance) applies. **Disclosure standards could be further strengthened and harmonised across the SOE sector** to ensure high quality and credibility of all SOEs' corporate reporting and not just of listed SOEs. A policy document could be developed setting a whole-of-government standard for what accounting, auditing and disclosure standards are applicable to SOEs, including any differences according to enterprise characteristics.

3.1.4. Equitable treatment of shareholders and other investors

- While it is entirely legitimate to offer to the public shares in an SOE that carry significant public policy objectives, **these objectives should be fully disclosed prior to the opening of the company's shareholding and updated if revised**. Non-state shareholders need to be able to make an informed decision on the SOE's likely future profitability to make investment decisions.
- **There is a need to improve internal processes that may limit the disclosure of BOD or GSM materials or communications with the major shareholder before BOD or GSM**. If SOEs conduct discussions with major shareholders, then minorities should also take part in such discussions. This is especially the case when non-core projects or expenses are financed by the SOE and can negatively impact minority shareholders.
- In the event that the state intends to instruct an SOE to undertake material transactions or alter their public policy objectives, **high standards of transparency and involvement of the non-state investors must be ensured.** One option might be to establish dialogue or consultation platforms with minority shareholders to preliminarily discuss key issues or transactions.

3.1.5. Maintaining a level playing field

- While the updates to the State Property Law enshrine some important basic principles related to SOEs' competitive position in the marketplace (notably by explicitly prohibiting unfair competition and abuses of monopoly), several elements could still distort the level playing field between SOEs and (actual or potential) private competitors, including the use of holding companies to facilitate intragroup financing among subsidiaries and shortcomings in the applicability of public procurement rules to SOEs as procurers, amongst other aspects. **Appropriate measures should be implemented to remedy concerns about a level playing field** and further align Kazakh ownership practices with the SOE Guidelines.

- **There is a need to further clarify SOEs' financial and non-financial objectives**: Guided by the overarching expectations of the state as an owner, Kazakh authorities should define unambiguous financial and non-financial goals for all SOEs. This process can commence with categorising SOEs based on whether they primarily serve a public-policy role, predominantly engage in commercial activities or operate as a hybrid of both. A structured mechanism should be instituted to establish and monitor tailored performance objectives for each enterprise.
- Too many variations of Corporate Governance Codes exist. **There is a need to streamline and create a national Corporate Governance Code that includes all corporate governance practices in Kazakhstan**. A clear methodology on how to assess the adherence to the Corporate Governance Code is needed which also clarifies which entity monitors its execution, and thereby increase controlling functions.
- Numerous laws targeting SOEs exist on top of laws that separately address SOEs and holding companies. This can create confusion, and ultimately lead to non-compliance with the laws. In the long-term, **it is recommended to streamline laws and abolish separate laws for separate entities**.

Annex A. Methodological note on data analysis

Legal definitions and main sources of information

SOEs in Kazakhstan are often referred to as *enterprises with public interest*. The legal definition of what is considered an enterprise with public interest is laid out in the law On Accounting and Financial Reporting No. 234/ 2007, and includes a range of sector- and operation-specific features.

There are certain pre-requisites an enterprise with public interest will need to fulfil in order to classify as such. For example, an enterprise with public interest may be a JSC whose operations are commercial in nature. However, there is no consistently applied classification system in Kazakhstan that provides the basis for what enterprise may be seen as commercial or non-commercial, and thus falling under the scope of what may constitute an enterprise with public interest in Kazakhstan. The Kazakh authorities shared plans to introduce such a classification system, though at the moment of analysis, such plans have not been realised.

Despite some ambiguity in the legal definition, the Ministry of Finance (MF), which is the main state body tasked with monitoring and analysing the performance of the quasi-state sector, maintains a repository of financial statements and auditor reports on all organisations considered as enterprise with public interest. Said repository serves as the primary source for data on the state-owned sector for the purpose of this review.

The total scope of the SOE sector

The overall scope of the quasi-state sector in Kazakhstan is very large and economically significant. Besides various legal entities such as JSCs, LLPs, state institutions and state enterprises, Kazakhstan also recognises the special status of 22 state-owned JSCs with additional management functions.

The overall legal understanding of what constitutes state and communal property is also different from what enterprises with public interest are, and the way in which this distinction is drawn in the monitoring mechanisms of the MF is not fully known. According to the MF,[1] the quasi-state sector includes 18 819 non-commercial bodies and 5 469 commercial enterprises – thus vastly exceeding the overall number of enterprises with public interest in the Kazakh economy.

According to information obtained from the World Bank, not more than 5% of the 5 469 organisations deemed as commercial in their nature of operations are in fact commercial. Roughly 95% of the 5 469 "commercial"-classed enterprises are in fact non-commercial entities – with the majority of their revenue coming from the state budget, or their activities being related to the provision of public services.

The SOE Guidelines note that "… any corporate entity recognised by national law as an enterprise, and in which the state exercises ownership, should be considered as an SOE" (OECD, 2015[1]). According to this definition, all 5 469 entities selected by the MF would be accepted as SOEs in the context of the state recognising them as corporate entities. However, given that the MF encompasses many enterprises that, in reality, are almost exclusively not-for-profit in nature, certain elements of the recommendations of the SOE Guidelines only apply to them in a limited capacity.

The data from the MF as of March 2023 finds that the state, directly and via state-owned holding companies, holds 700 enterprises at the central level of government. The first part of this review focuses its analytical work on the following group of enterprises:

- State property: 320 enterprises that are comprised of 132 JSC, 29 limited liability companies (LLC), and 159 state enterprises.
- State-owned holding companies (SOHC): 89 JSCs, 291 LLCs that are assigned to Samruk-Kazyna (178), Baiterek (12), Kazakhstan Engineering (17), social entrepreneurial corporations (96) and others (77).

Within the selected 700 SOEs, the state and holding companies own 50% or less shares in 139 of them, and thus hold a non-controlling stake in them. 58 of the 700 SOEs are non-commercial JSCs. Thus, the final selection of SOEs within the OECD scope of the analysis, include both non-commercial entities, as well as entities in which the state has non-controlling interest.

The largest 20 SOEs in terms of asset size

As established, the Kazakh quasi-state sector spans a variety of legal forms, covering both “commercial” and “non-commercial” enterprises and national (management) holding companies. For the purpose of facilitating the analysis, the OECD Secretariat reduces the overall amount of SOEs considered for more detailed assessments down to a pool of 700 SOEs that are held at the central level of government, thus excluding SOEs that are held at the regional *Akimat* level.

Certain sections of the SOE review of Kazakhstan, namely *Equitable treatment of shareholders and investors*, as well as *Disclosure and transparency*, necessitate a refined sample of SOEs to conduct detailed and qualitative analysis with. In past OECD reviews of the state-owned sector, the largest and most economically significant SOEs were typically selected for fine-grained analysis.

Though analysing the largest SOEs ensures that the review provides an apt description of the performance of the economically most impactful parts of the SOE sector, there are various reasons why such a selection methodology would not accurately reflect the SOE sector in Kazakhstan. Out of the 20 largest SOEs in terms of total asset size, 16 belong to either Samruk-Kazyna's or Baiterek's portfolio of state enterprises. This places 69% of the overall assets of these large SOEs in the management of national (management) holdings. Merely one of the largest SOEs in Kazakhstan is owned by a line ministry that reports to the government. The table below further showcases the ownership structure of the largest SOEs in Kazakhstan, and highlights that the top-20 largest SOEs do not accurately reflect Kazakhstan's state ownership structure.

Table A A.1. Overview of the ownership arrangements of the 20 largest SOEs

Ownership entity	Number of portfolio companies	Asset size, in bn KZT	Weight out of total assets
Samruk Holding	14	34 913	61%
Baiterek Holding	2	4 664	8%
Kazakhstan Engineering	1	12 229	21%
National Bank	2	4 769	8%
MIID	1	978 479	2%

SOEs that are managed by either Samruk-Kazyna or Baiterek comply with reporting expectations that are set, according to the Kazakh authorities, fairly independently. Both holdings require their portfolio companies to disclose information in accordance with their group internal Corporate Governance Codes.

Therefore, relying the analysis on them exclusively will give a one-sided perspective on the state-owned sector, mostly shining light on the part of it that is owned by larger holding structure.

SOHCs in Kazakhstan, in particular SWF Samruk-Kazyna, provide an entirely different institutional structure to house SOEs, often regulated and monitored separately than other branches and entities of the state which equally exercise ownership of SOEs. For this reason, it is important to consider a different selection method to arrive at the final sample of SOEs.

Selecting a stratified random sample of 20 SOEs

To obtain a balanced picture of the overall disclosure across different types of SOEs, the heterogeneity of the enterprises considered as state-owned in Kazakhstan must be considered in the sampling process. Therefore, the Secretariat analysis relies on a stratified sample of SOEs, where the overall amount of eligible SOEs is divided into three strata that are deemed to accurately reflect key characteristics of the Kazakh SOE sector.

The different strata cover 1) portfolio SOEs of holding companies Samruk-Kazyna and Baiterek; 2) financial SOEs; and 3) SOEs of different legal forms. SOEs that are classed as holding companies are excluded from the analysed sample to ensure comparability across portfolio SOEs. From the identified strata, a random sample of 20 SOEs was selected. The final sample of SOEs offers a more holistic perspective of the effect of the disclosure requirements applied conducive to the legal framework under which a given SOE may operate in. The final sample is detailed in the table below.

Table A A.2. Information on final sample of 20 selected SOEs

Full title of entity	Legal form	Ownership form	Owner
National Company "QazaqGaz"	JSC	SOHC	Samruk-Kazyna
KazTransGaz Aymak	JSC	SOHC	Qazaq Gas
National Company Kazakhstan Temir Zholy	JSC	SOHC	Samruk-Kazyna
Kazakhstan Railcars Building Company	LLC	SOHC	Kaztemirtrans NC
Kuryk Port	LLC	SOHC	Kazakhstan Temir Zholy NC
Fund on Entrepreneurship Development Damu	JSC	SOHC	Baiterek
Authority AIFC	JSC	State	National Bank
Banking Servicing Bureau of the National Bank	JSC	State	National Bank
Kazakhavtodor	LLC	State	KazAutoZhol NC JSC
International Airport Nursultan Nazarbayev	JSC	State	Ministry of Finance
Institute of Economic Research	JSC	State	Ministry of Finance
National Center for Neurosurgery	JSC	State	Ministry of Finance
SK-Pharmacy	LLC	State	Ministry of Finance
National Geological Exploration Company "KazGeology"	JSC	State	Ministry of Finance
Khabar Agency	JSC	State	Ministry of Finance
SEZ "Ontustyc" Management Company	JSC	SOHC	Social Entrepreneurial Corporation Shymkent
Plant after name of Kirov S. JSC	JSC	SOHC	Kazakhstan Engineering
Machine Building Plant named after Kirov S. JSC	JSC	SOHC	Kazakhstan Engineering
Republican Center for Space Communication JSC	JSC	State	Ministry of Finance
QAZEXPOCONGRESS National Company JSC	JSC	State	Ministry of Finance

Source: Information provided by the government of Kazakhstan to the OECD team.

References

OECD (2015), *OECD Guidelines on Corporate Governance of State-Owned Enterprises, 2015 Edition*, OECD Publishing, Paris, https://doi.org/10.1787/9789264244160-en. [1]

Note

[1] According to assessments of the OECD team, there are discrepancies in the amount of SOEs held by different ownership entities and reflected in the SOE data repository maintained by the MF.

Annex B. Selected SOEs – external auditing/ board compositions

Table A B.1. External Auditors of annual financial statements for 2012-2022 of the 20 selected SOEs

Audited SOE	2022*	2021	2020	2019	2018	2017	2016	2015	2014	2013	2012
National Company "QazaqGaz" JSC	Ernst & Young	Ernst & Young	Ernst & Young	Ernst & Young	Ernst & Young	Ernst & Young	Ernst & Young	Ernst & Young	Ernst & Young	Ernst & Young	Ernst & Young
KazTransGaz Aymak JSC	Ernst & Young	Ernst & Young	Ernst & Young	Ernst & Young	Ernst & Young	Ernst & Young	Ernst & Young	Ernst & Young	Ernst & Young	Ernst & Young	Ernst & Young
National Company Kazakhstan Temir Zholy JSC	Deloitte	Deloitte	Deloitte	Deloitte	Deloitte	Deloitte	Deloitte	Deloitte	Deloitte	Deloitte	Deloitte
Kazakhstan Railcars Building Company LLC	N/A	N/A	N/A	N/A	N/A	N/A	N/A	N/A	N/A	N/A	N/A
Kuryk Port LLC	AR Group Audit LLP	AR Group Audit LLP	N/A	N/A	N/A	N/A	N/A	N/A	N/A	N/A	N/A
Fund on Entreprenuership Development Damu JSC	PWC	PWC	PWC	PWC	PWC	PWC	PWC	PWC	PWC	PWC	Deloitte
Authority AIFC JSC	N/A	Russel Bedford A+ Partners LLC	Russel Bedford A+ Partners LLC	N/A	N/A	KPMG Audit	KPMG Audit	N/A	N/A	N/A	N/A
Banking Servicing Bureau of the National Bank JSC	N/A	CenterAudit Kazakhstan LLC	Almir Consulting LLC	Almir Consulting LLC	CenterAudit Kazakhstan LLC	CenterAudit Kazakhstan LLC	Kazakhstan Audit LLC	Serpin Audit LLC	Serpin Audit LLC	Serpin Audit LLC	Serpin Audit LLC
Kazakhavtodor LLC	N/A	AuditBukhCenter LLC	AuditBukhCenter LLC	AuditBukhCenter LLC	CenterAudit and S&M LLC	Elit Audit LLC	UHY Sapa Consulting LLC	UHY Sapa Consulting LLC	SKB Group-Audit LLC	N/A	N/A
International Airport Nursultan Nazarbayev	N/A	Crowe Audit KZ LLC	Audit Company Asia KZT LLC	Crowe Audit KZ LLC	Finex Standard LLC	Russel Bedford A+	Russel Bedford BC	Russel Bedford BC	Russel Bedford BC Partners	Nurteam Audit	KoshKal LLC

Audited SOE	2022*	2021	2020	2019	2018	2017	2016	2015	2014	2013	2012
JSC						Partners LLC	Partners LLC	Partners LLC	LLC	LLC	
Institute of Economic Research JSC	N/A	ARIP Consultng Group LLC	ProfUchetAudit LLC	Alma Audit LLC	E.S.T. Audit LLC	AltynAudit LLC	E.S.T. Audit LLC	SKB Group-Audit LLC	Audit Company Service Audit LLC	Audit Compan y Almas LLC	Astana Audit LLC
National Center for Neirosurgery JSC	UHY Sapa Consultin g LLC	BR Audit LLC	BR Audit LLC	Audit Company Asia KZT LLC	Audit Company Asia KZT LLC	GalAudit LLC	Ernst & Young	Ernst & Young	Ernst & Young	Ernst & Young	Ernst & Young
SK-Pharmacy LLC	N/A	ProgressAuditK Z LLC	Crowe Audit KZ LLC	Crowe Audit KZ LLC	Crowe Audit KZ LLC	Elit Audit LLC	CenterAudi t Kazakhsta n LLC	Russel Bedford BC Partners LLC	N/A	N/A	N/A
National Geological Exploration Company "KazGeology" JSC	N/A	Ernst & Young	Ernst & Young	Ernst & Young	Deloitte	Deloitte	Deloitte	Deloitte	Deloitte	Deloitte	Ernst & Young
Khabar Agency JSC	N/A	StarAudit LLC	StarAudit LLC	E.S.T. Audit LLC	ProgressAuditK Z LLC	Audit Company BagamAudi t LLC	Audit Company Asia KZT LLC	Russel Bedford BC Partners LLC	Russel Bedford BC Partners LLC	Russel Bedford BC Partners LLC	KoshKal LLC
Special Economic zone "Ontustyc" Management Company JSC	N/A	AiSer Consulting and Aidut LLC	Ordabasy Audit LLC	Ordabasy Audit LLC	Ordabasy Audit LLC	Consulting Company Expert-Audit-Capital LLC	Crowe Audit KZ LLC	Crowe Audit KZ LLC	KazAuditFinanc e LLC	N/A	N/A
Plant after name of Kirov S. JSC	N/A	Moore Kazakhstan LLC	Moore Kazakhstan LLC	Russel Bedford A+ Partners LLC	Russel Bedford A+ Partners LLC	Russel Bedford A+ Partners LLC	Russel Bedford BC Partners LLC	Russel Bedford BC Partners LLC	Russel Bedford BC Partners LLC	Russel Bedford BC Partners LLC	Russel Bedford BC Partner s LLC
Machine Building Plant named after Kirov S. JSC	A&Z Audit Consultin g LLC	Moore Kazakhstan LLC	Moore Kazakhstan LLC	Russel Bedford A+ Partners LLC	Russel Bedford A+ Partners LLC	Russel Bedford A+ Partners LLC	Russel Bedford BC Partners LLC	Russel Bedford BC Partners LLC	Russel Bedford BC Partners LLC	Russel Bedford BC Partners LLC	Russel Bedford BC Partner s LLC

Audited SOE	2022*	2021	2020	2019	2018	2017	2016	2015	2014	2013	2012
Republican Center for Space Communication JSC	HM Audit LLC	Audit Company Asia KZT LLC	Audit Company Asia KZT LLC	Audit Company Asia KZT LLC	AdiletAudit LLC	AdiletAudit LLC	AdiletAudit LLC	FinKamAudit LLC	N/A	N/A	N/A
QAZEXPOCONGRESS National Company JSC	N/A	KPMG Audit	KPMG Audit	KPMG Audit	KPMG Audit	KPMG Audit	KPMG Audit	KPMG Audit	KPMG Audit	KPMG Audit	N/A

Table A B.2. Board composition of selected Kazakh SOEs and holding companies

Full title of entity	Legal form	Type	Boards' structure and composition	Committees: **(I) Strategy Committee** **(II) Audit Committee** **(III) Specialized Committee** **(IV) Remuneration and HR Committee** **(V) Other Committee**
Selected holding companies				
Sovereign Wealth Fund Samruk-Kazyna JSC	JSC	Two-tier board	Board of Directors: Alikhan Smailov - Chairman, Prime Minister of the Republic of Kazakhstan Alibek Kuantyrov - Member, Minister of National Economy of the Republic of Kazakhstan Zhamishev Bolat - Member - Independent Director Luca Sutera - Member - Independent Director Mohamed Jameel Al Ramahi - Member of the BOD, Independent Director Nurlan Zhakupov - Member, Chairman of the Management Board of Samruk-Kazyna JSC Management Board: Nurlan Zhakupov - Chairman of the Management Board of Samruk-Kazyna JSC Aidar Ryskulov - Managing Director for Economics and Finance Saltanat Satzhan - Managing Director for Development and Privatization Ernat Berdigulov - Managing Director for Strategy and Asset Management Nikolay Kazutin - Managing Director for Legal Support, Counseling and Risks Yelzhas Otynshiyev - Co-Managing Director for Strategy and Asset Management	(I) Strategy Committee (II) Audit Committee (III) Specialized Committee (IV) Remuneration and HR Committee (V) Other Committee
National Management Holding "Baiterek" JSC	JSC	Two-tier board	Board of Directors: Alikhan Smailov - Chairman, Prime Minister of the Republic of Kazakhstan Roman Sklyar - Member, First Deputy Prime Minister of the Republic of Kazakhstan Timur Suleimenov - Member, First Deputy Head of the Executive Office of the President of the Republic of Kazakhstan	(I) Strategy Committee (II) Audit Committee (IV) Remuneration and HR Committee

Full title of entity	Legal form	Type	Boards' structure and composition	Committees: **(I) Strategy Committee** **(II) Audit Committee** **(III) Specialized Committee** **(IV) Remuneration and HR Committee** **(V) Other Committee**
			Yerulan Zhamaubaev - Member, Deputy Prime Minister - Minister of Finance of the Republic of Kazakhstan Alibek Kuantyrov - Member, Minister of National Economy of the Republic of Kazakhstan Marat Karabayev - Member, Minister of Industry and Infrastructure Development of the Republic of Kazakhstan Marie-Helene Berard – Member - Independent Director, President/Founder of MHB SAS an investment advisory company Daniel A.Witt - Member - Independent Director, the President of the International Tax and Investment Center (ITIC) Manfred Grundke - Member - Independent Director Vacancy - Member, Chairman of the Management Board of Baiterek Management Board: Nurlan Baibazarov - Chairman of the Management Board of Baiterek Nurbolat Aidapkelov - First Deputy Chairman of the Board Adil Mukhamejanov - Deputy Chairman of the Board Yersain Khamitov - Deputy Chairman of the Board	
Kazakhstan Engineering NC JSC	JSC	Two-tier board	Board of Directors: Azamat Beispekov – Chair, Vice-Minister of Industry and Infrastructure development, Erbol Akhmetov – member, Deputy Chairman of State Property and Privatisation Committee of the Ministry of Finance, Andar Shukputov – member, independent director, Kuat Kozhakhmetov – member, independent director, Kenzhebay Satzhanov – member, independent director, Serikzhan Zhakenov – member, independent director, Temizhan Abdrakhmanov – member, CEO of Kazakhstan Engineering Management Board: Temizhan Abdrakhmanov – CEO and Chair of the management board of Kazakhstan Engineering, Garyp Ismatov – Deputy Chairman, Kuanysh Kisikov – Deputy Chairman, Mosendz Artur – department director,	(I) Strategy Committee (II) Audit Committee (IV) Remuneration and HR Committee

Full title of entity	Legal form	Type	Boards' structure and composition	Committees: **(I) Strategy Committee** **(II) Audit Committee** **(III) Specialized Committee** **(IV) Remuneration and HR Committee** **(V) Other Committee**
			Sultan Seisengaliev – Managing Director, Kulaziya Chokusheva – department director, Issa Kairat – member	
Selected 20 SOEs				
National Company "QazaqGaz" JSC	JSC	Two-tier board	Board of Directors: Yelzhas Otynshiyev – Chairman, Co-Managing Director for Strategy and Asset Management of Samruk-Kazyna JSC Yernat Berdigulov - Member, Managing Director for Strategy and Asset Management of Samruk-Kazyna JSC Anatoly Tegisbayev - Member, General Director of the Regional Public Organization Veterans of the Oil and Gas Complex Omarkhan Oksikbayev - Member - Independent Director Nurlan Akhanzaripov - Member - Independent Director, independent member of the BOD of AstanaGaz KMG JSC, KEGOC JSC, and Areqet High-Tech Fund JSC Saya Mynsharipova - Member - Independent Director, Independent Director of Samruk-Kazyna Construction JSC, KazMunayGas NC JSC Mailybaev Eskendir - Member - Independent Director, Independent Director of KazPost JSC Sanzhar Zharkeshov - Member, Chairman of the Management Board of QazaqGas NC JSC Management Board: Sanzhar Zharkeshov - Chairman of the Management Board of QazaqGas NC JSC Meirbek Ikhsanov - First Deputy Chairman of the Board for production Aidyn Akan - Deputy Chairman of the Board on economics and finance Arman Kassenov - Deputy Chairman of the Board on marketing Akbar Tulegenov - Deputy Chairman of the Board for Strategy and Investments Relations Anuar Bitanov - Deputy Chairman of the Board	(I) Strategy Committee (II) Audit Committee (IV) Remuneration and HR Committee
KazTransGaz Aymak JSC	JSC	Two-tier board	Board of Directors: Arman Kasenov - Chairman, Deputy Chairman of the Board on marketing of QazaqGas NC JSC Daukei Serikbek - Member - Independent Director	(I) Strategy Committee (II) Audit Committee (IV) Remuneration and HR Committee

Full title of entity	Legal form	Type	Boards' structure and composition	Committees: (I) Strategy Committee (II) Audit Committee (III) Specialized Committee (IV) Remuneration and HR Committee (V) Other Committee
			Baurzhan Askarov - Member, Chairman of the Management Board of KazTransGas Aymak JSC Management Board: Baurzhan Askarov - Chairman of the Management Board of KazTransGas Aymak JSC Zhasulan Zhienbekov - Head of Legal Department	
National Company Kazakhstan Temir Zholy JSC	JSC	Two-tier board	Board of Directors: Aidar Ryskulov - Chairman - Managing director on economics and finance of Samruk-Kazyna JSC Kuat Irubayev - Member, representative of the interests of the Sole Shareholder Yernat Berdigulov - Member, Managing Director for Strategy and Asset Management of Samruk-Kazyna JSC Gibrat Auganov - Member, Managing Director for Public Relations and Change Management of Samruk-Kazyna JSC Ulf Wokurka - Member - Independent Director, member of the BOD of Nurbank JSC along with the position of an independent director in AIFC Administration JSC and NC KAZAKH INVEST JSC Schierhuber Alexander - Member - Independent Director, Global Head of Business Development of Superfund Asset Management Company GmbH, Board Member of Superfund Japan Co., Ltd. Jogn (Ian) McKay - Member - Independent Director, Owner Director of Otherhand Ltd, Board member of Stirling University Management School International, Independent Chair of Police Negotiating Board & SPCF Nurlan Sauranbayev - Member, Chairman of the Management Board of Kazakhstan Temir Zholy NC JSC Management Board: Nurlan Sauranbayev - Chairman of the Management Board of Kazakhstan Temir Zholy NC JSC Kanat Almagambetov - Deputy Chairman of the Board Anuar Akhmetzhanov - Deputy Chairman of the Board for Strategy Yerlan Koishibayev - Deputy Chairman of the Board for Logistics Ersaiyn Nagaspayev - Deputy Chairman of the Board for New Projects	(I) Strategy Committee (II) Audit Committee (IV) Remuneration and HR Committee

Full title of entity	Legal form	Type	Boards' structure and composition	Committees: (I) Strategy Committee (II) Audit Committee (III) Specialized Committee (IV) Remuneration and HR Committee (V) Other Committee
			Baurzhan Urynbasarov - Managing Director for Production Processes Dair Kusherov - Managing Director for Finance Serik Keulimzhayev - Chief of Staff	
Kazakhstan Railcars Building Company LLC	LLC	One-tier board	Supervisory Board: Yerzhan Kuangan - Chairman of the Supervisory Board, General Director of SMP Group LLC Berik Kyzdanayev - Member, General Director of TemirTransService Trading House LLC Talgat Lesov - Member, Director of Asset Management Department of KTT JSC Berik Tynyshtykbayev - Member, Director of Economy and Finance Department of KTT JSC Executive Body: Dauren Zhunusov - General Director of Kazakhstan Railcar Building Company JSC	The LLC law does not mandate the formation of committees.
Kuryk Port LLC	LLC	One-tier board	Supervisory Board: Baurzhan Urynbasarov - Chairman of the Supervisory Board, Managing Director for Production Processes of Kazakhstan Temir Zholy NC JSC Yerkin Baltabayev - Member, Head of the Group of Legal Support Department of Kazakhstan Temir Zholy NC JSC Amina Akmolda - Member, manager of the Department on Managing Assets, Division of Corporate Governance Management of Subsidiary Companies of Kazakhstan Temir Zholy NC JSC Executive Body: Serik Akhmetov - General Director of Kuryk Port LLC	The LLC law does not mandate the formation of committees.
Fund on Entreprenuership Development Damu JSC	JSC	Two-tier board	Board of Directors: Yerulan Zhamaubaev - Chairman, Deputy Prime Minister - Minister of Finance of the Republic of Kazakhstan Adil Mukhamejanov - Member, Deputy Chairman of the Management Board of Baiterek NMH JSC Timur Zhaksylykov - Member, First Vice Minister of National Economy of the Republic of Kazakhstan Galim Khusainov - Member - Independent Director, Independent Director of Bereke Bank JSC	(I) Strategy Committee (II) Audit Committee (III) Specialized Committee (IV) Remuneration and HR Committee

Full title of entity	Legal form	Type	Boards' structure and composition	Committees: (I) Strategy Committee (II) Audit Committee (III) Specialized Committee (IV) Remuneration and HR Committee (V) Other Committee
			Raimbek Batalov - Member - Independent Director, Chairman of the Presidium of the National Chamber of Entrepreneurs Atameken Elena Bakhmutova - Member - Independent Director, Chairman of the Council of the Association of Financiers of Kazakhstan Gaukhar Buribayeva - Member, Chairwoman of the Management Board of FED Damu JSC Management Board: Gaukhar Buribayeva - Chairperson of the Management Board of FED Damu JSC Farhat Sarsekeyev - Deputy Chairperson of the Board Bakhytzhan Makazhanov - Deputy Chairperson of the Board Yerbol Yeskakov - Deputy Chairperson of the Board Murat Bapaev - Deputy Chairperson of the Board	
Authority AIFC JSC	JSC	Two-tier board	Board of Directors: Renat Bekturov - Chairman, The Governor of AIFC Yernur Rysmagambetov - Member Kuanyshbek Yessekeyev - Member, Non-executive member Dr. Antonio Riera - Member, Independent non-executive director Meirzhan Yussupov - Member, Independent non-executive director Management Board: Temirlan Mukhanbetzhanov - Acting Chairman of the Management Board of Authority AIFC JSC Bakhtiyar Tleubekov - CFO and Head of Administration Daniyar Kelbetov - Chief Product Officer Yelena Pak - Chief of Communications Nursultan Serikbay - Chief of Staff	(II) Audit Committee (IV) Remuneration and HR Committee
Banking Servicing Bureau of the National Bank JSC	JSC	Two-tier board	Board of Directors: Vitaliy Tutushkin - Chairman, Deputy Chairman of the National Bank - Head of the Permanent Representative Office of the National Bank in Almaty Nurlan Kasainov - Member, Director of the Financial Technologies Department of the National Bank Abay Alpamysov - Member - Independent Director	(I) Strategy Committee (II) Audit Committee (IV) Remuneration and HR Committee

Full title of entity	Legal form	Type	Boards' structure and composition	Committees: (I) Strategy Committee (II) Audit Committee (III) Specialized Committee (IV) Remuneration and HR Committee (V) Other Committee
			Kuat Kozhakhmetov - Member - Independent Director Nurdaulet Maykotov - Member, Chairman of the Management Board of Banking servicing beaurau of the National Bank JSC Management Board: Nurdaulet Maykotov - Chairman of the Management Board of Banking servicing beaurau of the National Bank JSC Mikhail Lipov - Deputy Chairman of the Board Adilya Selimova - Managing Director - member of the Board	
Kazakhavtodor LLC	LLC	One-tier board	Supervisory Board: Zh. Tazhenova - Chairman of the Supervisory Board, Deputy Chairman of the Management Board of KazAutoZhol JSC S.Khamzin - Member, Deputy Chairman of the Management Board of KazAutoZhol JSC R. Sagyndykova - Member, Director of the Finance and Budgeting Department of KazAutoZhol JSC D. Sakanov - Member, Director of Exploitation Department of KazAutoZhol JSC O. Bekenov - Member, Director of Legal and HR Department of KazAutoZhol JSC Executive Boby: Serik Aydos - General Director of KazakhAvtoDor LLC	The LLC law does not mandate the formation of committees.
International Airport Nursultan Nazarbayev JSC	JSC	Two-tier board	Board of Directors: Talgat Lastayev - Chairman, Chairman of the Civil Aviation Committee of the Ministry of Industry and Infrastructure Development Bakhyt Tashenev - Member, Chairman of the Committee on State Property and Privatization of the Ministry of Finance Saltanat Aydarbekova - Member- Independent Director Gumar Dyisenbayev - Member - Independent Director Yerlan Absatov - Member - Independent Director Yergazy Zholdasov - Member, Chairman of the Management Board of International Airport Nursultan Nazarbayev JSC Management Board:	(I) Strategy Committee (II) Audit Committee (IV) Remuneration and HR Committee

Full title of entity	Legal form	Type	Boards' structure and composition	Committees: (I) Strategy Committee (II) Audit Committee (III) Specialized Committee (IV) Remuneration and HR Committee (V) Other Committee
			Yergazy Zholdasov - Chairman of the Management Board of International Airport Nursultan Nazarbayev JSC Ruslan Pyshtanov - First Deputy Chairman of the Board Marat Tuleshov - Deputy Chairman of the Board, Head of Aviation Security Service Dauren Tastambekov - Deputy Chairman of the Board for Special Missions	
Institute of Economic Research JSC	JSC	Two-tier board	Board of Directors: Alibek Kuantyrov - Chairman, Minister of National Economy Kairat Myrzakhmetov - Member, Deputy Chairman of the Committee on State Property and Privatization of the Ministry of Finance Danabek Kerimray - Member, Chief of Staff of the Ministry of National Economy Chingiz Kanapyanov - Member - Independent Director Khalida Azhigulova - Member - Independent Director Assel Sarsenbayeva - Member - Independent Director Ruslan Sultanov - Member, Chairman of the Management Board of Economic Research Institute JSC Management Board: Ruslan Sultanov - Chairman of the Management Board of Economic Research Institute JSC Kaisar Nigmetov - Deputy Chairman of the Board Kuanysh Beysengazin - Deputy Chairman of the Board Adil Kusmanov - Deputy Chairman of the Board	(I) Strategy Committee (III) Specialized Committee
National Center for Neirosurgery JSC	JSC	Two-tier board	Board of Directors: Mazhit Shaidarov - Chairman, representative of the Ministry of Healthcare Bakhyt Tashenev - Member, Chairman of the Committee on State Property and Privatization of the Ministry of Finance Gulnara Sarsenbayeva - Member, Deputy Director of the Department for Organization of Medical Aid of the Ministry of Health Kylyshbek Izbaskhanov - Member - Independent Director Andrei Golanov - Member - Independent Director Serik Akshulakov - Member, Chairman of the Management Board of National Center for Neirosurgery JSC	(I) Strategy Committee (IV) Remuneration and HR Committee

Full title of entity	Legal form	Type	Boards' structure and composition	Committees: (I) Strategy Committee (II) Audit Committee (III) Specialized Committee (IV) Remuneration and HR Committee (V) Other Committee
			Management Board: Serik Akshulakov - Chairman of the Management Board of National Center for Neirosurgery JSC Talgat Omarov - Deputy Chairman of the Board Asylbek Kaliyev - Medical Director Altyn Zhumabayeva - Nursing Director Aidos Doskaliyev - Director of Strategy and Science Aiman Baizhumanova - Financial Director	
SK-Pharmacy LLC	LLC	Two-tier board	Supervisory Board: Yuri Lavrinenko - Chairman - Independent Director, Deputy Chairman of the Presidium of the Union of transport and logistics organisations and associations KAZLOGISTICS, Chairman of the Supervisory Board of SK-Pharmacy LLP Vyacheslav Dudnik - Member, Vice Minister of Healthcare Bakhyt Tashenev - Member, Chairman of the Committee on State Property and Privatization of the Ministry of Finance Dauren Baimagambetov - Member - Independent Director, Financial Director and Compliance Director of the iKapitalist ltd Private Company Saida Taukeleva - Member - Independent Director, Head of the Public Control and Monitoring Republican Public Association Management Board: Yerkhat Yeskaliyev - Chairman of the Management Board of SK-Pharmacy LLC Gulnara Omarova - Managing Director Nurzhan Kansultan - Managing Director Mukan Uteuov - Managing Director Artur Kazhibaev - Managing Director	(I) Strategy Committee (II) Audit Committee (IV) Remuneration and HR Committee
National Geological Exploration Company "KazGeology" JSC	JSC	Two-tier board	Board of Directors: Kaiyrkhan Tutkyshbayev - Chairman, Deputy Chairman of the Geology Committee of the Ministry of Industry and Infrastructure Development Kairat Myrzakhmetov - Member, Deputy Chairman of the Committee on State Property and Privatization of the Ministry of Finance Dauletkhan Kilybayev - Member - Independent Director, Chief Investment Officer of Al Falah Capital Partners	(I) Strategy Committee (IV) Remuneration and HR Committee

Full title of entity	Legal form	Type	Boards' structure and composition	Committees: (I) Strategy Committee (II) Audit Committee (III) Specialized Committee (IV) Remuneration and HR Committee (V) Other Committee
			Mukhambet Kopeyev - Member - Independent Director Murat Perzadayev - Member - Independent Director Yeldar Tagash - Member, Chairman of the Management Board of Qazgeology JSC Management Board: Yeldar Tagash - Chairman of the Management Board of Qazgeology JSC Berikbol Khamzin - Chief Geologist Bakytzhan Nurmaganbetov - Deputy Chairman of the Board Mirzhan Bekmukhambetov - Deputy Chairman of the Board	
Khabar Agency JSC	JSC	Two-tier board	Board of Directors: Yerlan Karin - Chairman, State Advisor of the Republic of Kazakhstan Bakhyt Tashenev - Member, Chairman of the Committee on State Property and Privatization of the Ministry of Finance Kanat Iskakov - Member, Vice Minister of Information and Public Development Aiman Musokhadzhaeva - Member - Independent Director, Rector of the Kazakh National University of Arts Zinaida Zagoskina - Member - Independent Director, Director of the Internal Audit Department of Nazarbayev University Ichie Ishikava - Member - Independent Director, Senior Columnist for Japanese public broadcaster NHK Berik Uali - Member, Chairman of the Management Board of Khabar Agency JSC Management Board: Berik Uali - Chairman of the Management Board of Khabar Agency JSC Lyazzat Zhunusova - First Deputy Chairman of the Board Daniyar Menilbekov - Deputy Chairman of the Board Dauletkhan Zhienkulov - Deputy Chairman of the Board Eldar Bakpaev - Executive Director Zhaina Slambek - Director of TV Channel Khabar Nurbol Almanov - Director of TV Channel El Arna	(I) Strategy Committee (II) Audit Committee (IV) Remuneration and HR Committee
Special Economic zone "Ontustyc" Management Company JSC	JSC	Two-tier board	Board of Directors: Rasul Ilimbayev - Chairman, Chairman of the Management Board of Social Entrepreneurial Corporation Shymkent JSC	(I) Strategy Committee (II) Audit Committee (IV) Remuneration and HR Committee

Full title of entity	Legal form	Type	Boards' structure and composition	Committees: (I) Strategy Committee (II) Audit Committee (III) Specialized Committee (IV) Remuneration and HR Committee (V) Other Committee
			Bereke Duisebekov - Member, Head of State Institution Department of Entrepreneurship and Industrial and Innovative Development of Shymkent Yerbolat Sariev - Member, Deputy Chairman of the Management Board of Social Entrepreneurial Corporation Shymkent JSC Adilzhan Datkaev - Member - Independent Director, Acting Director of the Chamber of Entrepreneurs of Shymkent Aydyn Rakhymzhan - Member - Independent Director, Head of the Directorate for the Development of Industrial Infrastructure Kazakhstan Center for Industry and Export "QazIndustry" JSC Batyrbek Zhamanov - Member - Independent Director, Regional Director of Kazakh Invest NC JSC Nuraly Arginbayev - Member, Acting Chairman of the Management Board of Special Economic zone "Ontustyc" Management Company JSC Management Board: No data available in open sources	
Plant after name of Kirov S. JSC	JSC	Two-tier board	Board of Directors: Marat Dzhanikeyev - Chairman, representative of the Kazakhstan Engineering NC JSC Nursultan Smailov - Member, representative of the Kazakhstan Engineering NC JSC Nariman Absametov - Member - Independent Director Talgat Baidauletov - Member- Independent Director Almas Nurmagambetov - Member, General Director of Plant afte name of Kirov S. JSC Management Board: Almas Nurmagambetov - General Director of Plant afte name of Kirov S. JSC Didar Tasybek - First Deputy General Director Ainagul Rakhmetova - Deputy General Director for commercial and financial issues Dauren Kadyrov - Deputy General Director for strategic and new projects	The formation of committees was hindered by the financial constraints faced by the company.
Machine Building Plant named after Kirov S. JSC	JSC	Two-tier board	Board of Directors: Sultan Seisengaliev - Chairman, representative of the Kazakhstan Engineering NC JSC Dmitryi Maukebaev - Member, representative of the Kazakhstan Engineering NC JSC Azamat Smagulov - Member - Independent Director, Kairbek Kusainov - Member - Independent Director, Islam Akhmet - Member, General Director of MBP named after Kirov S. JSC	The formation of committees was hindered by the financial constraints faced by the company.

Full title of entity	Legal form	Type	Boards' structure and composition	Committees: (I) Strategy Committee (II) Audit Committee (III) Specialized Committee (IV) Remuneration and HR Committee (V) Other Committee
			Management Board: Islam Akhmet - General Director of MBP named after Kirov S. JSC Sayan Zhienbaev - Deputy General Director for commercial issues Kanat Meirman - Deputy General Director for economy and finance	
Republican Center for Space Communication JSC	JSC	Two-tier board	Board of Directors: Baubek Oralmagambetov - Chairman, Chairman of the Aerospace Committee of the Ministry of Digital Development, Innovation and Aerospace Industry Kairat Myrzakhmetov - Member, Deputy Chairman of the Committee on State Property and Privatization of the Ministry of Finance Dauren Rakhimzhanov - Member, Director of the Corporate Governance Department of the Ministry of Digital Development, Innovation and Aerospace Industry Rizat Nurshabekov - Member, Director of the "State Radio Frequency Service" Altai Aitmagambetov - Member - Independent Director, Professor of the RET Department, International University of Information Technologies Serikbek Elshibekov - Member - Independent Director Magzhan Madiyev - Member- Independent Director, CEO of the Corporate Fund "International Technopark" of IT-startups "Astana Hub" Malik Zhuyriktaev - Member, Chairman of the Management Board of the Republican Center for Space Communications JSC Management Board: Malik Zhuyriktaev - Chairman of the Management Board of the Republican Center for Space Communications JSC Vassiliy Leonov - Deputy Chairman of the Board Zhanatai Abdrakhmanov - Deputy Chairman of the Board Dauren Shaikhin - Deputy Chairman of the Board	(I) Strategy Committee (II) Audit Committee (IV) Remuneration and HR Committee
QAZEXPOCONGRESS National Company JSC	JSC	Two-tier board	Board of Directors: Serik Zhumangarin - Chairman, Deputy Prime Minister - Minister of Trade and Integration Kairat Torebayev - Member, Vice-Minister of Trade and integration Kairat Myrzakhmetov - Member, Deputy Chairman of the Committee on State Property and Privatization of the Ministry of Finance Nurzhan Alimukhamedov - Member - Independent Director, Independent director of DBK-	(I) Strategy Committee (II) Audit Committee (IV) Remuneration and HR Committee

Full title of entity	Legal form	Type	Boards' structure and composition	Committees: (I) Strategy Committee (II) Audit Committee (III) Specialized Committee (IV) Remuneration and HR Committee (V) Other Committee
			Leasing JSC and KazAgroGarant JSC Zhanarkul Koschanova - Member - Independent Director, Advisor to the Chairman of the Board on Legal Issues of KazPost JSC Kuat Zholdybekov - Member - Independent Director, Managing director, Commercial Director of BIO-LINE Group Allen Chaizhunussov - Member, Chairman of the Management Board of QazExpoCongress NC JSC Management Board: Allen Chaizhunussov - Chairman of the Management Board of QazExpoCongress NC JSC Daulet Yerkimbayev - First Deputy Chairman of the Board Baurzhan Bekeshev - Deputy Chairman of the Board Sansyzbay Zholdasbayev - Deputy Chairman of the Board Marlen Iskakov - Deputy Chairman of the Board Anna Lukina - Managing Director	
Listed SOEs				
Kazatomprom NC JSC	JSC	Two-tier	Board of Directors: Arman Argingazin - Chairman, Independent Director, member of the BOD of NC KazMunayGas JSC and Kazakhstan Investment Development Fund JSC Armanbay Zhubaev - Member, Independent Director, founder of the consulting company StrategyLab LLP, member of the BOD of NC Tau-Ken Samruk JSC, independent director of Samruk-Energo JSC and NC KazMunayGas JSC Nodir Sidikov - Member, Independent Director, partner at Fieldfisher LLP, member of the BOD - an independent director at Karazhanbasmunai JSC Yernat Berdigulov - Member, Managing Director for Strategy and Asset Management of Samruk-Kazyna JSC Yernar Zhanadil - Member, General Director of the Public Company Qazaq Green Power PLC Yelzhas Otynshiyev - Member, Co-Managing Director for Strategy and Asset Management of Samruk-Kazyna JSC Yerzhan Mukanov - Member, Chairman of the Management Board of Kazatomprom NC JSC	(I) Strategic Planning and Investment Committee (II) Audit Committee (IV) Nomination and Remuneration HR Committee (V) Production Safety (HSE) Committee

Full title of entity	Legal form	Type	Boards' structure and composition	Committees: (I) Strategy Committee (II) Audit Committee (III) Specialized Committee (IV) Remuneration and HR Committee (V) Other Committee
			Management Board: Yerzhan Mukanov - Chairman of the Management Board of Kazatomprom NC JSC Kuanysh Omarbekov - Chief Operating Officer of NC Kazatomprom JSC Dastan Kosherbayev - Chief Commercial Officer of of NC Kazatomprom JSC Alibek Aldongarov - Chief HR and Digitalization Officer of NC Kazatomprom JSC Yermek Kuantyrov - Chief Legal Support and Corporate Governance Officer of NC Kazatomprom JSC Mukhit Magazhanov - Head of Administration Office of NC Kazatomprom JSC	
KEGOC JSC	JSC	Two-tier	Board of Directors: Yernat Berdigulov - Chairman, Managing Director for Strategy and Asset Management of Samruk-Kazyna JSC Nurlan Akhanzaripov - Member - Senior Independent Director, independent member of the BOD of AstanaGaz KMG JSC, Areqet High-Tech Fund JSC, QazaqGas NC JSC Marat Dilkairov - Member - Independent Director, General Director of the Union of Power Engineers Damir Suyentayev - Member - Independent Director, President of the National Centre for Expertise and Certification JSC Almat Zhamiyev - Member, Head of Legal Support Department of Samruk-Kazyna JSC, member of Board of Directors/Supervisory Boards of Sekerbank, Bolashaq Investments Ltd, KNPP LLP, Samruk-Kazyna Business Service LLP, Samruk-Energy JSC Kanysh Moldabayev - Member Nabi Aitzhanov - Member, Chairman of the Management Board Management Board: Nabi Aitzhanov - Chairman of the Management Board Bakytzhan Zhazykbayev - Deputy Chairman of the Board Tolegen Safuanali - Managing Director for Legal Support and Risks Aigul Akimbayeva - Managing Director for Finance and Accounting Elvira Konakhbayeva - Managing Director for Strategy and Sustainability	(I) Strategy, Corporate and Sustainable Development Committee (II) Audit Committee (IV) Nomination and Remuneration Committee
KazMunayGas NC JSC	JSC	Two-tier	Board of Directors: Yernat Berdigulov - Chairman, Managing Director for Strategy and Asset Management of Samruk-Kazyna JSC Uzakbay Karabalin - Non-executive Member of the BOD, Representative of shareholder of Samruk-Kazyna JSC	(I) Strategy and Portfolio Management Committee (II) Audit Committee (IV) Nomination and Remuneration Committee (V) Health, Safety, Environment and

Full title of entity	Legal form	Type	Boards' structure and composition	Committees: (I) Strategy Committee (II) Audit Committee (III) Specialized Committee (IV) Remuneration and HR Committee (V) Other Committee
			Arman Argingazin - Member - Independent Director, member of the BOD of NC Kazatomprom and Kazakhstan Investment Development Fund JSC Armanbay Zhubaev - Member - Independent Director, founder of the consulting company StrategyLab LLP, member of the BOD of NC Tau Ken Samruk JSC, independent director of Samruk-Energo JSC and NC Kazatomprom Phillip Holland - Member - Independent Director Saya Mynsharipova - Member - Independent Director, Independent Director of Samruk-Kazyna Construction JSC and Qazaq Gas NC JSC Yelzhas Otynshiyev - Member, Co-Managing Director for Strategy and Asset Management of Samruk-Kazyna JSC Magzum Mirzagaliyev - Member, Chairman of the Management Board Management Board: Magzum Mirzagaliyev - Chairman of the Management Board Abdulgafarov Dastan - Deputy Chairman of the Board Zakirov Bulat - Deputy Chairman of the Board Lavrenov Vassiliy - Deputy Chairman of the Board Dmitriy Makeyev - Deputy Chairman of the Board Diana Aryssova - Deputy Chairman of the Board Brekeshev Serikkali - Deputy Chairman of the Board Kudaibergenov Kuanysh - Deputy Chairman of the Board Khasanov Dauletzhan - Deputy Chairman of the Board	Sustainable Development Committee
Kazakhtelecom JSC	JSC	Two-tier	Board of Directors: Baidauletov Nurzhan - Chairman, Representative of shareholder of Samruk-Kazyna JSC Auganov Gibrat - Member, Managing Director for Public Relations and Change Management of Samruk-Kazyna JSC Kazutin Nikolay - Member, Managing Director for Legal Support, Counseling and Risksof Samruk-Kazyna JSC Abdualiyev Asset - Member - Independent Director Zaika Dmitriy - Member - Independent Director Neupokoyev Artur - Member - Independent Director Yessekeyev Kuanyshbek - Member, Chairman of the Management Board	(I) Strategy Planning Committee (II) Audit Committee (IV) Committee for Personnel, Compensations and Social Issues

Full title of entity	Legal form	Type	Boards' structure and composition	Committees: **(I) Strategy Committee** **(II) Audit Committee** **(III) Specialized Committee** **(IV) Remuneration and HR Committee** **(V) Other Committee**
			Management Board: Yessekeyev Kuanyshbek - Chairman of the Management Board Berik Bitabarov - Chief Operating Efficiency Director Nurlan Meirmanov - Chief Innovation Officer Lyudmila Atamuratova - Chief Financial Officer Lyan Natalya - Managing Director for External Asset Management Alibek Indykbayev - General Director of the Corporate Business Division	
KazTransOil JSC	JSC	Two-tier	Board of Directors: Bulat Zakirov - Chairman, Deputy Chairman of the Management Board of KazMunayGas NC JSC Ardak Kassymbek - Member, representative of the shareholder of KazMunayGas Kazbek Kussainov - Member - Independent Director Glen Timothy - Member - Independent Director Hadrien Fraissinet - Member - Independent Director Talgat Kurmanbayev - Member, Chairman of the Management Board Management Board: Talgat Kurmanbayev - Chairman of the Management Board Temirkhan Abdirov - Deputy General Director for Production Erik Sagiyev - Deputy General Director for Transportation Amirzhan Ospanov - Deputy General Director for Economics and Finance Zhaydarman Issakov - Managing Director for Legal Affairs Gaziz Koshanov - Managing Director for Social and Labor Relations and General Issues	(I) Strategic Planning, Safety and Environmental Protection Committee (II) Internal Audit Committee (IV) Nomination and Remuneration Committee
Kcell JSC	JSC	Two-tier	Board of Directors: Alexey Buyanov - Chairman, Independent Director, and Independent Director of Bengala Investments S.A. Yermek Ramazanov - Member - Independent Director Timur Turlov - Member - Representative of shareholder Freedom Finance JSC, CEO of Freedom Finance Investment Company LLC, Advisor to the Chairman of the Board of Freedom Finance JSC, CEO of FFIN Brokerage Service, Independent Director on the BOD of FFINEU Investments, Chairman of the Supervisory Board of FFIN Bank LLC, Chairman of the BODof Freedom Finance JSC, Freedom Finance Life JSC and Freedom Finance Insurance JSC	(I) Strategic Planning Committee (II) Audit Committee (IV) Human Resource Committee (V) Committee on Sustainable Development

Full title of entity	Legal form	Type	Boards' structure and composition	Committees: (I) Strategy Committee (II) Audit Committee (III) Specialized Committee (IV) Remuneration and HR Committee (V) Other Committee
			Jere Calmes - Member - Independent Director Pietari Kivikko - Member - Independent Director, Managing Director at Fexcon Consulting Alexander Lezgovko - Member, Representative of shareholder Kazakhtelecom JSC Aliya Kishkimbaeva - Member, Representative of shareholder Kazakhtelecom JSC Management Board: Askhat Uzbekov - Member of the BOD, Chairman of the Management Board Malik Amardinov - Chief Digital Development Officer Azamat Uysumbaev - Chief Corporate Director Kirill Strashenko - Chief Technical Officer Daniyar Ibrayev - Chief Security Officer Olga Tsoi - Chief Commercial Officer Damir Mullashev - Chief Finance Officer	

Annex C. Kazakhstan's privatisation plans

Comprehensive privatisation plan for 2016-2020 (2015)

Key criteria (principles) for the formation of a list of state-owned and quasi-state sector objects to be transferred to private ownership:

1. the company carries out entrepreneurial activities that do not meet the conditions specified in paragraph 1 of Article 192 of the Entrepreneurial Code of Kazakhstan dated 29 October 2015.
2. the company is a small business in accordance with the criteria established by paragraph 3 of Article 24 of the Entrepreneurial Code of the Republic of Kazakhstan dated 29 October 2015.
3. the state owns a non-controlling block of shares (participatory interests), which do not provide the right to make strategic decisions regarding the most important aspects of the legal entity's activities. This criterion does not apply to legal entities whose activities are related to ensuring national security, the defense capability of the state, the use and maintenance of strategic and socially significant facilities.
4. the presence of individuals or private legal entities operating in this product market.
5. those who do not provide social services (in case of complete absence of competition or an insufficient number of private legal entities to fully meet the needs of the population in these services).
6. the activity does not affect issues of national security, the defense capability of the state or law and order

Comprehensive privatisation plan for 2021-2025 (2020)

Compliance with one of the following criteria is the basis for initiating the inclusion for a privatisation list after approval from industry specific public authorities and taking into account the economic interests of the country:[1]

1. carrying out entrepreneurial activities that do not meet the conditions specified in paragraph 1 of Article 192 of the Entrepreneurial Code of Kazakhstan.
2. compliance of the subject of the quasi-state sector with the criteria established by paragraph 3 of Article 24 of the Entrepreneurial Code of Kazakhstan (subjects of small, including micro-entrepreneurship).
3. the existence of a proposal from the antimonopoly body on the transfer to the competitive environment of state enterprises, legal entities, more than 50% of the shares (stakes in the authorised capital) of which are owned by the state, and legal entities affiliated with them.
4. ownership of a non-controlling block of shares (participatory interests), which do not provide the right to make strategic decisions on important aspects of the legal entity's activities.
5. non-implementation (from 0% to 39%) or inefficient implementation (from 40% to 54%) of the development plan, action plan on key performance indicators of the subject of the quasi-state sector over the past three years.

6. the payback period of the project, determined in accordance with paragraph 5 of Article 192 of the Entrepreneurial Code of Kazakhstan.
7. the onset of the period recommended by the antimonopoly authority for the presence in this commodity market of state enterprises, legal entities, more than 50% of the shares (stakes in the authorised capital) of which belong to the state, and legal entities affiliated with them.
8. receipt by the authorised body for state property or the local executive body or the office of the akim of the city of district significance, village, township, rural district of proposals from private business entities on the acquisition of the corresponding entity of the quasi-state sector.

Note

[1] These criteria do not apply to legal entities whose activities are related to ensuring national security, the defense capability of the state, the use and maintenance of strategic and socially significant facilities, as well as to facilities that are not subject to alienation in accordance with the laws, acts of the President and the Government of the Republic of Kazakhstan.

Annex D. Subsidiaries of SK and Baiterek

Table A D.1. Information on companies under the main holding companies Samruk-Kazyna and Baiterek

Subsidiaries of holding companies	Share of ownership, %	Number of companies at all levels within group, including subsidiaries of holdings	Sector
Samruk-Kazyna NWF JSC			
KazMunayGas NC JSC	87.42%	119	Oil and gas
Kazatomprom NAC JSC	75%	34	Uranium
Kazakhstan Temir Zholy NC JSC	100%	39	Railway transport and logistics
KEGOC JSC	90%	3	Power transmission
Kazakhtelecom JSC*	79.24%	9	Telecommunications
Kazpost JSC	100%	2	Postal and logistics
Air Astana JSC	51%	2	Aviation
Tau-Ken Samruk NC JSC	100%	14	Mining
Samruk Energy JSC	100%	20	Electricity generation
Qazaq Gas NC JSC	100%	15	Gas
Samruk-Kazyna Ondeu LLC	100%	7	Chemical
Samruk-Kazyna Contract LLC	100%	1	Procurement Services
Samruk-Kazyna Constraction LLC	100%	2	Real estate development
Samruk-Kazyna Invest LLC	100%	4	Investment
Samruk-Kazyna Business Service LLC	100%	2	Auxillary
Ekibastus GRES 2 JSC	100%	1	Electricity generation
Shulbinsk Hydroelectric Power Plant LLC	100%	1	Electricity generation
Kazakhstan Nuclear Power Plants LLC	100%	1	Electricity generation
Ust-Kamenogorsk Hydroelectric Power Plant LLC	100%	1	Electricity generation
Butadien LLC	25%	1	Banking
Aktau Sea Port NC JSC	100%	1	Port, logistics
Astana Gas KMG JSC	50%	1	Gas Transportation
Turkestan LLC	100%	1	Auxiliary
Baiterek			
Development Bank of Kazakhstan JSC	100%	6	Banking
Kazyna Capital Management JSC	100%	38	Investments
Damu Entrepreneurship Development Fund JSC	100%	1	SME fund
Kazakhstan Housing Company JSC	100%	1	Housing Construction Financing
Export Insurance Company Kazakh Export JSC	100%	1	Insurance
Otbasy Bank House Construction Savings Bank JSC	100%	1	Housing (mortgages)
Agrarian Credit Corporation JSC	100%	9	Agro Industry Financing
KazAgroFinance JSC	100%	1	Banking

www.ingramcontent.com/pod-product-compliance
Lightning Source LLC
Chambersburg PA
CBHW061217240926
51846CB00006B/1258
9789264497184